DANCE ON THE EARTH

a memoir

BOOKS BY
MARGARET LAURENCE

FICTION
This Side Jordan (1960)
The Tomorrow-Tamer (1963)
The Stone Angel (1964)
A Jest of God (1966)
The Fire-Dwellers (1969)
A Bird in the House (1970)
The Diviners (1974)

NON-FICTION
The Prophet's Camel Bell (1963)
Dance on the Earth (1989)

FICTION FOR YOUNG ADULTS
Jason's Quest (1970)
Six Darn Cows (1979)
The Olden Days Coat (1979)
The Christmas Birthday Story (1980)

ESSAYS
Long Drums and Cannons: Nigerian Dramatists
and Novelists 1952–1966 (1968)
Heart of a Stranger (1976)

TRANSLATIONS
A Tree for Poverty: Somali Poetry and Prose (1954)

MARGARET LAURENCE

DANCE ON THE EARTH

a memoir

M&S

CANADIAN CATALOGUING IN PUBLICATION DATA

Laurence, Margaret, 1926-1987
Dance on the earth: a memoir

ISBN 0-7710-4746-0

1. Laurence, Margaret, 1926-1987 – Biography.
2. Novelists, Canadian (English) – 20th century –
Biography.* I. Title.

PS8523.A86Z53 1989   C813'.54   C89-094981-6
PR9199.3.L39Z47 1989

Design by T.M. Craan

Set in Stempel Garamond by The Coach House Press, Toronto

Printed and bound in Canada

McClelland & Stewart Inc.
The Canadian Publishers
481 University Avenue
Toronto, Ontario
M5G 2E9

For Jocelyn and David
with faith, hope, and love

ACKNOWLEDGEMENTS

My thanks to my daughter, Jocelyn Laurence, for editing this book, and to my son, David Laurence, for the portrait photograph of me.

A very special thanks to my friend Joan Johnston, whose enormously generous help in every way, including the typing of the second and third drafts of the manuscript, enabled me to bring this work to near-completion.

Margaret Laurence
Lakefield, November 1986

CONTENTS

PREFACE

My mother first decided to write her memoirs around 1984. When she told me, I was distinctly apprehensive about the whole idea. Didn't she think, I asked her, that she was much too young to be undertaking such an endeavour? After all, she wasn't yet sixty, and presumably had farther to go before she slept. Weren't memoirs kind of, well, final?

She listened to me with her usual patience and said she'd think about it. Next thing I knew she was on the phone, announcing that she'd started a draft but it wasn't working out. She'd written pages and pages merely to get to the point where she turned eighteen, and she was bored silly. I made suitably sympathetic (albeit slightly hypocritical) noises, secretly relieved that she would now presumably give up the project and move on to something else.

She didn't, of course. My mother had more gut-level determination than almost anyone I've known. She conceived of a new structure, one in which she could not only incorporate the facts of her own life but also touch upon the lives of her three mothers, as she called them – her biological mother, her aunt, who became her stepmother, and her mother-in-law. This new approach allowed her momentary digressions, too, into the issues that most concerned her: nuclear disarmament, pollution and the environment, pro-choice abortion legislation. Suddenly, her interest revived. And with the memoirs now definitely under way, I was forced to admit to myself that I had a superstitious feeling about the damn book. It was altogether too bounded, with a beginning and a middle and presumably an end. It had nasty implications of mortality. I realized I hadn't wanted her to write her life story because

I couldn't allow myself to believe her life could ever be over.

My mother always claimed she had Celtic second sight. She finished writing the first draft of these memoirs just before her sixtieth birthday on July 18, 1986, and was diagnosed as having terminal cancer a month later, on my thirty-fourth birthday. (Some small measure of the love and consideration she always had for her children is demonstrated by the fact that she waited until the next day to call me because she didn't want to spoil my birthday.)

It's perhaps appropriate here to say a brief word about her writing methods, since my small part in this book came about as a result of her illness and therefore her inability to write the book in the way she wrote her others. She always wrote her first draft in longhand, with subsequent drafts done on the typewriter. (She prided herself on being an excellent typist; years of pounding away on a manual ruined her back and gave her a fearsome grip that could crack bones.) She would normally write at least three drafts of a manuscript, and sometimes as many as five. She would also occasionally put a manuscript to one side and come back to it months or, in a few cases, years later.

None of this was possible with *Dance on the Earth*, though God knows she tried. She'd been in hospital only a couple of days when she had a friend bring in the manuscript, her typewriter, and some paper. The nurses set up a typing table and she sat on the edge of the bed, tubes coming out of the incision in her chest, and launched herself into the second draft. But much to her annoyance, she tired quickly. Writing is physically hard work. It's also psychically exhausting. She was all too aware of just how much she had to do and how little time and energy she might have to accomplish it. Her cheerfulness and resolve when I spoke to her on the telephone were, of course, deceptive. When I came up to Peterborough to take her home from the hospital for a few hours, she was sitting in a chair next to the window, dressed, holding her purse on her lap, and for the few seconds before she realized I was there, she looked tiny and lost and discouraged, a small child in a world she couldn't cope with and didn't really understand.

That didn't last. She had a renewed burst of energy immediately she was allowed to go home (she had refused any long-term treatment). And then her friend Joan Johnston came up with the idea of dictating the next drafts of the manuscript on tape. Joan gamely volunteered to type out each tape as it was completed; my mother would then correct the typescript and return it to Joan for one further draft.

Eventually, the system worked splendidly. At first, my mother was somewhat reluctant to try such an unaccustomed method of writing. It felt as if the work was somehow out of her hands (which, of course, it was) and she had never been comfortable with machinery. (It had taken her years, and much persuasion on my part and my brother's, before she decided to buy even an electric typewriter.) Pretty soon, though, she was hunkering down at the kitchen table every day, dictating like a mad business-woman. She started taping September 11, and by October 6 Joan had finished the first typed draft.

Throughout this process, I would get progress reports almost daily; not, this time, gauged in terms of how many pages she'd completed but calculated in terms of how many tapes she'd done. She knew, however, that she likely wouldn't have time to get the book to the stage where it was publishable. This new way of writing worked up to a point, but my mother had a good enough ear to realize that the manuscript would still need fine-tuning before she could submit it. She was also professional enough not to want to hand anything to a publisher that was less than her best.

At that point, she and I began talking about my editing the book. We had, in fact, worked together once before, on a piece on censorship that I'd asked her to do when I was working as an editor at *Toronto Life* magazine. (The article appears at the back of this book, along with a few other short pieces of writing that she chose as being relevant to the main text.) On that occasion, once we'd both overcome our slight initial awkwardness at having our relationship temporarily turn from a personal to a professional one, we actually had a lot of fun. We had, after all, spent years together discussing the process of writing and the role of the editor and when it came to putting those conversations into practice, we discovered we already had a shared language that was completely natural to both of us.

I had hoped, of course, that we could also work on the book together, but it gradually became apparent that my mother simply didn't have the strength. She would often say to me about the book, "Oh kid, it's going to be so hard for you," and I would insist, with a confidence born of ignorance, that it wouldn't be difficult at all. But she was right. After she died, it was six months before I re-read the manuscript and another six months before I began to work on it. It wasn't that the book needed much alteration. My role was simply to smooth out some portions and eliminate any repetitions that inevitably arise from the spoken rather than the written word. My mother and I had talked about the manuscript in general terms, and thanks to those discussions, I felt I was making changes that we had both agreed were necessary.

No, the hardest part was listening to her on the page. Of all her books, *Dance on the Earth* is, for obvious reasons, the one most literally written in her voice. It is, in that sense, an unusual book, since the way in which she spoke, the rhythms and idiosyncrasies of phrasing, the choices of language and emphasis, are integral not only to the book but to the actual process of writing it. Hearing my mother's voice so accurately made it easy to remain true to her original intent, but it was also painful at times to hear stories – and remember others – that she would never again tell me in person.

I miss her greatly, of course, and almost constantly, as people do miss parents whom they love. I have often found myself wishing she were still here, although I like to imagine she is around in spirit if not in body. But it is at times like this, when her final book is near completion, that I particularly wish she could be present to receive praise for her undoubted achievement.

Jocelyn Laurence
Toronto
July 1989

I

FOREWORDS

I have heard it said that war is for men what motherhood is for women. I find this appalling, and essentially quite false. I realize, however, that it is more true for some men than most of us, both women and men, would like to think. But to compare (on an intensity-of-experience scale? on a devotion scale? on a commitment scale?) the giving and nurturing of life to the violent and brutal and senseless taking away of life seems to me to be an ultimate obscenity. Yet we live in an increasingly violent society. Films filled with war and violence are immensely popular. Pornography – violence mainly against women and children – is a profitable and proliferating industry, the products of which, films and videotapes and photographs, some men are said to "need," even though women almost uniformly find this supposed fact frightening and enraging. War is still portrayed as ennobling, engendering a male camaraderie unparalleled in other human relations. Even among some men who have actively fought in wars, the horrors tend to fade with the years. Out come the tales of daring and courage, the amusing tales that, when they happened (if indeed they actually did happen), were no doubt born of a desperate survival humour.

I have heard these stories from contemporaries of mine, men who fought in the Second World War. But this telling of old tales is by no means universal. I have also known men who never spoke of their war experiences. My father fought in the First World War, and although I was nine when he died, I do not remember him ever talking about his war. Women have to be very careful. We must never talk of "men's responses" to war, or to anything else, as though there were only one set of responses in the entire

3

male population. This seems a blinding glimpse of the obvious, but it is not. Not only among feminists, of whom I count myself one, but also among non-feminist women, of whom, alas, there are plenty, it is all too common to say, "*Men* are like this" or "*Men* are like that." And yet we properly resent it when we hear a man say, "Oh well, you know, *women* drivers" or "She knew she couldn't win the argument so she turned on the tears . . . they do it every time." No generalization should be the rule for either women or men. This is not easy; in fact, I often find it excruciatingly difficult.

The fact remains, however, that war is a popular and time-honoured subject of novels, histories, poetry, films, painting, and sculpture, whereas birth and mothering have scarcely been subjects at all, or at least not recognized and honoured subjects of art and history and philosophy, until comparatively recent times (another generalization, of course, for which numerous exceptions, including ancient ones, can be found). But this is scarcely surprising in a world in which communications and the arts have been dominated by men and herstory either ignored, condescended to, or forgotten. To my personal knowledge, this downgrading of women in every field has been changing considerably for the better, although still too gradually, over the past forty years or so, but some memories come back bitterly.

Those of us who are old enough to remember the Second World War song "Rosie the Riveter," for example, also recall how, just after the war's end, the New Look in female clothing came in, ostensibly because lots of lovely clothing materials were newly available. In reality the message was clear, although few of us read it correctly then – "Back to the kitchen, girls" (which women in fact had never left; they simply added domestic duties to their war work). Wearing our long hobble skirts, peplum jackets with awkward shoulders and miserably pinched-in waists, and crippling spike-heeled, pointy-toed shoes, we weren't going to be doing much competing with men in the labour market. I married in 1947. My going-away outfit (how strange the words sound to me now) was a navy-blue suit with a tight skirt down nearly to my ankles and a cumbersome gold-braided puff-sleeved jacket that must have made my slender twenty-one-year-old body look like a dirigible. High-heeled shoes, of course. A natty little navy-blue felt hat, tri-cornered, with a huge pink ribbon bow, fashioned by Miss Phipps, the local ladies' milliner in my home town. I thought it was just wonderful. My husband Jack and I spent our honeymoon at my family's cottage at Clear Lake, in Riding Mountain National Park. We were driven there, on the evening of our wedding day, by friends of my mother's. If a bear had shown up as we were getting out of the car, I couldn't even have sprinted the couple of yards to the cottage, clad as I was in that outlandish outfit.

Writing by women, in those and the following years, was generally regarded by critics and reviewers in this country with at best an amused tolerance, at worst a dismissive shrug. It still makes me angry how thoroughly I had been brainwashed by society, despite having been greatly encouraged by two of my male professors at college, whom I bless to this day. But when I first submitted poems to the University of Manitoba student paper, *The Manitoban,* I sent them in under the name of Steve Lancaster. After the Lancaster bomber, and I had always liked the name Steve. I cringe with shame to recall it now. Later, I dared to use my own name, but it was J.M. Wemyss, I think, not Jean Margaret. In one of my early stories, published in the United College magazine, *Vox,* I actually used a first-person narrative, but the narrator was a man. How long, how regrettably long, it took me to find my true voice as a woman writer. In my first novel, *This Side Jordan,* published in 1960, I described the birth of Miranda Kestoe's child from the point of view of Johnnie Kestoe, the child's father. How could I have done? How could I have been so stupid, so self-doubting? I find it hard to understand. At that point I had borne two children, but women writers had virtually no models in describing birth, or sex, from a woman's view. We had all read many women writers, of course, but I had found no one who described sex or birth as they really were for women. I, who had experienced such joy with sex, such anguish and joy in the birth of my children, not only didn't have the courage to describe these crucial experiences; it didn't even occur to me to do so.

One of the reviews that appeared when *This Side Jordan* came out has stayed in my mind all these years. "Ho hum," the male reviewer said (or words to that effect). "Why must we always have the obligatory birth scene in novels written by women?" Unwittingly, that dolt helped me begin a kind of self-liberation in the area of writing. I was furious. It was fine for male writers to portray unending scenes of violence, blood, and gore in the service of destruction and death. It was swell for some male writers to drone on interminably about the boring masturbation of their protagonists, or how they screwed a multiplicity of faceless women. But it was not all right, apparently, for a woman writer to speak of the miraculous beginnings of human life. Obviously, something was pretty crazy here.

My novels are not exactly dotted with birth scenes, but after that I never hesitated to write about birth, and I never did so again except from the viewpoint of the mother. I like to think that in some ways my generation of women novelists may have helped younger women writers to speak with women's voices about sex and birth.

Still, there are areas in my mind and memory that I have not been able to write about fictionally. *The Diviners* came closest to being not precisely an autobiography, but certainly a spiritual autobiography. I have tried over the past years to write another novel. In fact, I have tried many times. I have not succeeded. It has finally become clear to me that the novel I thought I wanted to write was simply

6

not there to be written. I prophesied this at the end of *The Diviners*, but I didn't know how much it would hurt.

I decided to write my memoirs, even though people usually wait until they are somewhat older. That didn't work out either. After hundreds of handwritten pages, I had got myself to the age of eighteen. I was bored. I knew what was going to happen next. There was none of the mysterious excitement that one feels in writing a novel. Furthermore, I knew I didn't want to write the entire story of my life, for numerous reasons, one of them being that it *is* mine and from the start I recognized that there were areas I wasn't prepared even to try to set down. I wanted to write more about my feelings about mothers and about my own life views. I realized finally that this could only be done by coming as close as I could bear to my own life, but in such a way that I could also deal with broader themes that interested and absorbed me.

I am a fortunate woman. I had three mothers and I am myself the mother of a grown daughter and son. Two of my mothers (my stepmother and my mother-in-law) were very strong women who endured a lot and overcame a lot, and who gave me in large measure such strength as I now possess. They helped me, far more than they knew, to deal with my own life and to go on writing. The third, or rather my first and birth mother, I hardly knew. I am so much older now than she ever became. Sometimes I think of her as my long-lost child. I was brainwashed, as I have said, by the society in which I grew up and lived as a young adult. I was less brainwashed in this way by my mothers, and by my aunts, my mother's sisters, although I now see how that era and that society affected their own considerable talents and afflicted them in individual ways. I grew up among determined women, intelligent and talented women. My own young mother was a pianist. Two of my aunts were nurses. My aunt Velma was a public-health nurse, much beloved in the B.C. communities in which she worked over many years. My aunt Ruby was the first head of the Nursing Division in the first Public Health Department in Canada, in the province of Saskatchewan. She was the head of the Canadian Nurses' Association for some years and eventually received the OBE. (I have a very touching photograph of her, resplendent in lace dress and broad-brimmed picture hat, about to receive her medal at Buckingham Palace. How the years have changed Canadian perceptions: the Order I am proud to bear is the Order of Canada.) My aunt Margaret, who became my stepmother, was a high-school teacher whose great love was English literature. I don't recall that there was anything any of these women ever suggested I couldn't achieve because I was a female. But all these women had themselves been hampered. Their father, my grandfather Simpson, was a male chauvinist of the first order. I know they drew strength from their mother, my gentle and, I think, long-suffering grandmother, and from one another. In their struggle to proclaim their lives, to be their own persons, they must have gone through pain that I can only guess at.

I was not a person for the first three years of my life. It was only in 1929, because of the enormous and valiant efforts of such women as Nellie McClung and Emily Murphy, that Canadian women were finally legally recognized as "persons." Of course, at three, I wasn't aware that I had suddenly been promoted into personhood. Certainly, my mother and aunts never saw themselves as inferior, or non-persons, whatever the asinine law might have said.

There are so many women I would like to honour – to tell them, even though many of them are no longer alive, how much I owe them, how much *we* owe them, how much my own daughter and son are their inheritors. But this is a book about my mothers and about myself as a mother and writer. Only by implication and some references can I include all those women, even in my own family. My two grandmothers and four great-grandmothers, some known to me through old photographs, eight great-

great-grandmothers, all virtually unknown, and back and back in time, until the familial ancestors become all our ancestors, the ancestors of us all. Yet they are here, too, in my mind and my dreams. All those women back to the ancient Picts of Scotland (from whom my father's family, Wemyss, is said to be descended), and to the Irish from whom my mother's family came.

In our culture, our genealogical descent is always in the male line. Where the mothers come from, what their names are, is always where their fathers came from and what names they carried. A woman who keeps her own family name when she marries still bears the name of her father and his father. Women have no surnames of their own. Their names are literally sirnames. Women only have one name that is ours, our first or given name. I value my own given name and that of others. I'm sure this is important to everyone, but perhaps more so to women. When I was divorced, I would never have dreamed of resuming my own family name of Wemyss. Laurence had been my name at that point for more than half my life, and it is the name of my children. I know many divorced women take back their family name, and that's fine. I actually feel more at ease with Margaret than with any surname, but on the other hand, I think of my full name as Margaret Wemyss Laurence. I would never repudiate my familial name nor the married name I took on so many years ago, with love, and which is borne by both my children and my books. To repudiate either last name would be in a sense to repudiate all those lives, stretching far back, through which I and my children came to be ourselves.

I think, then, about my mothers and myself in terms of our given names, but also in terms of the surnames we all bear. Verna Simpson Wemyss. Margaret Simpson Wemyss. Elsie Fry Laurence. Margaret Wemyss Laurence. Many histories are contained in those combinations of names. My mothers are long dead, but I continue to miss them all, even my own young mother whom I hardly knew. I wish they were here. I wish I could explain myself to them, and they to me. When the very beloved mother of my close friend the writer Adele Wiseman was dying at the age of eighty-odd, she was perfectly lucid and very aware, as she always had been, of the young. Yet she sometimes called out, in her pain, for her mother. The first cry of life, perhaps, and the last. So it is that I write this book, for my mothers and for my children. I write as a child and as a mother.

My mothers were white women in a predominantly white society, and thus in some ways greatly privileged. Nevertheless, two of my mothers were daughters of a stern, authoritarian pioneer father. The other, my mother-in-law, was the daughter of an English parson. Two of them coped somehow with the Depression and drought of the thirties. One died very young. For my stepmother and my mother-in-law, life was filled with troubles and hard work, relieved by their determined humour and, I believe, by the existence of their children. All of them were talented artists in their various ways – music, teaching, writing. All of them might have, under other circumstances, pursued careers that fulfilled their talents, as well as marrying and having children. I mourn that loss, even as I rejoice in the riches they gave their children, no matter how hard up they were for money.

Beyond and behind them are their mothers. I never really knew, I only know about, Jane Bailey, my grandmother, the mother of Verna and Margaret Simpson, my two mothers. A gentle, quiet woman who bore eight children, a woman overshadowed by her domineering husband, a woman greatly loved by her children and grandchildren. Do I idealize her? Certainly. It is easier to idealize grandparents (or devilize them, as I did for years with my grandfather Simpson, whom I hated and feared)

10

because we usually don't know them as well as we do our own parents.

I wish I knew more about Jane Bailey. All I have is a photograph of each of her parents, very rigid and posed, saying little except respectability; one picture, very faint and faded, of Grandmother and Grandfather in winter coats outside their brick house; a number of childhood memories. Her family had been United Empire Loyalists, who moved from the States at the time of the American War of Independence to Amherstburg, Ontario. A long time later that branch of the Baileys moved west, to Portage la Prairie, Manitoba. Jane Bailey met my grandfather, John Simpson, in Portage, and married him there. He was a young cabinet-maker who had come from Milton, Ontario, to Winnipeg by Red River steamer and then had walked to Portage, plying his trade along the way. After they married, my grandparents moved to Neepawa and raised their family there.

How I wish I had known my grandmother as a young woman. When I was a child, she always seemed so very old to me. I remember she always had a great stone cookie jar full of homemade cookies and whenever I visited, which was often, for Grandmother and Grandfather lived just at the other end of our small town, she would let me play with her button bag, a big cloth drawstring bag full of what seemed like millions of fascinating buttons. There were ordinary ones, of course, like the small pearl buttons used on men's shirts or women's blouses, but the true treasure trove was a strange assortment – several brass buttons from a First World War uniform, oddly shaped mother-of-pearl buttons, china buttons painted with tiny violets.

Grandmother gave me my first (and indeed only) Bible. It is inscribed (in my stepmother's handwriting): "Jean Margaret Wemyss May 5th, 1935 Grandmother." I have carried it around the world with me for more than fifty years. It is tattered now, and the soft black leather cover is

11

held together with tape. It is full of pen markings, where I have noted passages I wanted to be able to find again easily. In fact, it's the only Bible in which I can find anything. I think of my grandmother whenever I open it.

I didn't realize until long after I was grown up that my grandmother was an artist. The works of her art were all around us in the Simpson house, and remained so long after she died, but I scarcely noticed them except as comfortable household objects. She made hooked rugs from strips of old stockings, which she bleached and then dyed in all sorts of colours. My two aunts' white nurse's stockings must have been welcome since they could be dyed in light and peacock shades, whereas darker stockings, even if they were bleached, would take only darker shades. The patience those little rugs must have taken! The patterns on them ranged from flowers to houses set about with trees. My grandmother made quilts, too. Some of them were patchwork, with intricate designs put together from the scraps of the dresses she sewed or the many aprons she made for herself and as gifts. These quilts, done in some of the traditional patterns she must have learned as a girl, looked old and uninteresting to me when I was a child. They probably seemed the same to my mother and aunts. Quilts were viewed in those days not as works of art but as practical and affordable necessities. I am quite sure my grandmother never thought of herself as an artist or even a craftswoman. Just as my grandfather prided himself on being a good provider, so she took satisfaction (pride was not one of my grandmother's attributes) in being a good housekeeper.

But artist she was. I must have been six or seven when she made a quilt for me. She had begun making appliqué quilts since not as many scraps of material were around. Her daughters were grown up by that time and no longer wanted homemade dresses. So she bought pastel cottons for her creations, although I suspect my grandfather thought it a terrible waste of money. My quilt was the most beautiful I had ever seen and in my memory it remains the most beautiful. It was called "Wild Rose" and consisted of stylized pale pink roses with pastel green leaves on a white background. I had it for years, but when I was about thirteen, I decided I didn't like it any more. It was homemade, never a desirable quality to a thirteen-year-old, and old-fashioned. I envied my best friend Mona's bedspread, chenille in three shades of blue. The barbarity of youth.

My grandmother's quilt may be irretrievably lost, but the patterns and colours are clear in my mind. She died before I had mentally rejected it, but she had been dead many years before I came to recognize her artistry. I wish I could tell her. I can never bring myself to believe in a personal immortality, but if there is, even in such places as the various heavens of our imaginings, I am sure my grandmother is there. I hope she is chatting to the generations of women who grew gardens and made quilts and told stories and sang songs and wove baskets and did all the other unrecognized and unsung work. I would like to reach back and back into time gone, and embrace these women as a mother embraces her grown children, with loving respect, as a grown child embraces a mother. These women are an integral part of the Holy Spirit.

In fact, it has become more and more important to me to recognize the female principle as part of the Holy Spirit. This may seem unconnected with the subject of these memoirs – my mothers and foremothers, and myself as child and mother – but there is a deep connection. I am a Christian, or at least aspire to be, although perhaps not an orthodox one. I have spoken to many women within the Christian Protestant faith, several of them ordained ministers, who have very similar feelings to my own. There are also quite a large number of Roman Catholic women, some of them nuns, who feel that women must be allowed to take a full part in the church and become ordained priests if that is their calling.

I know, however, that there are many people of various faiths who find abhorrent the very idea of a female principle being part of what we call God. It is a highly controversial subject, and that saddens me immeasurably. Not all women, perhaps not even a majority, feel as I do. Many would get angry at the suggestions I make here. I find it increasingly disturbing, though, probably because I notice it more than I did years ago, that so much of the Christian ritual is male-oriented. Women are just not there in our hymns (apart from a few modern ones and some American spirituals) except, of course, for Mary, the one constant – and virginal – representative of our sex. Look at all the old and noble hymns that so many of us have loved all our lives: "Rise up, O men of God!" "Faith of our fathers!" "Praise, my soul, the King of Heaven . . . " Not to mention that it is always "God the Father, God the Son, God the Holy Spirit." A United Church minister, a woman, once told me that she always thought of the female principle as being part of the Holy Spirit, and I have thought of it like that ever since. I often find it easier to say Holy Spirit rather than God, because this means to me not only God the Father and the Mother, but a kind of holiness in life itself, in trees and rivers and the earth and all creatures. When I sing "Praise, my soul, the King of Heaven," I sometimes substitute "mother" for "father," as in "Praise him for his grace and favour / To our fathers in distress . . . " Why not mothers? Weren't they in distress fully as much as our fathers, and frequently more so? The opposing argument, that the word "fathers," like "mankind," really means all parents and is an inclusive term, seems specious to me. The third verse of the hymn is this:

Father-like he tends and spares us;
Well our feeble frame he knows;
In his hands he gently bears us,
Rescues us from all our foes.

14

Does that sound, especially the first three lines, like a father (at least more traditional fathers, with some honourable exceptions)? Or does it sound more like a mother? This is not to malign fathers, but we can only begin to understand, a little, the Holy Spirit by thinking in the terms we have, human ones, which is why we make comparisons with the human family. Even in hymns as stirring as this one, to leave out all mothers and daughters indicates something I do not like at all. I love these hymns; I love their music. Yet when I sing them I feel left out, deprived.

Some other religions, some of the polytheisms, recognize this. Some of those very religions that early Christian missionaries believed so evil had and still have the concept of a god unseen and above all other gods, a god both male and female, mother and father, earth and sky. Women have been intentionally excluded from so many of the rituals and practices and words of Christianity, and the same is true of the other monotheisms. I believe this exclusion cannot go on. It is precisely because of our memories of some of our "mothers in distress" – our foremothers who laboured and suffered and did without in order that their children and their children's children might be brought into life and cared for – as well as our own sense of worth as women that so many of us now, both inside the churches and outside, feel that the recognition of the female principle in faith, in art, in all of life must come about much more fully than it has done.

A few years ago, a magnificent sculpture called "Crucified Woman," by the Canadian sculptor Almuth Lutkenhaus, was displayed over the Easter season in Bloor Street United Church in Toronto. It was a very courageous and sensitive act on the part of the church. A great many people, both women and men, were extremely moved by the sculpture. A photograph of it appeared in the newspapers and I was so struck by it, so awed, that I managed to meet Almuth Lutkenhaus and to see the statue, which was then in her own home. (It has now, I am happy to say, been cast in bronze and is on permanent display outside Emmanuel College, the United Church theological college at Victoria University in Toronto.)

Some people, especially fundamentalists, were outraged, and stormed around crying, "How dare she say Christ was a woman!" "Heresy!" and so on. This, of course, was beside the point. "Crucified Woman" shows a naked and somewhat stylized female figure, slender, almost emaciated, with outstretched and slightly elongated arms. She is in cruciform, her arms reaching out in a gesture that to me speaks both of an anguished appeal and of an attempt at loving consolation. Her head is bowed to the right, and on her face and in her eyes is an expression of such suffering and such compassion that it is difficult to understand how anyone could see it and not be moved to joy and tears. There is no cross. The woman herself, with her outstretched arms and her long legs reaching as though for the earth, forms a cross. She is simply there, suspended in the air but close to the earth, perhaps even with her feet touching an earth unseen. To me, she represents the anguish of the ages, the repression, the injustice, the pain that has been inflicted upon women, both physically and emotionally. "Crucified Woman" also speaks to me of the comfort and help I have known from my mothers and the unconditional love I feel for my own children.

She says something else to me, too. I think of "Lord of the Dance," a modern hymn by Sydney Carter. The first verse and chorus of this splendid hymn go:

> I danced in the morning when the world was begun,
> And I danced in the moon and the stars and the sun
> And I came down from heaven and I danced on the
>   earth –
> At Bethlehem I had my birth.
>> Dance then wherever you may be;
>> I am the Lord of the Dance, said he,

I'll lead you all, wherever you may be,
I will lead you all in the Dance, said he.

Women, as well as men, in all ages and in all places, have danced on the earth, danced the life dance, danced joy, danced grief, danced despair, and danced hope. Literally danced all these and more, and danced them figuratively and metaphorically, by their very lives. "Crucified Woman" is almost dancing, on the earth, the life dance of pain and love.

Dancing, both as metaphor and as actuality, has always been part of my own life. When I was a young woman I loved to go dancing. One of my greatest pleasures when my husband and I lived in Ghana was to dance in one of the African nightclubs in Accra, to West African high-life music with its counterpoint rhythms of the drums. I was pretty good at it, too. When young African men asked me to dance, I was honoured – they didn't ask just anyone. When my children were little, I used to dance with them sometimes and that was pure joy, as their small bodies whirled and spun and occasionally tripped and righted themselves, laughing, and the dance went on. Later, during some of the most difficult times of my life, when I was alone with the children, I often used to dance to my favourite music – "Zorba's Dance," African high life, some of the jazz or boogie from the forties. I danced alone in my study, when the kids were asleep, dancing pain, worry, loneliness. And the dancing helped. I don't dance any more. I don't feel the need when alone, and in public . . . well, when you have once been very good at something, it is no pleasure to do it badly, and the body ages even as hopeful dignity remains evergreen. It does not worry me nor cause me regret not to dance now, for I know there are many ways of dancing other than the literal ones. These other ways, of friendships, of work, of stubborn hoping in a terrifying world, I pray to be able to go on with until my own dance ends and I leave the earth.

I never saw my maternal grandmother dance, although I think she must have, both ballroom dancing and square dancing with a fiddler and a caller in country schoolhouses. In her quilts and hooked rugs she also danced some of her perseverance, her gentleness, her hard work, her pain, her life. I never saw any of my mothers dance, although I feel sure that they did, and that my own young mother perhaps even danced with me when I was a very young child. My mothers must have danced the dances of their youth: the waltz, the Charleston, the two-step. No, I never saw my mothers actually dancing, but they all danced in the other ways, the ways that are different from the dance observed as dance. Twice, not so long ago, my daughter and I danced, a stately dance, not the exuberant rhythms of my past or her present, a graceful easy dance, at a slight distance from each other, hands touching lightly, a dance with no name.

A dance is lifelong, and its measures are quick, slow, frenetic, quiet, worried, painful, joyous, women's dances everywhere. I wrote a sort of song a few years ago, called "Old Women's Song." Part of it goes like this:

> I see old women dancing
> dancing on the earth
> I hear old women singing
> singing children's birth
>
> > great is their caring
> > strong is their measure
> > dancing and singing
> > life's frail treasure
>
> I see old women dancing
> dancing even here
> bleakworld and wanworld
> world of fear

I see old women dancing
dancing children's breath
I hear old women mourning
mourning children's death

I see old women dancing
dancing in their grief
singing of the sorrow
singing of belief

I see old women dancing
dancing through all lands
foremothers with them joining
all of their hands

    dance on, old women,
    dance amidst the strife,
    sing out, old women,
    sing for life

I am one among them
dancing on the earth,
mourning, grieving, raging,
yet jubilating birth.

I had three mothers. I have countless foremothers. I never
saw my mothers dancing. But now I know their dance.

II

VERNA

The kitchen of the Big House, my Simpson grandparents' home, is vast to my very young eyes. It is lined with cupboards and the long cabinet where my grandmother so frequently kneads bread and rolls out cookie dough. In this cabinet, at the bottom on one side, is a large and fascinating pull-out bin that I am not allowed to meddle with, for it contains flour and a tantalizing scoop. The huge black woodstove, with "McClary's Range" in silver letters on the warming oven on top, dominates the place. The back stairs open off the kitchen and are very steep and curved. This is hard work, getting my new – my first – tricycle up those stairs. But we manage it, my aunt Marg and I, and I feel I am really doing most of the pulling, for she is very tactful with her help. Finally we achieve the upstairs. This is a great moment for me. My first real bike and I am going to show it to my mother. I am not really sure why she is in the bedroom in the Big House, in what I think of as my aunt Vem's room, instead of at home in her own and my father's bedroom in the Little House at the other end of town. My aunt Velma, whom we all call Vem, is a nurse. She is home from Winnipeg right now. I guess that my mother is just visiting her, probably. This bedroom is magical to me. It contains, among other marvels, my aunt's silken pyjama bag in the shape of a floppy doll, and a little wooden container that holds camphor ice for chapped lips and is shaped like a smiling and bulbous dwarfwoman.

We wheel the splendid green-and-silver trike along the back hall, past the bathroom with its huge, deep, claw-footed bathtub that I love and don't often get the chance to bathe in. Around the corner is the linen cupboard where, along with all the sheets, carefully ironed and folded, and the towels of all sizes and colours, my grandmother keeps the spare quilts, the patchwork coverlets she has made. Then we are there, and I happily run to my mother, excitedly telling her about the new trike, how great it is, how I can ride already, and my feet *do so* reach the pedals.

My mother, lying in the grey-painted double bed, smiles at me. Her face is white and her dark hair is spread out across the white pillowcase. She touches my face, my hair.

It is unlikely she knew she was dying. Or perhaps she did know, or suspected, and it broke her heart to leave us, my father and me, and her sisters and beloved mother. I hope she didn't know. But I have no memory of anything more complicated than her look of love for me. I never saw her again.

This memory is my first conscious one, my own memory rather than the imagined memories of infanthood and early childhood that were based on what was told to me later on. My mother died a few days later, of an acute kidney infection, after only a week's illness. She was thirty-four. My father was thirty-six. I was four.

It is only now, writing this, that I look up my mother's death in the old Simpson family Bible, a large, battered leather-bound book. In the few pages between the Old and New Testaments, and on pasted-in pages, the family births and deaths have been entered since 1803. There is an entry for Verna's death: July 20, 1930. I have always known I was four when she died, but it is only now that I realize she died just two days after my fourth birthday.

I was not told of my mother's death at once, although it was probably only the next day that I learned of it, and not in the way that my father must have intended. He and my aunts must have been immersed in their own immediate and shocked grief and simply couldn't cope with telling a four-year-old right away and answering the inevitable young queries about when my mother would be coming back. Children are widely believed not to understand death at that age, but children almost always know more than they are supposed to. I don't think I asked that question. When I found out, I think I knew.

I am back home at the Little House and I am playing outside with my friend from across the road. We are tramping around in our rubber boots, in a ditch that contains a few inches of rain-water. The muddy, weed-filled water is a sea. Neither of us has ever seen a sea, but probably it is just like Clear Lake, where my family's cottage is. My friend is a year older than I, and so of course much smarter. I follow her lead gladly, proud that she will play with a little kid like me. Suddenly she looks at me strangely, almost with a frightened expression.

"Your mother's dead," she says.

She has undoubtedly been told not to say this to me. She is five years old, and not at an age for keeping secrets.

I stare at her. Then I get very angry.

"She is not! You're telling a lie! Liar! Liar!"

I run inside the house. Someone is there, my aunt Marg or my father. I have no memory of who told me that my friend was not lying. My mother is dead. I might not have known precisely what "never" meant. But I think I understood I would never see her again.

After that, I have no conscious memories for about a year. In the small book, which I still have, called "Mother's Record of Baby," the entry for Fourth Birthday Anniversary is in my aunt Margaret Simpson's handwriting. Among the six gifts listed is "Bicycle." Somehow this book has weathered and survived the many journeys of my life. Possibly I've kept it all these years because it is the only tangible link I have with my mother. I have photographs of her, but only one taken with me, a family group picture, and I can't see her face. The baby book records her feelings about me. The entries (except for this fourth-birthday one and the fifth birthday, when the book stops, babyhood over) are in my mother's handwriting, so much like my own sprawling penmanship and so unlike the even and beautifully formed handwriting of her sister, my aunt and stepmother.

I am said to be like Verna in some ways, the ways of laughter and lightheartedness. The part of me that remains young and even clowning, that retains a childish sense of humour, that writes funny verses to dear ones, I probably owe to her. How much of the other side – the anxious, worried, sometimes deeply depressed side – I owe to the Black Celt in me, and to the terrifying world we live in, and how much that may have begun to grow within my spirit at my mother's death, I can never know.

Verna was born in 1896, the second-youngest child of seven children of John and Jane Simpson. John was a cabinet-maker who had also become an undertaker, a combination of trades common at the time. The demand for furniture in a small prairie town was limited, but the demand for coffins was constant. My grandfather was a stern man. He always seemed ancient to me, and chances are that he appeared that way to his children.

I remember the brick house, the Big House as we called it, so clearly. I can see the screened veranda with its canvas curtains, brown and beige striped, to be rolled down against the sun or at night if you were sleeping out there in the worst heat of summer. In the winter, safe from cats and dogs and light-fingered passersby, the veranda was used, as was the unheated summer kitchen at the back of the house, for storing pies and sausage rolls and stone crocks of mincemeat. When I think of the Big House, though, I think of myself visiting there as a child, and later, living there with my young brother and our mum. I can't visualize my mother and my aunts and uncles there when they were young. There were four bedrooms. Where, I used to wonder, did they all sleep? The biggest bedroom would have been the parents'. The three boys must have shared one room, and three of the girls the other, with the fourth girl, probably the eldest, Ruby, having the small back bedroom to herself. I don't see how else they could have arranged things, although by the time Vem, the youngest, was born, Ruby was already fourteen, so there wouldn't have been many years when they all lived together in the house.

My mother was the youngest until she was six years old, when Vem was born. What must it have been like for Verna, growing up with three older brothers and two older sisters? I wish I knew how she had gotten along with all of them: Stuart, the eldest of the family, smart, handsome Stuart, who wanted to be a lawyer but who instead ultimately went into the undertaking business with his father; diminutive Ruby, quick-witted and quick-tongued, who later became a distinguished nurse; Margaret, tall and slender, in childhood and young womanhood very beautiful, perhaps the most intellectual of the family, determined to make her own way in the world, denied university because she was female; Jack, easily the best-looking, charming in manner and speech, wicked Jack of the practical jokes and the hordes of female admirers, who grew up just as charming and handsome and ne'er-do-well, a brave officer in two world wars (his natural milieu), Jack who moved to California, was one of the horsemen in the old film *Lives of a Bengal Lancer* and who married three, or was it four, wives (although not simultaneously), some of them, luckily, wealthy; and finally spectacled Rod, quiet and self-effacing, who was not a swashbuckling officer in the First World War but a rank more lowly, and who became a pharmacist and married a girl in Oregon. What an assortment they must have been, even as children. The family was complete with Vem's birth, Vem who was likely the darling of them all when she was a kid, who grew up to be a public-health nurse and, in my eyes, my zany flapper aunt with the great sense of humour.

They are all listed in the yellow-brown pages inserted into the family Bible, the ink faded. There is one last and pathetic entry that ended my grandmother's seventeen years of childbearing: "Baby Simpson, born January 29, 1904. Died February 2, 1904." Grandmother must have been about forty-two, not old by today's standards, but no doubt considerably aged by so much childbearing and work.

I wonder if John Simpson had mellowed a little by the time my mother Verna came along, if he was less severe with her, and with Vem, than he must have been with the older ones. I suspect I know the answer. Unless he went through some unlikely period of relative mildness around the age of forty, he was probably just as irascible, as demanding, as undemonstrative of affection, as I remember him when I was a child and he was an old man. Perhaps Verna was relieved when a younger sister arrived. The oldest and the youngest in a large family are so noticeable.

I have a picture of Verna taken with her younger sister. She must be about ten and Vem about four. Vem is standing on an upholstered armchair, clad in a frilly ruffled dress. Verna stands beside her, one arm protectively around the youngster, her own dress ruffled and trimmed with lace (I look at this and can't help imagining my grandmother having to iron those dresses with flat-irons heated on the woodstove). Verna's hair is in ringlets, gussied up with a bow. Her mouth is smiling slightly, but her eyes look faintly sad.

In another picture, this one of Verna by herself, she wears a dark middy top and her hair is done up neatly. She looks so grave, and beneath her rather heavy eyebrows her eyes are large and shadowed. Yet Mum always spoke of how happy Verna ("your other mother") was. I look at the old pictures carefully, wanting them to tell me more than they possibly can. Perhaps if I look hard enough, things will be revealed that I never knew about her.

I knew my father, Robert Harrison Wemyss, for five years longer than my mother, although in some ways he is as mysterious to me as she is. He was born in Neepawa, Manitoba, in 1894. My father's grandfather had been a tea merchant in Edinburgh in the 1870s. Family oral history has it that his partner cheated him, so he packed up and headed for the colonies, settling in Raeburn, Manitoba, with his wife and a bunch of young children. His eldest child, John, my paternal grandfather, stayed on at Glasgow Academy and was to have joined his uncle, Sir John Wemyss, as an apprentice lawyer in India. Before young John graduated, however, Sir John died in the northwest provinces of India in 1878, and young John ended up joining his family in Canada.

He arrived in 1881 and articled with a law firm in Winnipeg, afterwards moving to Neepawa, where he was the town's first lawyer. He married Margaret Harrison, daughter of Dr. D.H. Harrison, and they had three children: Robert, my father; John; and Norma. My grandfather Wemyss died about two weeks after my own birth. He was the only person in Neepawa at that time, and possibly at any other time, who could read the Greek tragedies and comedies in the original ancient Greek.

My father, Bob Wemyss, must have known Verna slightly as a child, for their younger sisters were friends and both Verna and Bob attended public school in Neepawa. He was a year and a half older, though, so they likely ignored each other until much later on. Bob was sent to St. Andrew's College, a private boys' school, then in Toronto, now in Aurora, Ontario. As a product of the Scottish school system, my grandfather Wemyss probably believed that a small-town prairie high school could not provide an adequate education for his elder son, who he hoped would follow him into the legal profession. One family legend, perhaps apocryphal, had it that Bob was something of a hellion and was sent to St. Andrew's because the local teachers couldn't handle him. I always hoped myself that was the real reason.

He stayed at St. Andrew's for three years. I visited the school once, to meet the Grade Twelve and Thirteen students who were studying some of my books. I accepted principally for the sentimental reason that it had been my dad's old school. I didn't expect to find any trace of him there. He had attended before the First World War and the school had moved since. But to my amazement, the headmaster had found my father's records and gave me a photocopy of them. These two sheets of paper are one of the few links I have with the man who died when I was nine and my brother was only two. The later entries prove that he couldn't have hated boarding school, for he kept in touch sporadically over the years. A note was jotted down on the second page each time one of his communications arrived. The final entry reads: "July 18 / 26 – birth of a daughter, Jean Margaret; (Wemyss & Wemyss, Neepawa, Man.)." It amused me to see that he seemed to have neglected to inform the school of his marriage, although a decorous hand had added "Married" above the announcement of my birth, but he had taken the trouble to write to his old school and tell them about me. I felt, reading this entry, as though he were speaking to me across the long years that had separated us since his death.

I have a lot of pictures of my father as a child, into boyhood and young manhood. The depictions I have of him in uniform, with the Canadian Field Artillery, are among the most eloquent statements about war I have ever seen. He and his younger brother Jack had joined up together, Bob at twenty-one and Jack at eighteen. Jack had the sight of only one eye, having been blinded in the other eye by an accident with a BB gun. My father had fired the gun, and I think he must have felt protective towards his younger, sight-handicapped brother. They managed to stay together throughout their whole time in the army. They had a picture taken in Winnipeg when they joined the CFA in 1916, kids, prairie kids, with cheerful smiles and hopeful looks, spiffy in their new private's uniforms with brass buttons and peaked caps with the regimental insignia. The second picture was taken in France in 1918. It is a studio photograph, with a stiff backdrop of painted trees. By then, they had been in the trenches for months. The only traces of a uniform are the clumsy puttees on their legs and their tin hats (gone were the smart peaked caps). Jack is wearing a saggy, thick jacket with a filthy canvas or oilskin overvest. Bob is wearing the same jacket, but over it he wears a sheepskin, wool side out, tied with rope around his waist. Around their necks they each carry a small battered bag containing a gas-mask. But it is in their faces and their eyes that the greatest contrast with the other picture is evident. Their expressions are wary, bitter. They are no longer young men. They look old. Back home in Canada they will regain some of the appearances of youth, but these will be appearances only. They will not talk, later on, of what they have seen, of what they had to do, in the blood and mud, in the trenches of France, amongst the wounded and dying, amongst the dead, in the gunfire. They have become old men at twenty-one and twenty-four. But they are two of the privileged, the fortunate. They survived.

I have my father's copy of *The 60th C.F.A. Battery Book*, published in 1919. He and Jack are listed there. My father, gentle man that he was, was a gunner. My one-eyed uncle was a driver. In the valedictory at the end appear these words: "To die worthily is better than many years of life, and it is well if we are remembered by what we leave behind. No man has seen tomorrow; perhaps a higher civilization may be built upon the ruins of the old, and some of us think we see a light upon the horizon which is not the light of bursting shells."

I could weep with grief and rage as I read these words, as I remember the boys I knew when I was growing up in Neepawa, the boys who were killed or taken prisoner at Dieppe, or who died in their burning tanks at the last onslaught in western Europe in the Second World War. The light upon the horizon turned out to be the bombing of London, the burning of Dresden, the decimation of the Russian people, the stench and smoke of the gas chambers in the death camps, the slaughtering conflagrations and blinding deathlight of Hiroshima and Nagasaki, the Agent Orange of Vietnam.

My own son is now over thirty. Both his grandfathers fought in the First World War when they were younger than he is now. To me, the noblest causes or the conquest of the whole world would not be worth the life of my son. I realize I live a privileged life in a (thus far) privileged place. I think of people struggling against oppressors and torturers and exploiters and purveyors of brutality and racism in so many other places in the world. I think, too, of the escalation of the nuclear arms race, and of the fact that both America and Russia now have enough nuclear weapons to destroy all life on this planet *many times over*. I think of the way I love my children and I know, with no shadow of doubt, that mothers everywhere feel the same.

I hate the men who make wars. I hate the old statesmen, the old politicians, the old military men, who talk of "megadeaths" and "acceptable losses." I hate them with all my heart and soul and voice. I hate oppression and brutality and the demeaning of the human body and spirit whenever they occur. I've often heard the specious rejoinder, "Oh sure, everybody's against those things. But that's just a motherhood statement." *"But"* like hell. Everybody *doesn't* hate these things. That's the whole trouble. And the label "a motherhood statement" is more accurate than any accusers realize, although in a way that they may find difficult to comprehend.

When my father and uncle finally returned from the war that supposedly would end all wars, Bob finished articling with his father, who then took him in as partner in his law firm. He and Verna Simpson became engaged in 1922.

They wrote a letter together, taking turns, to my aunt
Norma, Bob's sister, announcing the news.

Dear Norma:

Verna is sitting on my knee so please excuse the
scrawl. I should have told you "Nous sommes
engagé," if you can guess what that means.

Curtains please – you've got a nut of a brother,
haven't you, Norma, but nevertheless am forced to
admit am most awfully *keen* on him. Am not really
sitting where he said I was.

She is! We are both broke but happy. For the love of
pete don't show this letter to the neighbours. Are you
glad, Rusty? [Norma had red hair.] Your affec.
brother and sister-in-law-to-be.

Bob and Verna.

Write us the odd note and tell us what you think of it.

I have a picture of Verna taken around this time. She is
standing beside a Manitoba maple. It must be spring
because the leaves are not yet out. She is wearing thick
stockings, sensible shoes, a tweed coat, belted, a long
woollen scarf that shows at the neck and protrudes slightly
at the bottom of the coat, a knitted hat with a roll brim.
Not the sexiest of outfits. But her face is so happy. There is
not a trace of sadness in those eyes, and the smile can only
be called loving. Perhaps my father didn't take it. Perhaps
it wasn't her true love she was looking at when the picture
was taken. I still like to think it was.

Theirs was a fairly long engagement. They had to wait
for several years until they had some money saved and their
future home (and my birth home) was built. My father was
a good amateur carpenter and painter. He did a lot of the
inside work himself: built-in kitchen cupboards, painted
apple green; a built-in china cupboard in the living-dining

room, painted cream; built-in main bedroom clothes-cupboard, painted mauve – built-in everything was very modern and innovative.

Traditionally, women married young, had their children right away, and went on having them. My mother's age, twenty-six, was just about over the hill. But the war had disrupted the pattern of their ways. The men who survived came back and many had to learn a trade or profession, get a job, and somehow get back into the unhelpful system. Verna was twenty-eight, Bob thirty, when they married on July 25, 1924.

I was born two years after my parents married. Folk wisdom (folk folly, more likely) held that although a woman might go on bearing children for years and years, she had better have the first one before she was thirty. I myself was an inheritor of this skewed socio-medical misinformation. I believed it was absolutely necessary to have my first child before I turned thirty. In retrospect, thinking of all the women I have since known who bore their first children in their thirties or even early forties, this seems quite crazy. However, my mother had two miscarriages before she had me and I can imagine, given the misconceptions of the times, my parents' concern.

I was born on July 18, 1926, at the Neepawa General Hospital, at 7:30 a.m. on a Sunday. My mother must have felt, as I did when I had my own children, the truly miraculous nature of birth. A new human being. What an astounding process it is. My mother must have felt blessed, even as I in my time felt blessed by my children.

My mother and I were lucky. I often think, however, of the children born with birth defects. Their parents are by necessity heroes, caring for and loving their children, refusing to give up, coping somehow under stresses that I have never known and feeling, despite all the terrible difficulties, that their lives have been immeasurably enriched by the life of their child. Also feeling so often, or so I would imagine, that sense of being overwhelmed and defeated by the sheer awful presence of need: so much care, so much strength, when human strength even at its utmost is limited. I stand in awe of those victories of the human spirit, while at the same time I wonder at a society where the caring parents of disabled children, and the children themselves, are so inadequately helped.

Feeling so strongly and positively, as I do, about birth and parenthood, it could be asked why I then publicly support, as I also do, such causes as the Canadian Abortion Rights Action League (CARAL). I don't believe anyone, including myself, is pro-abortion. I am pro-choice because there are times when abortion is the least damaging course. Those who would give to the fertilized egg the same rights as a born child seem to me to have precious little regard for those children once they *are* born. Nor do the anti-abortionists show much concern over the rights and life of the mother. I have never met a woman who has had an abortion flippantly or easily or without searching her heart and her soul. No doubt such women do exist, but I believe they are in a small minority, and should be cared for, for their shadowed pain. As for the young girls – terrified children, really – who have been molested, subject to rape or incest, or simply, out of desperate need, have sought what they mistakenly believed to be love and caring, I think it is wicked to force them to bear the children of such frightening unions, of such traumatizing and wounding encounters. I do *not* think, of course, that abortion should be used as a form of birth control. But when children are forced to bear children, or the middle-aged woman, worn out with much childbearing and child-rearing, becomes pregnant again despite all care, or a young woman realizes she will have to raise a child alone with no help, financial, physical, or emotional, and cannot face that – in short, when a woman for any reason at all, and the reasons are many and never frivolous, feels she simply cannot bear the child she is carrying, I do not think she should be forced by a punitive, authoritarian society to do so.

Our society is all too willing to place a life sentence upon a woman for an unwanted pregnancy, to make her "go through with it," to tell her she can either have the child adopted or rear it herself for some eighteen years. Certainly, our mothers often had large families, often "went through with it." In the days of their youth they had no choice at all, and I am saying it is wrong not to have a choice.

I also feel it is wrong that only women are faced with this dilemma, while the mechanics of abortion and the research for safe, reliable birth control methods are largely in the hands of men, men for whom it is acceptable to have sexual experiences without the responsibility of caring for children. It has never been a recognized part of any culture for women to have the same right, to have sex without responsibility.

I do not accept any of this. I think it is outrageous that men are recognized as sexual beings whereas women are often left with either a burden of guilt over an abortion, or a burden of guilt over an adoption, or a burden not only of guilt but of eighteen and more years' work trying to raise a child alone with damn little help from anyone. In the years of my youth, young women who became pregnant were frequently helped by their families – correction, by their mothers. I knew more than one person who was reared by a grandmother whom she or he called "mother." This attitude – that women must be punished for having sex outside marriage, particularly if it results in a pregnancy, or that women must be punished for inadequate birth control methods – is almost as prevalent today as it was fifty years ago. The fires at the Morgentaler Clinic in Toronto, the bombing of various abortion clinics in America, the harassment of women entering these clinics – all these demonstrate to me not a concern for the sanctity of human life but, on the contrary, a deeply aggressive and punitive attitude towards women on the part of a basically male establishment.

This frightens me, but it also stirs me into action on behalf of all of us, all women. Naturally, I also believe that young people, girls and boys, should be given much better sex education and information on birth control and on the responsibilities of procreation. Better education on the realities of parenthood might make some young women think again before they take on the awesome task of parenthood.

My own mother was fortunate. She had a loving husband and was able to be a loving and devoted mother. As I look again at my baby book, I see that under the heading "First Conscious Notice" my mother wrote, "Noticed music." My little mother, the musician. She must have been delighted, and of course more aware of my alertness to music than to anything else. She was the only one in the family with a real talent for music. She studied with Eva Clare for a time, and I believe she gave a few concerts with Miss Clare in Winnipeg. Eva Clare, also from Neepawa, went on to become a distinguished pianist, studying in Berlin and New York. She ultimately became the first director of music for the University of Manitoba in 1937, and then director of the University School of Music, established in 1944, until her retirement in 1949. She never married. I'm certain my mother thought of herself as the luckier of the two. If she had lived, however, it is entirely possible she might have regretted her lost career in music. Even if she had tried to do everything – to be wife, mother, and professional musician – it would have been virtually impossible for her to have achieved professional status without wealth and a great deal of domestic help. A few women did succeed, of course, but given the demands of a concert career it seems unlikely that most women musicians or singers were able, in those days, to combine their careers with raising a family. If they had a vocation, they chose not to marry. Naturally I'm glad my mother chose to have me, but had

37

she lived to see me into adulthood, I can't see that she could have failed to feel some regrets for that other self of hers, her own self of music.

It is still enormously difficult for a woman to have both a marriage and a family, and a profession. I often become angry when I think of this injustice, of having to choose between the talent that was born in you, your lover / husband, and your children. What a terrible choice society has always forced upon women. For most women throughout history, there was in fact no choice. The poet in them was unvalued and unrecognized by their society. Milton spoke of "that one talent that is death to hide / Lodged with me useless." But it wasn't lodged with him useless. Difficult though it must have been, the blind poet sang. He dictated his greatest works to – who else? – his daughters.

A number of women of my generation have managed to do their own work and raise their children, not infrequently as single and breadwinning parents. I have done both myself, and I am profoundly grateful to have been able to do so. But it was accomplished at an enormous cost – a cost, I should add, borne not just by myself. Do I regret it, even sometimes? No, I cannot. I confess I wonder how gifted women who were silenced managed not to go mad. (Of course, some did, or took the more socially discreet route and became invalids.) And I can't help but wonder about my own mother, what course her life would have taken, what frustrations she might have had to hide or forget as she played the piano for herself, for friends, or at church concerts.

My mother's idealization of her perfect child, me, is amusing and touching. My "First Creeping" was "to reach a flower." Naturally, what else? Under "First Confession of Wrong-Doing" and "First Punishment" are conspicuous blanks. I should hope so. Can you imagine a young mother writing, "Baby confessed to poking dog in eye with baby spoon"? On the "First Christmas" page, underneath a bandy-legged, excessively pink, diapered baby holding a giant striped candy cane, my mother recorded that for my first Christmas I received yet another brush and comb set (I'd been given three when I was born) and a powder puff.

Among the pages is a yellowed envelope. In it are a few locks of pale brown-gold hair. Mine. In my own jewel box, among the very few remaining things there, is a lock of blonde hair, my daughter's, from when she was two. The harmless archives of love.

Of course I learn more about my young mother from this baby book than I do about myself. How I want to hear her own words, though. She writes, "At 1½ was very fond of listening to little rhymes. At twenty-two months knew several by herself." "At 2½ exceptionally fond of being read to." Echoes of a long-gone way of life are here too. At two years old, "Took her first motor trip (a distance of fifty miles) to Brandon, in August. Had her first picnic in September, 50 miles away and drank out of a lovely clear brook."

Fifty miles was a long way then. And in those days, children could safely drink out of brooks. I do not say this with any sentimental nostalgia. I say it with enormous rage and anger at the chemical pollution by commercial firms committed to making money (never mind anything else) that now makes it almost impossible for anyone to drink from or even bathe in natural waters. All this in the name of making a buck. Water killed. Earth killed. What will these men do with their money, when everything is dead around them? Mine was possibly the last generation of children to have known what it was to swim in rivers and lakes, to drink from brooks, to have known the land before it was ruined. I feel passionately that we must repair the damage before it is forever too late. But although I keep on, although I yell and roar, I suppose in my heart I sometimes believe it may well be too late. It is unconscionable. I feel so angry, so helpless. The whole earth *ruined* so that a few people can make something they call money. What a travesty. What a tragedy.

When I was a child, of course, I – and my parents – knew nothing of what was to come. I must, however, have learned the gift of the gab at quite a young age and my mother was obviously delighted: "At thirteen months trying to say practically everything." And "At two years, telling us she was crazy about beet greens."

The last entry in my mother's handwriting moves me the most of all. It is under the stunningly corny heading "Sayings of Baby." This page was used by my mother to jot down things over my first three and a half years of life. The last entries are:

Informed us she had a "bad little twinkle in her eye."
Said to her mother, in speaking of a bad night she had had: "Don't let's mention it, mummy."
A great imagination. Speaks a lot of her "funny" house, where Paper Slim, and Mr. and Mrs. Slim live, also sister Polly, of whom she speaks, and plays Three Bears a lot, with herself as Tiny, her mummy as Mammy Muff, and her daddy Father Bruin. Starts her stories always, "Once upon a time."

My mother must have seen pictures of me, like the one with my friend Mona at two (she just two weeks older than I), together in a box sleigh, wearing bulky coats and mittens and wool bonnets, mine down right around my eyes. Those two little kids, me and Mona, have known each other now for sixty years. I wish my mother had known that Mona and I would give support and caring to each other over our whole lives. I also have the snapshots of the Little House around that time, with its screened veranda, where I used to sleep sometimes in the heat of summer, and its flowers – all around it, my father's flower gardens, the gladioli, the geraniums, the portulaca, the sunflowers. I have always wondered if his passion for growing things, making things, recording houses and families in his photographs (in the days when not everyone took photographs) might partly have grown out of his young man's experience of death in the First World War. He was by nature a builder, not a destroyer.

For most of my knowledge of my mother, I had to rely on tales told to me by Mum and by my aunts Vem and Ruby. Mum never hesitated to talk about her and in fact referred to her as "your other mother." She was always a part of my life, even though Mum was my mother from the time I was four until she died when I was thirty-one. Mum told me once that Verna was sometimes so engrossed in playing with me when I was a baby that she forgot to make dinner for my dad.

I have always known how fortunate I was to have Mum bring me up, and how fortunate both my brother and myself were to have her there after our dad died, when Bob was only two and I nine. It must have been so hard for Verna, having to leave her child and husband and go into death. I used to think I was the unfortunate one, losing my mother when I was four. I see it slightly differently now that I have had my own children and have been able to see them grow into maturity. Now I grieve for her, for Verna, for her having to leave.

All the same, it is strange that the pain of her death, which I had long, long forgotten or thought buried too deeply ever to be touched again, surfaced in 1981. A very dear friend, Anne, who was like a young sister to me, died of cancer in her thirty-fifth year, leaving her husband Don and their five-year-old son, Daniel. I had seen her in hospital only the day before, and I knew she must soon die. I was in Toronto, staying as I usually do with Adele Wiseman and Dmitry Stone and their daughter Tamara. Annie's mother phoned me there to tell me. That, of course, would be the worst thing possible, the death of one's child. I can hardly believe how people find the strength to go on. I remember putting down the phone that morning, going to the kitchen and having coffee. I suddenly put my head on my folded arms and cried as though I could never stop.

Adele, Dmitry, and Tamara put their arms around me and comforted me. I was grieving for Anne, for Don and Daniel. And more than I could ever have believed possible I was grieving, I realized later, for my mother who also died at just about the same age, with a child almost the age of Daniel.

I mourn that young mother of mine still, and always will. Yet she passed on marvels to me. Humour. Music, although my music has been made with words. She danced on the earth, in her way, in the time that was given to her. Danced laughter, danced youth, danced love, danced hope in a child. She passed her dance on to me.

III
MARG

I don't remember a time when I didn't call her Mum. Even my one real memory of my own mother doesn't seem to negate this. But of course for the first four or five years of my life, she was my aunt Marg.

Margaret Campbell Simpson was born March 15, 1890, the third child of John and Jane Simpson. She had an older brother and sister, and subsequently two younger brothers and two sisters. No doubt she had to look after the young ones a lot. I suspect it was a role she never really cared for. I have a studio picture taken with her older sister, Ruby, and her younger sister, Verna, my mother. Margaret must have been about eight and Ruby ten, although Margaret is the taller. Verna, about two, is sitting in a wicker push-chair with huge, spindly back wheels and small front ones. She is smiling a bit shyly. Ruby and Margaret, both with their dark hair parted in the middle and falling in long ringlets, are wearing identical gingham dresses with high collars, lace-trimmed butterfly-like projections at the shoulders, long lace-edged cuffs, and sashes at the waist. Both girls have solemn expressions, but whereas Ruby looks slightly diffident, Margaret stares at the camera with wide-open eyes, as near to hostility as she dares.

Ruby, Margaret, Verna, and Vem were jointly known as the Simpson Girls. Margaret hated this label. She didn't want to be known as one of the Simpson Girls. She was always, in her own eyes, clearly herself and only herself. In another snapshot, however, there they are, the four of them together, Margaret, Verna, and Ruby as young women, Vem possibly twelve or thirteen. Everyone except Vem is wearing an enormous hat with feathers or artificial flowers. Vem wears a clumsy-looking woollen toque. All are clad in heavy winter coats and carry huge fur muffs. The Simpson Girls.

It took Margaret a while to get away, but she made it. When she graduated from high school in Neepawa, she got the highest marks in the province of Manitoba. She was obviously a likely candidate for university, but her father, John Simpson, didn't believe in education for women. Ruby and Vem ultimately became nurses. That was acceptable. Verna was allowed to study music for a time. But my grandfather couldn't see the use of a general arts course for a woman. Marg took teacher training instead.

She loved teaching, as it turned out, and ultimately took a teaching post in Calgary. I've often thought, though, that in another, later era she would have gone to university, stayed on for her master's and doctorate, and become a professor of English literature. She had a passionate and enduring interest in literature and a real love of education, of knowledge, of learning. She might have encouraged a whole new generation of women academics and scholars, as some of our finest women professors have done and are doing. Like some of them, she might also have struggled for the teaching of more books by women writers and by Canadians. In fact she had a lifelong interest in Canadian writing and gave enormous encouragement to the girl and young woman who was to become a Canadian novelist: myself.

When she was thirty, Marg went to Bermuda for a year's exchange teachership. A snapshot dated December 3, 1920, shows her in an ankle-length white dress and white shoes, smiling as she leans with one hand against the ringed trunk of a feathery palm tree. That year away must have been a great adventure, and an unusual step for a young woman from a small Canadian town. Her father undoubtedly ranted and stormed over her departure. I can just hear my grandmother saying in the placating way that I remember so well, "Now, John, now, John," her hands fluttering in distress.

With or without her father's blessing, Marg left for a year. She retained clear and colourful memories of Bermuda ever afterwards. When I was young, she would sometimes tell me of the markets, of her amazement at the foliage and flowers, the roads with no motorcars, the native women with their bright head scarves, taking their laundry to the river. I wish now I had asked her more about Bermuda, not just when I was growing up but also after I had lived for some years in Africa. What was her perception of the colonial regime? Did she hate it as much as I did, in another country so much later? It's unlikely, for she was never particularly aware of racism or of the oppression of colonialized people. I wish, too, that I had asked about what happened to her there, so far from home. Did she fall in love? I used to wonder, but I never asked.

Marg returned to Calgary and continued teaching there. Many years after she died, I found three inspectors' reports on her classwork, dated 1922-23, 1924-25, and 1928. She'd kept them carefully stashed away among her important papers. At the time of her death, I was too full of grief to want to read them, but when I finally did, I was astonished. I had always thought she had been a high-school teacher of English, simply because I don't recall her ever mentioning teaching anything else. Literature was her great interest. The 1922-23 report, however, is from the Victoria Prevocational School in Calgary, a school in which students apparently took only half a day's ordinary schooling, the other half being spent on "cooking, sewing, etc." Margaret Simpson taught Grade Eight girls spelling, writing, history, penmanship, composition, literature, arithmetic, and geography.

One of the inspectors of schools noted, "A number of the pupils are overage and are apparently retarded." Another commented, "Miss Simpson . . . is progressive in her viewpoint and inspires confidence on account of her grasp of her work . . . There is a definite effort being made to teach penmanship." (Alas, she never succeeded in teaching penmanship to either my brother or me.) "Teaching of literature seeks to bring out a literary appreciation." "Pupils are taught to think and to discuss the subjects with teacher."

Marg stayed at this school from 1921 to 1930, when she went back to Neepawa for the summer holidays. That was the summer my own mother died. Marg stayed on to look after me and did not return to teaching again. Just over a year later, she and my father were married. He was thirty-seven and she was forty-one. She told me, long afterwards, that they had gone to Brandon, Manitoba, to be married in a civil ceremony. She added, with that wry, somewhat bitter amusement so typical of her, that she was married in a green dress and that some of the good ladies of Neepawa had kindly informed her that green was an unlucky colour to be married in. More to the point, she said that some of the more religious (I use that word ironically) folk in the town maintained that in Christian practice, a man was not supposed to marry his deceased wife's sister. That kind of comment was always made oh so casually, or in the guise of someone else's remarks: "Of course, *I'd* never say this in a million years, Marg, but *some* people are saying it." It must have hurt her dreadfully, to the point where all these comments remained with her, even years after Dad had died. I remember with total clarity that when she told me, my reaction was a strong impulse to wring the necks of those self-appointed keepers of the community morals with my bare hands.

When Marg married my father, she had no engagement ring. She had a plain gold wedding ring, although my father later gave her a silver ring with a small sapphire and tiny diamonds, and a gold ring, yellow gold from India, containing a single, beautiful pearl, made from one of a pair of cuff-links that had come down to my father from his father

1. Great-grandmother Wemyss.

*2. Great-grandmother Wemyss, in
Scotland, with three of her children.
Grandfather Wemyss is on left.*

3. Great-grandparents,
D.H. Harrison and wife,
Grandmother Wemyss' parents.

4. My paternal
grandmother, Maggie
Harrison Wemyss.

5. Grandfather John
Wemyss at college in
Scotland.

6. *Jack Wemyss and my father, Bob Wemyss (right).*

7. *Jack Wemyss and Bob Wemyss (right) just after joining up in W.W.I.*

8. *Jack (left) and Bob Wemyss after they had fought in the trenches.*

9. *The Simpson girls – (left to right) Margaret, Verna, Ruby, Velma – c. 1913.*

10. *My mother, Verna Simpson, as a young woman.*

11. *Margaret Simpson, my stepmother, about age 16.*

12. *Myself at 5 months.*

13. *Four generations: Great-grandmother Wemyss, my dad, Grandmother Wemyss, and myself.*

14. My father, Bob Wemyss, 1932.

15. Grandfather John Simpson.

16. *Myself (left) and my friend Mona, both of us about 2 years old.*

17. *Myself, age 6, on my first day of school.*

18. *Mum, myself, and Dad, 1933.*

19. *My brother, Robert, in his highchair, and myself, 1933.*

20. *Myself, my brother, Bob, and Rufty, 1939.*

and had belonged to Sir John Wemyss. She never wore Verna's diamond engagement ring, but she gave it to me in 1947 when I became engaged.

She told me when I was older that she and my dad were so pleased and relieved, not to say grateful, when at about five I began naturally, without prompting, to call her Mum. I cannot say that Mum stepped into the vacuum left by my mother's death. A measure of my own pain and bewilderment is that total gap in my memory of at least one year. She was familiar, I knew her as my aunt, and, after a while, she became Mum to me. She was rightly described, in one of the school inspectors' reports, as being progressive in her viewpoint. Never did she close off my sense of my own mother, never did she pretend that mother had never been. That year, between my mother's death and the time I naturally began to call my aunt Mum, must have been hard for her. I probably had bad dreams. Likely I was difficult in many ways. I probably kicked up fusses that were an expression of my pain and inability to absorb the enormity of what had happened to me. I did know the finality of death, though. I knew I would not see my mother again. No one had to tell me. Frankly, given all the deaths in my family, I think it is a miracle I'm as steady as I am. The miracle, of course, was a gift given to me by my stepmother, by Marg, by Mum, who quit her teaching and came back to look after me, and then to look after both my brother and me for so many years after our dad died.

I can only guess at how she felt. I know she loved me, her sister's child. I also know she had been committed to her own life, to teaching. Her marriage to my father couldn't have been love's young dream, as Verna's marriage was. Bob was a young lawyer, left alone with a four-year-old daughter. He needed support and help. Margaret Simpson gave it. She gave up a lot for that. She was not simply a teacher, her vocation was teaching. At forty, she probably wasn't expecting to marry. She was an intelligent woman who couldn't pretend to be otherwise. It was a problem she shared with my other aunts, Ruby and Vem, the nurses – Ruby, who never did marry, and Vem, the youngest, who married quite late and never had children.

I imagine Bob and Marg living in the same house, the Little House, for a year, he sleeping in the bedroom where he and Verna had slept and she in the little back bedroom, me in my attic room. I imagine them saying after about a year, "This is ridiculous. We'd better get married." It may not have been a marriage of youth, but I don't believe it was a marriage of convenience either. After Verna's death, they must have comforted each other and come to know each other. I like to think of their marriage as a marriage of comrades. I was the unknowing catalyst whom they both loved and for whom they wanted the best, but they liked each other and could talk together. They joined in a marriage that was marked both by mutual need and by mutual respect and deep affection. Mum once said to me, when I myself was about to get married, "Your father was a kind man. Kindness is a valuable quality. We don't see too much of it." They were kind to each other. They married not just to look after me but to look after each other.

I have often wondered why tales and jokes about wicked stepmothers are so much a part of our culture. They are such a putdown of women who, like Mum, take on the sometimes difficult role of loving and caring for children not their own. Is it to assign a lowly place to a woman who has not borne children herself? Or is it perhaps to say that only a birth mother can really be brought under society's control because a stepmother may be a more independent woman?

In fact, in my eyes, Mum was never my stepmother. She was just my Mum. In a picture taken before my brother was born, when I was about six, the three of us are sitting on the chesterfield in the Little House. I'm between them. Mum looks serious and Dad a bit amused, a cigarette-holder in his left hand. The end table holds books propped up with brass book-ends, and behind the table, a lamp is shining down on us. My expression is interested, even studious, as Mum and I peer at a book together. The pictures taken earlier, about a year after my own mother died, are quite different. One shows me with my dad, his arm around my shoulder, me small and sad in the garden at the Little House. In another, of grandmother Wemyss, Dad, and me, I'm still not smiling. Shortly after Mum and Dad married, the pictures change. In those pictures, I am a perfect little poser but I'm always grinning quite self-consciously. Here I am on the lawn of the Little House, wearing a white frilly hat and a short embroidered white dress, holding a book in my hand. A book! What a small phoney. And here I am again, swanky in white overalls and skipper's cap, about to trundle off with my four-wheel wagon.

Dad kept on taking snapshots. One I'm fond of shows me and Mum around 1932, standing beside one of the old barnstormer planes. These tiny planes used to come to the country fairs and take people up for rides at about fifty cents a whirl. Up and around, over the fairgrounds, and down again in fifteen minutes. In the photograph, the pilot with his leather cap is sitting in the cockpit of the biplane. Mum is holding her hair against the wind with one hand. I'm next to her, a little kid in a short dress and coat, white socks and black-buttoned shoes, who's just had her first flight. The picture reminds me of the time my own son was about five and I took him up the Grouse Mountain chairlift in Vancouver, our legs dangling and unsupported, miles above the forests. I clung to my young son, terrified, while David said cheerily, "This is the happiest day of my life," then, turning to me in puzzlement, "Why have you got your eyes closed, Mum?" My Mum probably felt the same.

Another picture I like was taken on my first day at school. I'm standing outside the door of our house, neatly turned out in a short little dress, white socks, black shoes, a woollen tam, my straight hair held by a barrette, clutching a notebook under one arm. I look shy and hesitant. In fact, as family legend has it, I had been sick, having eaten some green tomatoes the day before. Maybe tomatoes, maybe nervousness. I managed to survive my first day at school, however. My one memory of the event is that I was pretty annoyed I didn't learn how to read after one whole day.

My brother, Robert Morrison Wemyss, was born in May 1933, and was named after our dad. I had been an only child for seven years. A baby brother! I was over-joyed. Overjoyed, that is, until I realized that a baby is a demanding creature, and that your mum has to spend a lot of time looking after this kid. You're not the only one around any more and your mum worries about the slightest thing having to do with this baby. He is *her* baby. She thinks he's great, so you look at him. Gee, he really is swell. Look at those tiny fingers and toes and his cute grin. You have mixed feelings. I was glad to have a baby brother, but I had been used to having centre stage. How come, I must have thought, I have to share everything? Precious, adorable me and this kid, so admired by one and all. Mum might have been more nervous about him when he was a baby than she would have been if she had been a younger mother. She was in her early forties when he was born, after all. Yet every concerned mother has to think first of the well-being and safety of the youngest child. I've done so myself. Never, however, do I recall feeling that she loved me any less because of Bob. I have passed her mes-sage on to my own children: love is not a loaf of bread. If you give a lot to one person, there's still just as much for another.

Only once do I recall doing something really mean to my baby brother, though there must have been quite a few other times. He was outside the Little House in his baby carriage and I was put on guard for a few minutes while Mum got organized to go out. I looked at my adorable baby brother and I pinched him, hard. Naturally, he roared. Mum came tearing out of the house. "What's the matter, is Bobby all right? Peggy, what's happened?" I leaned nonchalantly against the wicker baby carriage. "Gee, I don't know." She never questioned me.

When I was a mother of young children, I was a worried mother too. You care so much. You want everything for your kids to be fine. And of course you can't promise or guarantee that. You can't make it happen. It was only when I had my own children that I could understand Mum's nervousness and her fright as an adjunct of her love for me and Bob. In our early childhood, though, she didn't have much to worry about. We were in many ways happy, privileged kids. A picture of us when I was eight and Bob was one shows me in my wrinkled tunic and sweater, my straight hair cut short, standing beside my kid brother in his high chair. Bob is encased in layers of woollen clothes. We're both beaming, our eyes full of laughter.

That picture must have been taken in 1934, the year we moved into the big red-brick house, the Wemyss house, Dad, Mum, me, and Bob. The Little House had become too little. My grandmother Wemyss had recently moved to Winnipeg to live with her daughter, Norma. We were only in that house for just over a year and a half and I was glad to leave. I never liked it much. It was too large, too imposing – our father's house, not really ours.

The house had been built by John Wemyss in the late 1800s and by the time we moved into it, it needed quite a few repairs. My best friend Mona and I, two small girls, used to watch closely while a young man from the north end of town, a Ukrainian, repaired drains and eaves-troughs. Mona and I stood beside him, admiring him, his physical strength and his know-how, wanting him to notice us, to admire us. Unfortunately, brainwashed as we had been, not by our parents particularly but by the stratified society in which we had grown up, we tried to get his attention in a horrifying way. "Hunky, hunky, hunky," we chanted to this Ukrainian boy from the other side of the tracks, one of the people whose parents and grandparents had come to Canada at the beginning of the century, as Mona's Irish and my Scots ancestors had. What repulsive little kids. What a lot we had to learn and overcome. He looked at us very, very straight and said, "Don't you ever say that again." I don't think we ever did.

The front of the Wemyss house was covered with Virginia creeper. Upstairs, there was a rose window, round, with strange coloured-glass patterns, and the front door had set in it a pane of glass with wonderful colours. My brother's and my bedrooms were at the back of the house, our parents' bedroom at the front. The house seemed very grand to my eight-year-old eyes. Mum, of course, had to cope with the huge, old-fashioned kitchen, which originally had been staffed by servants. No servants in our days, although occasionally we had so-called hired girls from farms. One was Scots, a Salvation Army lassie, who loved my little brother and taught him and me a lot of the old hymns. I still remember Scotty belting out:

> Will your anchor hold in the storms of life?
> When the winds unfold their wings of strife,
> When the strong tides lift and the cables strain,
> Will your anchor drift or firm remain?

I don't imagine Mum was quite so thankful about all this loudly proclaimed religion. She counted herself a Christian, but didn't think it suitable to announce it quite so flamboyantly.

The living room in the Wemyss house was more or less out of bounds to Bob and me. It was there that our mother held her afternoon teas. In those days, teas had to be given by women of the community at regular intervals. Bob was too little to know about the mysteries of afternoon teas, but I was old enough to notice the four kinds of sandwiches and six kinds of cake that had to be offered. I would glimpse the ladies, sitting in the living room with the Chinese carpets and the antique furniture and the chairs that no kid was supposed to sit on.

54

The study was Dad's, but we used it much more than we ever used the big living room. It had a fireplace and bookshelves holding all Dad's *National Geographic* magazines. Over the mantelpiece hung a bronze curved sword, sent from India to Scotland and then to Canada by some distant Wemyss ancestor.

The one Christmas we spent in the Wemyss house was the last Christmas I had with my father and it was quite marvellous. It was during the Depression, when no one had any money. Dad had always liked to do woodwork and fix up old furniture. My gift that Christmas was my first desk, a tiny one. He had found it in the attic and had repaired and painted it turquoise-blue for me. It was possibly the most beloved desk I have ever owned. It had chains on either side that let down the writing board and pigeonholes to hold important stuff. My brother's present was a rocking-horse Dad had made himself, with a seat in the middle flanked by wooden horses painted cream and flecked with green. Bob loved it.

On January 13, 1935, our father Robert Wemyss died of pneumonia. I have written about this in a story called "A Bird in the House." The story is fiction, but in that particular story, fiction follows facts pretty closely. It was a flu epidemic. One week after Dad died, Mum's eldest brother, Stuart Simpson, died, also of pneumonia. He was survived by his widow, Bertha, and their daughter, my cousin Catherine. Mum had been married less than five years and was left with two children to bring up alone. It must have been unbelievably hard.

My father had been sick for only a few days when I asked Mum one evening if I could sleep with her. I was uneasy. She was sleeping in the guest room and I didn't know why. She agreed. Dad was in his and Mum's room, attended by two of our local doctors. When I woke up in the middle of the night, my mother was crying, and I knew my father was dead.

I remember in the days that followed feeling very helpless. I was only nine but I wanted to protect Mum, somehow to protect her against – against what? Maybe against the sympathetic community. I remember being angry at the minister who came to give his condolences and support. It has taken me many years to come to see how difficult it must be for ministers to try to comfort people. How can anyone say with any conviction that the death of a beloved person was wanted by God? I feel sorry now for my young and ignorant anger at that minister, who really couldn't comfort Mum even though I'm sure he wanted to and certainly tried. I've written about this aspect of faith a number of times, about ministers who, under certain circumstances, despite their own efforts, even despite God's grace, perhaps, find they cannot minister. And yet they may minister more than they know. All I knew when I was nine was that my dad had died, my Mum was bereft, and my brother was still just a baby, too young, really, to understand. It was difficult to return to school and be stared at by the other kids, and hard to have to accept my teacher's expression of sympathy. I was desperately afraid of crying and so must have seemed merely sullen and withdrawn. When my piano teacher said how sorry she had been to hear about my father, I just ignored her. That surly, often angry mask was my only defence. I could not, would not break up. I and Mum had to carry on somehow. I have very few other memories of that time, apart from not wanting to let Mum out of my sight. I remember the two of us together. I don't remember very much about anybody else.

We didn't stay in the big red-brick house for long, but we were still there when the polio epidemic happened. Perhaps I make this sound as though my childhood years were rife with medieval plague, death right, left, and centre. It wasn't like that at all, of course. I remember a lot of very happy things. In fact, none of us kids were alarmed by the polio epidemic. Our mothers sprayed our throats daily with a bitter-tasting yellow concoction that was supposed to prevent the disease but I'm sure was totally ineffectual. Its only real virtue was that it gave our mothers some sense of protecting their children against what was then called infantile paralysis. Those who survived were nearly always crippled for life. Mum must have been terribly frightened. First her husband and her eldest brother died of pneumonia and now this disease threatened her children.

Our neighbours on the other side of the giant birch tree in our garden had two sons who were only a few years older than I. They were mean kids, or at least mean to girls. I recall virtually all the boys I went to primary school with as being mean and cruel. They were probably just shy, scared of girls, brought up in families who put a high premium on male strength and dominance. Little boys didn't cry in my town; they played hockey instead. Girls were supposed to behave like natural victims and accept their meanness. Mum had helped give me a fighting spirit, as had my aunts, but it was difficult nonetheless. Girls and women were trained to want people to like them, but sometimes I had to wage a kind of war against the two boys next door, when they threatened me and my perch in the birch tree. And they did, with mockery and the threat, rarely carried out, of physical harm.

I had learned something, however, from my father's death. Sometimes your pain is so great, although possibly unacknowledged, that you have nothing to lose; you are fearless because you don't care what anyone says or does to you. In my own life, I have rarely known what it was to have nothing to lose. I am not by nature a revolutionary but rather a natural-born reformer. I realize that if I had been born a black woman in South Africa, I would feel differently about my passionate belief in non-violence. I have never resolved this and I think I never will. Some of my ambivalence goes back to the seemingly trivial, but to me important, time in my childhood when the boys next door seemed very cruel. I didn't attack them or retaliate physically. How could I? I was younger and I was a girl. But I had a kind of burning fury that was sometimes enough to scare the two of them off. Then one of them, Gavin, got infantile paralysis and died.

I remember how I felt, exactly. I had been afraid of those kids and had managed to drive them off, but I wouldn't have wished or imagined either of them dead. Kids like me didn't die. But they did. They do. I had scared Gavin away and he had died. It was a great shock.

Somehow this incident is linked in my mind with my mother selling the Wemyss house. It was bought by a local doctor and his family, who really didn't care about the house. They had it covered with yellow stucco. It made me very angry. I had no right to be angry. It was no longer our house and in any event, I hadn't actually loved that house at all. I loved the garden but not the house itself. But I vented my bewilderment and rage at fate by refusing ever to walk down that street in Neepawa again.

In fact I was glad when we moved back to the Little House. I got my favourite attic room back and installed my blue desk in the corner where it had always belonged. Things could never be the same, though, even in this beloved house. We were fewer now. There was just Mum and Bob and me.

Mum must have had endless financial worries, on top of dealing with her grief. She was committed, now, to raising two children alone. She had moral support from her own mother and her sisters and from close friends. A network of helpful women existed in the town, and no doubt without them life would have been much more difficult, but it was hard enough as it was. I was aware of this. In those days, middle-class children were popularly believed to be incapable of understanding the woes of the world until they were eighteen, a ridiculous underestimation of children's intelligence and perceptions. Mum protected me from financial worries, but I instinctively understood the situation of a woman who had lost a sister only a few years before, had married, had taken on the responsibility of raising her sister's child, had had a son, had grown to love her husband, had lost both her husband and a brother in a single month, and who was left alone with us, with me and Bob.

Although we were hard up, we weren't in any sense as hard up as many. Mum worried, though, for the rest of her life, but despite her real concerns, she remained vitally interested in life and in books. She had a keen mind and a witty one. Our house was never shrouded in gloom. Mum wasn't about to give up. Much of her pain she kept to herself and it was only because children do have a kind of sixth sense that I knew of it. Like all the Simpsons, however, including myself, she was a fairly volatile person. Her concern for Bob and me could, under stress, boil over into anger. She may have been essentially an intellectual, but she was also emotional and could yell at her recalcitrant kids with vigour and even venom, chastising us for being so difficult. Once, when I was talking too loudly, she told me I had a "carrying voice." She could summon up a pretty good carrying voice herself. Even deadlier were her quiet sermons when things became so rough that yelling wouldn't cut any ice. Any time she bawled me out for misdemeanours, however, or for the sheer bloody-mindedness in which I specialized when I was young, it was done with correct grammar and no vulgarisms of speech. She had been a high-school teacher, after all. She had a saying she lived by and that I tried to use in bringing up my own children: "Let not the sun go down upon your wrath." Parents do get angry at their children, and children at their parents. Life can be abrasive. Often we strike out at whoever is handiest or whoever is least able to hit back. We do indeed hurt those whom we most love. It's important, though, to say we're sorry if we've been angry or unreasonable. My Mum had that one rule, and we always kept it. It might have been difficult to talk about what was bothering us, but we always made up before the day was done. She never left us comfortless at night when we were children. She may not always have liked what we did, but she loved us without qualification.

I recall much of my childhood as being basically very happy. There were many diversions that have since disappeared and that might seem pretty simplistic now, I guess. Those were the days of the radio serials. We all had Little Orphan Annie secret codes and badges and rings and other enchanting junk. We also had the Big Little Books. My particular gang used to make up our own codes and our own hand-sewn books. We had secret hiding places and buried treasures. One of my possessions I remember with great pleasure is a gift that Miss Johnson, the superintendent of the Neepawa hospital and a great friend of our family, gave me. It was a child's first-aid kit, fitted into a big old square wooden cigar box. She'd painted the box red with a white cross on the top. It held real stuff from the hospital: rolls of bandages, absorbent cotton, scissors, a thermometer, Mercurochrome, which was later proven to be only slightly more efficacious than vanilla but which had a reassuringly violent crimson colour. Mona and I and our friends made great use of this kit in our games. At this point, my ambition was to be a nurse, and naturally I needed no persuasion to treat the slightest scratch on my young brother or my friends.

Miss Johnson also got the local carpenter to make me a child-size tool bench, complete with a vise. She had furnished it with simple, basic tools – screwdrivers, hammer, pliers, fret saw, coping saw, and the like. Girls were supposed to be strictly interested in dolls, but I wasn't alone in my love of carpentry. Some of my friends thought it was more exciting to make things than to play with dolls. Only later, in high school, were we expected to toe the line and happily labour over a stove in the Home Ec room while the boys learned how to use a lathe in Shop. I loved that tool bench. I turned out a number of bread boards in the shape of a portly and simplified pig and made gaily painted scenes from what I imagined to be life in other countries – a Dutch windmill, a Chinese pagoda – my imagination tearing around a world that I had not yet seen. I was writing, too, all the time. Clumsy, sentimental poetry, funny verses, stories, and once a highly uninformed but jubilantly imaginative journal of Captain John Ball and his voyages to exotic lands, complete with maps made by me of strange, mythical places.

At about eleven, I got my first two-wheeled bike, bought second-hand from Bert Batchelor, the milkman and a great buddy of mine. His daughter had outgrown it. I walked out the several miles to his farm to pick it up and Bert showed me how to ride it. I practised around the yard a few wobbly times. Then he pointed me in the right direction, gave me a little shove, and I was off. No one has ever learned to ride a bike more quickly. By the time I reached home, I had pretty well mastered the art. What I had forgotten, though, was how to stop, but a ditch near our house solved the problem. One of my knees bears the scars to this day. That was more or less the way my dad had taught me to swim when I was just a tad. He had taken me into the shallow water in Clear Lake, supported me with his hands for a minute or so, then removed his hands and said, "Okay, now swim." He was not an unkind man, quite the contrary. He simply thought that was how you taught kids to swim, and I must say it worked.

Around the time I acquired my bike, I also had my first long train trip to Toronto. Aunt Ruby was going to a conference in Quebec, so she stayed with me until she had to change trains. From then on, I was on my own, all the way to Toronto, where my aunt Norma and uncle Mord met me and took me to their home in Newmarket. Almost all Canadians of my age and older have had a lifelong love affair with the railways. The long steel was what would carry us out of innumerable ruts in small towns during the Depression, into what we imagined to be the vast glamour and ease of other places, other lives. For a child, that first overnight trip fulfilled every expectation of excitement. Meals in the dining car, the porter making up the bed at night, the dizzy climb on the portable ladder to the upper berth. What if you had to go to the bathroom in the middle of the night? The steady clank, clank, clickety-clank of the wheels, stopping at mysterious stations and finding they looked just like the one in your own home town. More land and water than you had ever dreamed might exist, and the awesome thought that Winnipeg to Toronto was only a part of the entire journey across your vast country.

I was glad to be going to see my aunt Norma, my father's sister. She was a connection to my father. I remember her warmth and how she loved to tell funny family tales. I felt something near reverence for my uncle Mord, who had been one of the famed bush pilots in northern Manitoba. During that visit my little cousin Terry, who was just about my brother's age, unwittingly helped me not to feel homesick or nervous, especially since we all had to cope with the somewhat stern and commanding, not to say demanding, presence of my grandmother Wemyss. I remember, too, that we saw two car accidents on the way back to Newmarket. My aunt was terrified that the bodies and blood would mark Terry and me for life. We sped on, but it didn't seem real to me at all. Only deaths in the family seemed real.

In May 1936, grandmother Simpson died. She had been ill and my mother had been looking after her at the Big House. I went over one day after school. As I reached the veranda, my grandfather came out. He said, "Peggy, she's dead." I couldn't take it in for a moment. What shocked me terribly was that grandfather Simpson was crying. I had never seen him cry before. I don't think I had believed it possible.

For Mum, this latest death must have been almost unbearable. Grandmother Simpson had been a very religious person. I don't mean she was a proselytizer. She quite simply lived by her faith. She was gentle and, I used to think as a child, docile, because she never argued with Grandfather. I see now that was wrong. It would have been futile to argue with him. In his opinion, there was only one point of view – his. All else was heresy. She was far from spineless, however. She must have listened patiently to her husband's diatribes and then gone on and done things according to her own conscience. She also must have had her ways of communicating strength and passing it on to her daughters, for they loved her greatly and were indeed strong themselves.

For reasons of practicality and finances, my mother and brother and I moved to the Big House. I don't suppose we could have afforded a housekeeper for grandfather Simpson, but even if we had been able to buy such a luxury, I can't imagine any person in the world willing to be housekeeper to that irascible old man. Mum, of course, had no choice. So we moved again.

I felt very odd about that move. I had loved that house all my life, but it was for visiting, not for living in. It was my grandfather's stronghold and he ruled it like Agamemnon ruling Mycenae or Jehovah ruling the world. It had its secret corners, its fascinations, but it was his domain, not mine. It did become mine, in time. We moved there when I was ten and it was there I lived until I left home for college, eight years later. In fact when I think of my childhood home, it is that one more than any other that comes to mind.

Years before, when I was a small child, my father had built me a play-house. It wasn't a tiny little Peter-Pan-and-Wendy effort. This was the real thing. It had a sloped roof and was about the size of a largish woodshed, big enough for an adult to stand up straight in. Dad had even equipped it with windows that opened and window boxes planted with various perennials, plants that later died, I regret to say, under my negligent care. The play-house had moved with us to the Wemyss house and again, after Dad's death, back to the Little House. Now it moved to the Big House of my grandfather Simpson. I really was too old for a play-house, but the little building was set in the back-yard, beside the high, grey-weathered wooden fence that separated Grandfather's property from his neighbour's and just beyond the huge and lengthy woodpile, Grandfather's pride, that stood in three straight, military-like ranks, the long cordwood sticks of poplar and birch for the furnace, the shorter stove wood, and the kindling for the kitchen range.

At the Big House, my play-house changed its function. It became my study, my refuge, my own private place. Even in winter, although the little shack wasn't heated, I used to go there to brood upon life's injustices, to work off anger, or simply to think and dream. In summer, I would climb up to the roof and lie there, hidden from view by the big branches of the huge spruce trees that bent over the gently sloping roof, and read for hours. It was there that I read Arthur Conan Doyle's *The White Company,* Kipling's *Kim,* Robert Louis Stevenson's *Treasure Island* and *Kidnapped,* Mark Twain's *Huckleberry Finn.* I didn't entirely spurn girls' books – I loved L.M. Montgomery's *Anne of Green Gables* and *Emily of New Moon* – but a lot of girls' books of that and an earlier era, my mother's and aunts' old books, were just plain awful. In fact, I read quite indiscriminately, including the romances of Ethel M. Dell and a syrupy tale called *Cecelia of the Pink Roses.* I read anything I could get my hands on: Dickens, Gene Stratton-Porter's *A Girl of the Limberlost* and *Laddie,* over which I wept, while Mum gently suggested that some people considered it rather sentimental. My favourites were adventure stories. I don't think it ever occurred to me that such adventures could never happen to me, a girl. I never pretended, in fantasy, to be a boy. I saw myself as myself, doing deeds of high bravery on the high seas and the low moors. I was the female version of Alan Breck. Yet what a pity that the girls of my generation had so few women role models in fiction who were bold and daring in life and work.

An activity that I found far less thrilling than reading was piano lessons. I really had no musical aptitude whatsoever, but my mother conceived the brilliant notion that if I didn't wish to play the piano, perhaps I would fare better with the violin. A strange, rather touching couple had come to town, advertising lessons in both guitar and violin. The lady was young and shy and white, the man was handsome and dashing and what used to be called mulatto. The group music lessons were given in the Oddfellows' Hall on Tuesday and Thursday evenings. Individual lessons could be arranged. The teachers drove all the way from Brandon twice a week so lessons in winter could not, I imagine, have been guaranteed. Prairie people are optimists, though, and in spring prefer not to believe that winter will indeed return with its impassable, snowed-in roads. Numerous kids' parents signed them up for guitar lessons. Country-and-western was called cowboy music then, and this was what these budding guitarists wanted to learn to play. Alas for the teacher, who wanted to teach them classical guitar, in which their interest was somewhat less than zero. He felt hurt and so did his young wife, who did piano accompaniment when required but otherwise did not herself teach. After a time, or so Mona reported to me – she was one of the guitar sign-ups – he gave up and taught them "The Old Chisholm Trail" and "The Yellow Rose of Texas." Often, however, his genuine love of what were to him the pure aspects of music broke through and he would wistfully try to impart some of it to these little prairie sow-thistles who wouldn't have known a flamenco from a wiener roast.

Mum considered the guitar vulgar. I was the only one who signed up for violin. Oh, the mortification! I took my weekly lesson alone in the vast emptiness of the Oddfellows' Hall, the chairs stacked around the walls. My adamant Mum bought me a cheap violin and an adjustable music stand. I practised the Minuet in G standing in our living room, squinting at the music (I didn't yet have glasses and lied about my poor eyesight). I would try to quiver my left wrist to achieve what I believe is called vibrato. The sounds that ensued must have been ear-boggling.

I hated that damned violin, but what kept me from saying so was that my Mum put such stock in my learning how to play. I wasn't so stupid that I didn't know why. I knew her real need was to give me every opportunity – oh dire phrase – to show I had inherited my other mother's musical talents. I also didn't want to hurt the young couple's feelings, the teachers. Their pupils in the guitar class rapidly dropped off. They needed the money, and you didn't have to be adult or very perceptive to realize such things. It wasn't that I was a young philanthropist or a musical martyr, but I couldn't bring myself to reject a couple who were obviously true music lovers, who wanted to communicate this love to prairie children, and who were also obviously hard up. Her dowdy clothes, his well-pressed serge suit, shiny with wear. They had their dream: to do what they loved best and earn a living while doing it. How could you tell them it was no go? I had no idea. I felt guilty, embarrassed, and furious by turns.

Then winter descended. By that time I was the only pupil left, and the weekly drive from Brandon wasn't worth the couple of bucks my Mum paid for the lesson. The young couple reluctantly gave up on Neepawa. Mum, however, did not give up. She found that one of the local jewellers played violin very well and asked him if he could continue to give me lessons. He agreed. All that winter I trudged over to his house, feeling idiotic as I struggled through simple classical pieces adapted for beginners.

Spring came. I retreated as often as possible to another refuge I had found, the loft of what had once been the stable on my grandfather's place and had then become the garage, housing his old McLaughlin Buick until he became too old to drive it and it too old to be driven. There was an outside staircase to this loft, and I had discovered that I could hide away better there than in the play-house. It was more inaccessible to the adult eye. I used to cheat on my violin practice and whip up to the loft, where I kept my five-cent scribblers in which I was writing a novel entitled "The Pillars of the Nation." I don't know when I decided on a confrontation with my Mum. It must have been during my first year in high school because, for that one year, I was a truly undistinguished member of the collegiate orchestra of which there were, I think, six members. I had joined in the hope of becoming socially acceptable. One day I confessed to Mum that I really wasn't interested in the violin; in fact I hated it, I wanted to quit. All I was interested in was writing. She accepted it. Maybe she even welcomed it. She had done her best by her dead sister. I had shown I was not musically inclined. From that time on, I think she could accept without guilt that my chief interest was very close to her own. Writing was where she could help me the most and, over many years, she did. The end of my music lessons marked the beginning of her realization that writing might be the important area of my spirit.

The loft was not just a retreat for me. It was also a theatre, a stage. I had read Willa Cather's *Shadows on the Rock* and *Death Comes for the Archbishop,* both given to me by Mum. The loft became a kind of forbidden theatre. It was because of Willa Cather and my fascination with the apothecary in *Shadows on the Rock* that I decided to grow herbs, but it must have been because of my canny Scots background that I decided to market them. I grew sweet basil, sage, summer savory, borage, horehound, dill. My grandfather's house had a huge garden at the back in which

I worked as little as possible, but the herbs were different. I dried them in big bunches strung up on the rafters in the loft and when they were dry, I crumbled them and bottled them in jars with tops I had painted a deep rose, with labels devised by myself. I sold them for moderate prices, mostly to my mother's friends. It was my first and only venture into sales. I also looked up herbs in the Encyclopaedia Brittanica and discovered some of their medicinal uses. For a while, I entreated my Mum and young brother to swallow horrendous concoctions of sage tea as a cure for colds. They never took to it very kindly.

In summer, I used to write up in my loft, leaving the little door open for light and filling scribblers with stories, one of which I recall took place in a nineteenth-century inn in Quebec, a place and time about which I could scarcely have known less. Inspired again by *Shadows on the Rock,* I constructed, as I fancied, an apothecary shop in the loft. Sometimes I managed to recruit Mona and one or two others to play this fascinating game. We had jars of dried herbs on the makeshift shelves, plus jars of cheap, one-cent candies, bought with my meagre allowance, old candleholders, small brass postal scales that I'd found in the attic, an assortment of old chairs and apple boxes, and various other treasures. The loft was very dark, having no windows, and was suitably spooky. We were, of course, forbidden to have candles there. If the place caught fire, as my grandfather rightly pointed out, it would go up like tinder. We naturally ignored this order and regularly lit candles until one day my grandfather invaded the sanctuary and discovered the candle stubs. He raged for days. After that, it was nothing but flashlights.

We had a number of so-called hired girls at the Big House in those days, among whom was a strapping Ukrainian girl from Riding Mountain who knew how to work a ouija board and scared me half to death by making a small table tap with messages from the beyond. She also knew how to use fresh, light snow as a substitute for eggs in a cake. I developed jaundice at one point and was confined to bed for nearly a month. She would lift me up in her arms and carry me downstairs so I could lie on the chesterfield and listen to the radio. Many illnesses were nursed or treated at home. I had my tonsils out in hospital, but when I needed to have my adenoids out, the doctor did it in my bedroom, unassisted. I can still feel my terror and queasiness beforehand, as I lied that I had to go to the bathroom one more time in order to postpone, for another five minutes, the dreadful descent of the chloroform mask over my face.

During the first year in the Big House, there must have been a lot of suppressed unhappiness and bewilderment in my mind. I used to walk in my sleep sometimes, and woke one night to find myself beside the linen cupboard at the end of the hall, taking out a clean sheet. I've never forgotten that feeling of panic as I wakened and thought that perhaps I was going mad. We had very little money and Mum was constantly worried. She had close friends, but she must have felt dreadfully alone, responsible for two children and an old, very difficult father. I overheard her saying on more than one occasion to one of my aunts or to a friend, "He'll outlive me." There was such desolation in her voice that I could hardly bear it. I had fantasies of becoming rich and famous (in a pinch, rich would do) and saving my mother from anxiety forever. I felt helpless and sad or silently angry a great deal of the time.

There were many compensations, however. I needed and did have an unusual amount of privacy in order to think and write. I had my special places for this – the play-house, the loft, my own bedroom. My bedroom had been my grandmother Simpson's and at first I felt strange there. But Mum had it repapered and I chose the paper myself, a soft green patterned with apple blossoms. She moved the heavy old furniture out and found a little dressing table with a mirror. There was also a bedside table and another table with drawers that served as my desk, for I had outgrown my first small desk. These she painted white. I had a low bookcase under the bay window on top of which I placed an old bathroom medicine cabinet, also painted white, in which I kept my best treasures: the clothespeg dolls I had made, a small *cloisonné* jar, a blue glass Cinderella slipper that had been my other mother's, a pair of real Chinese lady's shoes, tiny and embroidered, set upon rope and plaster platforms, that my great-uncle George had brought from China, a white bookmark enclosed in a blue ribbon with the cross-stitched words "No cross, no crown," and some old diaries and letters that had belonged to my grandfather Wemyss.

There was a small room off mine that once had served as a dressing room to the master bedroom. In my time, it contained a couch. We called it a Toronto couch and it could be used as a bed. There was also a dresser and a cupboard excitingly full of old books, many of which had been my mother's, aunts', and uncles' when they were young. It included, which I'm sure Mum wasn't aware, two texts called *What Every Young Married Man Should Know* and *What Every Young Married Woman Should Know*. From these I gained my first "scientific" knowledge of sex. I still recall one sentence from the young married woman book: "Fortunately for the survival of the race and of civilized society, women do not need to feel any physical interest in sex." Even at that tender age, I suspected the writer of the manual, a man of course, might be wrong on one or two points.

My mother gave me a small microscope and Mona and I set up our laboratory on the dresser in the little room off my bedroom. We laid out all the first-aid stuff from my kit plus the microscope, glass slides, tweezers, and other bits of equipment so necessary to the scientist in her pursuit of higher knowledge. We used to prick our fingers, smear the blood on the glass slides, and look at it under the microscope.

Grade Seven, when I was twelve, was an exciting year. Our teacher was a man who actually cracked jokes in class. We adored him. He was our hero. It was he who introduced me to Conan Doyle's *The White Company*, and he used to read some of my stories and give me kindly criticism. When I was about fifty, I met him again, stared at him, and said, "My God, you're not much older than I am." It turns out he was only in his early twenties when he taught me.

That same year, 1938, was the year Frank Sinatra hit the world. Many of the girls would imitate what they had heard on the radio or read in the movie magazines. They'd go around fainting and swooning, crying, "Frankie!" I longed to join them, but I was much too proud and shy. That was the year, too, when Walt Disney's *Snow White and the Seven Dwarfs* came to Neepawa. Mum made me take my young brother, then five, along with me, and I resented it terribly, since I was sure he'd fidget, thus distracting me from this masterpiece we had all read about and were now about to behold with our own eyes. My brother, of course, remained as riveted to his seat as I did, even through the scary bits. Maybe he was petrified. I know I was, although I'd have died rather than admit it.

That film seized my imagination and I immediately began work on constructing my own dwarfs' house, a wooden apple box into which I clumsily fitted an upstairs. I built a sloped roof and added hinged doors at the front so the house could be opened to view. I made tables out of spools, chairs from matchboxes, bowls from acorn cups. I painted the furniture, snipped bits of cloth for bedspreads, used some of the miniature china jugs from my collection, and had a wonderful time. That dwarf house remained on the chest of drawers in my bedroom, gathering dust but still beloved, for several years.

My childhood could be said to have ended in 1939, the summer and autumn I was thirteen. That summer I visited a much-loved cousin and his family on their farm, north of Riding Mountain. It was a sad visit in many ways. I was dreadfully homesick. I knew my cousin well because he had gone to high school in Neepawa, but I didn't know his brothers and sisters or his mother. Although they were all very kind, I felt shy and lonely except when Bud and I went to the hayfields beside the vast lake. He would talk to me there when his work was finished, and tell me of his dreams for the future. He had originally wanted to go to university, but this was the Depression and he'd been forced to return to the farm. He still hoped somehow, sometime, to get out of his present situation. I didn't know what to say. We both knew there was no money and no likelihood of any. I felt inadequate, too young to say anything to help or even comfort him, yet old enough to understand his tragedy, the tragedy of so many young men and women in those years.

His eventual release was only another enslavement. He joined the army. That September, I was visiting two of my friends, Bob and Elizabeth, who lived in a nearby town but came in to Neepawa to visit their grandparents. Elizabeth was a couple of years younger than I, and Bob a couple of years older. Although I was a bit in awe of him because of his age, I had known him all my life and he didn't scare me the way most boys did. Elizabeth and I were sitting out on the screened front porch when Bob came running out of the house. "Guess what?" "What?" we asked cautiously, thinking he was probably working up to a practical joke at our expense. But no. "We're at war against Germany." For a moment, none of us spoke. We didn't know what war would mean. In a vague way, we felt tremendously excited. Certainly not frightened. What would happen now? We didn't have the foggiest notion.

So on September 5, 1939, my world changed out of all recognition, forever. It had not been an idyllic world. It had had its terrors, its nightmares, but compared with the world in which my children grew up, it had been a small

72

and rural world, upon which the vast outside impinged relatively little. That simplicity would never be possible again.

In a sense, though, these changes only became apparent to me slowly. I didn't know that day that my friend Bob would be killed in France five years later, in 1944, a member of the Canadian Army, in the final European push against the Nazis. He died in a burning tank. Meanwhile, I was still young and I had my own concerns. In the summer of 1940, I visited my aunt Ruby in Regina, where she was director of nursing services in the Department of Public Health, with an office in the legislative buildings. I had just completed my masterpiece, "The Pillars of the Nation," which filled two or three scribblers and was the story of pioneers. I believe it was in that story that the invented name Manawaka first appeared. The only part of the story I recall was a sensational scene in which the young pioneer wife delicately communicates to her husband that she is pregnant by the tactful device of allowing him to arrive home and witness her making a birch-bark cradle. (I guess if I'd stuck to birch-bark cradles in my fiction, the book-banning elements loose in Canada wouldn't have hit on me as a target.) I desperately needed my manuscript typed so I could enter it in the *Winnipeg Free Press* junior writers' contest. My aunt's secretary very kindly performed this service for me and only once, when I entered the office unexpectedly, did I catch her and my aunt mildly chortling.

"The Pillars of the Nation" got an honourable mention and I was ecstatic. A few months later, a story of mine called "The Case of the Blond Butcher" was actually printed in the young people's section of the Saturday *Free Press*. It was a murder story in which it turned out that no murder had been committed after all. (In those days I favoured happy endings. I still do – who wouldn't? But nowadays they're not always possible.) With "The Blond Butcher," I also received my first fan letter. It was written in purple ink and it was from a boy in Winnipeg. I was so embarrassed I didn't know what to do, so I threw it in the kitchen woodstove before Mum could see it and I never told a living soul.

I was fourteen that summer and about to enter high school. I learned that I would be able to take typing in high school, as an extra, and had got my first typewriter. My aunt Ruby found it, a small second-hand Remington that cost $14. Mum put up half and I paid the other half by earning money babysitting. In some ways I was being very practical in equipping myself to be a writer, although outwardly, and I suppose inwardly as well, I still planned to be a nurse like my aunts and like our beloved friend Miss Johnson at the Neepawa Hospital. The following episode sounds unlikely, but it is perfectly true. Sudden revelations aren't supposed to happen, whereas in truth, they happen quite a few times, or at least they have to me in my life. I was fourteen and I was walking up the stairs in my grandfather Simpson's house, towards my bedroom. I can see myself, with my hand on the dark varnished banister, staring at the ugly etching of "The Stag at Eve" that hung on the stairway wall. A thought had just come to me, with enormous strength: I can't be a nurse; I have to be a writer. I was appalled and frightened.

What frightened me was not the writing itself. It would only be much later that I would realize what a long, tough apprenticeship this trade called for. No, what scared me was how, if I wasn't going to be a nurse, I would earn a living. Through high school and college I thought I would be a journalist, and indeed I did become one, at least for a year. It never occurred to me that I might be able to earn a living from writing. Just as well, for I never had any unreal expectations of large financial rewards and, in fact, was a professional writer for many years before I could earn a living by the practice of my trade. Even then I was lucky, simply because my timing happened to be right. The generation of writers before me – Hugh MacLennan, Morley

Callaghan, Ernest Buckler, Sinclair Ross, and all the others – were unable, for much of their career, to earn a living from their writing. They were Canadian writers and the home product wasn't valued at home for a long time, not even, as happened in their cases, when it was valued in England or America. I had no idea how many difficulties there would be, but I don't think it would have made a scrap of difference if I had known. What I realized that day was that I had a life commitment and could do no other.

I may have discussed what I wanted to do with my life, but, like most fourteen-year-olds, I was excruciatingly shy and tried to conceal it under a somewhat loud-mouthed exterior. I had a thirty-two-inch bust at a time when Betty Grable had made it a shame, if not a downright disgrace, for girls not to have breasts like overripe cantaloupes. A currently popular song went, "The girl that I marry will have to be / As soft and pink as a nursery," and it ended, "A girl I can carry, the girl that I marry, must be." How I hated and detested and feared that song. I was five-foot-six and although I was slender, no young man could have carried me far without straining a muscle.

All through the time I spent in high school, you could see increasing contrasts in society's attitudes towards women. As the war progressed and more women were needed in industry, in weapons and airplane factories, it was conceded that women could do "men's work." Women joined the Women's Auxiliary Armed Forces and strode around in tailored uniforms. At the same time, what our brave boys in uniform, and many of our boys still too young to go to war, obviously wanted was a dumb, pink, fluffy female, loaded with makeup and light on brains. It was a tough life for some of us, like myself, who not only knew that we could never fit this image but who, in our private hearts, detested it. Girls were supposed to flirt, to play hard to get, while all the time wangling the chosen male into their perfumed clutches. Maybe if I had been better at the game, I wouldn't have hated it so much. However, I thought it was demeaning then and I still think so. Like some of my friends, I had been reared in a home where I was expected to be intelligent. If you have brains, how the hell are you supposed to hide them? And how cruel to have to try. All of us girls who didn't look exactly like one of the glamorous Hollywood movie stars (and who ever truly did?) would try desperately to fix our hair in fashionable, stiff, sausage-roll curls, getting sore scalps in the process from the nightly application of tightly rolled tin curlers.

In 1940, the now notorious War Measures Act was brought into force and a wave of racial and political prejudice was unleashed in this country. England stood in danger of invasion by the Germans. The so-called phoney war was getting hotter. It's almost unbelievable, but I was only very dimly aware of these events. My friends and I had to register at the post office the minute we turned sixteen, I think so the government would know where we were in case of a national emergency and could make use of our individual skills. Where could I possibly have been except Neepawa? And I didn't have any individual skills, at least not any the government would have found useful in an emergency. When my registration hour struck, I put down as one of my skills "plain cook." I couldn't even boil an egg.

The chief joys of high school, and they remained so for four years, were being able to work on the school newspaper and studying English literature. I remember practically nothing that I learned in other courses. Mathematics, geometry, algebra were my nemeses and I barely scraped through. History was composed largely of the kings and queens of England or what felt like the endless laws and acts of the governments of Canada. I studied the Manitoba School Act of the late 1800s without having the faintest idea of what it actually meant, namely that in my own native province, some of my ancestors had been responsible, directly or indirectly, for depriving the quite large French-speaking populace, both whites and Métis, of their language rights, not only in provincially supported schools but also in the provincial legislature and the courts.

I was unaware of how terrible this was. I expect my teachers were as unaware as I. History was taught from the anglophone point of view, the view that presented Louis Riel and Gabriel Dumont, Big Bear and Poundmaker, as rebel villains. It was the Upper Canadian, white Protestant interpretation of our history and it was dreadfully distorted. I had no idea that both Big Bear and Poundmaker, those proud and courageous men, virtually the last of the old independent Cree chieftains, had, after their defeat in 1885, been incarcerated, humiliatingly, in the Stony Mountain penitentiary in my own province, and that both had died of the experience soon after their release. When I think of what I learned of Canadian history, I feel cheated, not by my teachers but by the society in which I grew up.

English literature was something else. Of course literature meant British literature, although in Grade Twelve we studied – oh fascination – Euripides' *Electra* in the Gilbert Murray translation. Virtually nothing Canadian was taught, but when I began high school in 1940, a great deal of what we think of as contemporary Canadian literature had not yet been written or published. I was enchanted with Keats, Wordsworth, and Shelley, and in Grade Eleven, when Miss Mildred Musgrove began teaching some of Browning's dramatic monologues, such as "My Last Duchess," I felt as though a whole series of doors were opening in my mind. I still have the *Pocket Book of Verse* that we used for the two final years of high school, with the poems marked that we studied, among them some of Shakespeare's lyrics and selections from the Bible. These included the "Song of Songs," without, however, the accompanying comment on that great love poem found in my grandmother's Bible: "Christ's marriage to the church." We read Gray's "Elegy"; some of Blake's shorter poems; quite a lot of Wordsworth; Coleridge's "Kubla Khan"; Shelley's "Ozymandias"; Keats's "Ode to a Nightingale" and "Ode on a Grecian Urn"; Fitzgerald's "Rubaiyat"; Tennyson's "Ulysses"; Matthew Arnold; A.E. Housman; Yeats; de la Mare; Robert Frost and Sandburg; Vachel Lindsay; Rupert Brooke; Stephen Vincent Benet. As a collection for high school, it still seems pretty good to me. At the back of my tattered pocket book, I copied, in handwriting now scarcely recognizable to me as my own, the following quotation from W.E. Henley: "In the fell clutch of circumstance I have not winced nor cried aloud / Under the bludgeonings of chance / My head is bloody but unbowed." Bloody but unbowed, indeed. Ah, youth. Maybe Henley never winced nor cried aloud but, if so, he must surely have been unique among humankind.

Composition was a subject that, naturally, I enjoyed. We had to write either an essay or a story for the exam, and I always chose the short story. I took the precaution, though, of composing one in my head well before the exam and would, through nimble mental and verbal juggling, manage to connect it with one of the given titles. Then I was off and away.

Our school newspaper was called *The Black and Gold*. Every month or two I, among others, cranked out an edition on an old mimeograph machine, getting covered with pungent and gooey black ink in the process. For the last couple of years of high school, I edited that paper. I don't think anyone else wanted to and I certainly needed no urging. Mildred Musgrove was the guiding spirit behind this publication, with the help of Connie Offen, another teacher of mine. Both women gave me so much, and both have remained lifelong friends.

One of the big social centres in Neepawa was the skating rink. We used to go skating about three evenings a week. If you were a girl, and lucky, boys would ask you to skate with them and hold hands. If a boy liked you a lot, or even some, he might ask you to go for coffee or a Coke afterwards in one of the cafés and then walk you home. After the second or third time, unless he was fresh and tried the first time, he might kiss you. After the fifth or sixth time, you would stand on the doorstep, the pair of you, doing such necking as was physically possible, given a temperature of 30 to 40 below, Fahrenheit, and the vast amounts of heavy clothing you both wore. No one's virginity was seriously threatened on those winter evenings, but we were a hardy lot and managed slightly more proximity than anyone hailing from softer climes would have believed possible.

My first boyfriend lived on a farm with his aunt and uncle and a girl cousin, who was in my grade, about five or six miles from town. I thought he was heroic because he had a black stallion that he used to ride to school, day after day, month after month, in all seasons. He was a couple of years older than I was. As soon as he was old enough, he joined the RCAF and that was that.

Before the happy, if brief, advent of my first boyfriend came the gruelling and ghastly experience of the first high-school dance. Dances were pretty prim affairs, heavily chaperoned by teachers. If one of the boys (never, ever a girl) came in with breath even faintly indicating beer, out he went. In my third year of high school, in the company of several of my peers, I was caught at a high-school dance smoking a cigarette in the library. For weeks afterwards, I trembled at the real possibility of public disgrace and expulsion. But at my first dance, I was fourteen and petrified. For a start, I didn't know how to dance. Mum had been touchingly eager, as always, to help her tender prairie crocus. Just before I entered high school, she had had the nifty idea that, to be socially successful, a girl should learn ballroom dancing. This was worse than violin lessons, much worse. I was chivvied off to yet another hall in one of the town's old hotels, the King Edward. Some lady from somewhere – these anonymous ladies proliferated in that period of history in our town – was teaching ballroom dancing to the offspring of the genteel, if relatively broke, middle class. (There was, of course, no upper class in our town.)

"One, two, three, one, two, three, don't watch your feet," the intrepid lady would shrill, while the geriatric gramophone ground out "The Blue Danube" in the nearly empty and decidedly tatty room. And I, who could skate to the same music with no trouble at all, lithe and graceful, fell over my own feet and hers. There were few boys in this civilizing class, just one or two, younger than I by a year and shorter by a head, who were going through the horrible process that made them likely candidates for the role of suitors-to-be. They and the other girls were as embarrassed as I was. This torture lasted about two sessions, after which I informed my Mum that not only had I no desire to learn ballroom dancing, I planned to spend the rest of my life resisting any knowledge of it. Mum, who believed, as an honest and indeed basically feminist woman, that it wasn't how you looked but what you were, readily agreed to my quitting. I thought she was trying to fit me into the mould of social acceptability. I later saw that in fact she feared I would grow up feeling different and wanted to do all in her power to assure me a sense of belonging in the world I would be entering.

I had mixed feelings about the dress I wore to my first dance. My aunt Ruby was friends with a doctor and his wife who had considerably more money than we had. Their daughter was a year older than I and, through my aunt, they sent me her outgrown clothes. It was kind. It was sensible. But I hated them with a passionate hatred. My pride rejected those dresses, even though many of them were quite nice. I didn't hate the family that bestowed this munificence, nor my aunt nor my Mum. I just hated the garments themselves, because they weren't really mine.

I wore one such dress to that first high-school dance. It was green, a dark moss-green, made of a rather heavy, rayon-type material. Along the square yoke at the neck there was a strip of embroidered braid, red and gold. I thought I should wear makeup with it, at least a little bit of powder and lipstick. My mother thought otherwise. Her daughter was going to succeed socially, was going to look like a million bucks, but by heaven, she sure wasn't going to look cheap. Gussied up in the hand-me-down, off I went. It was a grim experience. I didn't know how to dance, and only one boy asked me anyway, a guy who was the president of the student council, an older boy in Grade Twelve, who (I still think of it as such an act of kindness) asked a number of the Grade Nine girls such as myself to dance.

The following year, in June 1941, the Germans invaded Russia. Six months later, on December 7, the Japanese bombed Pearl Harbor. Russia and the United States were now in the war. On the same day, two thousand Canadian troops were sent into battle to defend the ill-prepared British garrison and colony of Hong Kong. More than a quarter of them died and a large number spent the remainder of the war in Japanese prisoner-of-war camps under appalling conditions. We had begun to learn, at least a little, about what war meant.

After Japan joined the war on the Axis side, people on the west coast of Canada fell prey to panic of the most paranoid kind. Reinforced by the racial prejudice already in existence there, they turned against the large community of Japanese Canadians, a group who were mainly industrious fishermen, market gardeners, fruit farmers, and small businessmen. Some of them had been born in Japan, but by far the larger proportion had been born in Canada. This land was the only one they knew. They had no other country. All the same, the Canadian government, in one of the most shameful chapters of our history, yielded to the hysteria of some of British Columbia's white population and invoked the War Measures Act. More than twenty thousand Japanese Canadians were forcibly removed from the west coast, most of them to camps in the interior of B.C.

Many families were split up when the men were sent to separate work camps. The property owned by these thousands of Canadian people was supposed to be held in trust by the government. In fact, it was confiscated and sold at auction for a fraction of its value. A number of B.C. land speculators realized a very tidy profit and the Japanese Canadians received virtually no compensation after the war. Even personal belongings, things like family photograph albums, had been seized and lost. None of them ever recovered anything like the full value of their property, and there can never be any real compensation for what had been done to them in psychological and emotional terms.

The whole story was told, movingly but with great restraint, by Ken Adachi in his definitive history of the Japanese in Canada, *The Enemy That Never Was.* Ken and his wife, Mary, have been friends of mine for more than twenty years. Mary is a third-generation Canadian, Ken a second-generation Canadian. Both of them spent time in the camps when they were children and they are both younger than I am. Our country has much to answer for. Not one case of sabotage or subversion was ever brought against any Japanese Canadian. This means that in a war in which we were supposed to be fighting for democracy, twenty-one thousand innocent people were imprisoned for years and their possessions stolen. After the war, the Canadian government admitted that a mistake had been made, but in a sense it was too late. Years of labour had disappeared overnight, property had been sold off and a whole group of people damaged. It should be added, for those Canadians who like to feel we are somehow morally superior to the Americans, that the Japanese Americans received better treatment than did their ethnic cousins in Canada.

It seems odd to me now that I should have been so ignorant. Most of us in the rest of Canada, however, were barely aware of what was going on, although there were a few people, such as F.R. Scott and Edith Fowke, who tried nobly but without success to gain justice for the Japanese Canadians. Like most people's, my early teenage years were self-centred. I edited the school paper, worried about my appearance, agonized over whether I would get a date or not, wrote long patriotic poems of dreadful banality, skipped basketball at which, like all sports, I was totally untalented, and hid out in the furnace room exchanging stories with the janitor who was a godsend to the unsportsmanlike me. Although I read about the war in the papers, it remained remote to me until August 19, 1942. That was the day of Dieppe.

I suppose it could not have been until the next day, or maybe the day after, that the full news broke in Canada, and I guess it must have been a few days later that the casualty lists came out. Five thousand Canadian troops, from seven regiments, had charged the beaches at Dieppe. The Germans were waiting for them. A total of 3,100 Canadians were killed, wounded, or captured, to remain in camps for the rest of the war. I read about Dieppe in the *Winnipeg Free Press,* sitting in the big oak armchair in my grandfather Simpson's house. One of the prairie regiments to take part in that battle was the Queen's Own Cameron Highlanders, or, as they were called, the Camerons. I remembered when the Camerons had marched through our town in their dress kilts, led by pipers, just before they went overseas. A lot of the Neepawa boys were in that regiment. They were such a brave sight. I was sixteen that year, and for the first time I knew, really knew, what war meant. It meant that young men from your own town, your friends or brothers of your friends, boys only a couple of years older than yourself, had been mutilated and killed. Boys of eighteen, nineteen, twenty years old. I think it was only through that knowledge that all the other dead and suffering people from all the wars became finally and forever real to me. Before, despite my father's experience, they had been appalling statistics, but they were not statistics any more. They were boys I had known. They were a part of me.

The limitations of the perceptions one permitted oneself were abruptly shattered once and for all with Dieppe. In one sense, for me, Dieppe perpetually has happened only yesterday. It runs as a leitmotif through all my so-called Manawaka fiction and, in a way, it runs through my whole life, in my hatred of war so profound I can't find words to express my outrage at these recurring assaults upon the human flesh, mind, and spirit. How dare we call our species *Homo sapiens*? The whales and dolphins, whom we are rapidly destroying, are surely superior in every way that counts. I do believe in some kind of a Creator. I believe in the Holy Spirit. I think there is an informing spirit in the whole of creation but I also believe we have some kind of free will. The sorrow of a creator spirit, having formed mankind with a degree of free will and then observing how we persist in misusing it for destruction, is impossible for our minds to comprehend.

When I was in Grade Eleven, there were only two boys in our class. By Grade Twelve, there were none. They were all at war. In those days, Saturday-night entertainment was parking in Mona's dad's car on the main street and watching the world go by, the uniformed boys home on leave, farmers and their families in town doing their weekly shopping. An RAF training base was built just outside our town by a firm of contractors from the Maritimes, and some of the younger workers would turn up at school dances, sophisticates of eighteen or nineteen showing the local girls how to jitterbug and boogie to "Chattanooga Choo Choo" and "The Boogie Woogie Bugle Boy." Now that the Yanks were in the war, a proliferation of American war songs marched relentlessly into our lives. We sang the U.S. Marines song, "From the Halls of Montezuma to the Shores of Tripoli." Canadian songs were mostly notable through their absence. We had always looked south of the border for our pop music, but the war seemed to step up the process. I worked Saturdays for a local clothing store and spent every cent I earned on satin underwear, never to be seen by anyone other than myself, and, when I had saved enough, dresses to wear to the Saturday-night dances at the town dance hall, which I was permitted to attend in the company of a group of girlfriends.

It was around this time the man from Miramichi entered our lives. Mum – out of financial need, not patriotic concern – took in a boarder, a man who worked with the construction company building the airport. Mum moved into the back bedroom and my brother moved into the half-size makeshift bedroom, the dressing room off mine. My grandfather went around muttering about "that fella" in the poor guy's hearing. Everyone was miserable. Mum tried to make polite conversation at meals, with no help from either her children or her father. Bob and I totally disliked that guy. We didn't want him. We didn't care that she needed the money. The unfortunate boarder stayed only a few months, after which the airfield and training school were completed and he left town. My brother and I were delighted to see him go, and Mum never took on another boarder. Instead, knowing how much Bob and I had hated having somebody in our house who was not family, she supplemented our meagre income by doing the accounting and secretarial work for the local hospital.

Those must have been lonely and anxious years for her. Often I couldn't face the fact that she had problems. I could only cope with my own, and I didn't even cope with those very well. The RAF had hit town. Suddenly a huge influx of young Englishmen, in air-force-blue uniforms, arrived. The Saturday-night dances took on a whole new dimension. No longer did girls have to dance with one another because of the shortage of boys. We danced to all the sentimental songs of parting and of future hopes: "I'll Be Seeing You," "Skylark," "When the Lights Come On Again All Over the World." Alice Duer Miller's book of prose / poetry, *The White Cliffs*, came out and I wept over it, as it proclaimed the sentiments that a world without an England wouldn't be worth living in.

If the Nazis had won, that would probably have been true, but thinking back on it as a Canadian, I realize that England has never been of all-consuming importance to me. During the war, however, we felt close to the beleaguered "old country" none of us had ever seen. Even though England wasn't in fact the "old country" for everyone, we all sang "There'll Always Be an England" like a hymn. From the RAF boys we learned English methods of dancing, English songs, English expressions, and our mothers, delighted, invited the boys from the station in for Sunday dinners.

I fell in love with an RAF man when I was seventeen years old. He was not only handsome and ten years older, he was also well read. He introduced me to some of the contemporary English poets such as Stephen Spender and W.H. Auden. None of the boys I had ever gone to school with would have given poetry the time of day, but here was an older man who not only could quote reams of the stuff, he also (could it really be?) wanted to spend time with awkward, shy, nervous, clever, often loud-mouthed me. I include clever because I knew I was smart, but I certainly didn't regard it as an asset. It was more of a millstone around my neck. I couldn't believe my good fortune. There was Derek, with all those remarkable qualities, interested in me.

One of his remarkable qualities that took me a while to discover was that he was a compulsive and quite classy liar. We had all learned, of course, the term "shooting a line." Englishmen in Canada did it with Canadian girls, the Canadian boys in the forces in England did it with English girls. Canadian boys might tell English girls about the huge ranches their fathers owned in Alberta, while the Englishmen claimed they were descended from aristocratic families. Some Canadian girls not only believed these boys but married them and went over to England to find out the unfortunate truth, in the same way that many English war brides came to Canada.

I met Derek at a dance, one of the Saturday-night dances Mum always hated me going to because she thought they were rowdy. She was absolutely right. There were always a few beer bottles flung around and the occasional fight. There were the usual brash girls, some of them from our town, in their CWAC (Canadian Women's Army Corps) uniforms, loudly flirting with the RAF boys, who were only too willing to be propositioned. There was the usual complement of drunks and half-drunks, both men and women, uniformed or civilian. And a number of high-school girls, such as myself, in our party dresses, with our stiff imitation curls, wearing our blood-red lipstick and nail polish, smiling, smiling, dreading the ever-present danger of not being asked to dance.

Looking back on it, it seems a bit like a cattle market, but at the time, it was Life and Excitement. Each dance we had to sit out was our very own, personal failure. We would retreat to the ladies' powder room to avoid being seen without a dancing partner. Many of the young men must have been nearly as uncertain of their own manhood as we were of our womanhood, but it didn't look that way to us at the time.

That was the era of the big bands, and even our small-town band captured something of the smoothness of Guy Lombardo and his Royal Canadians or the beat of American jazz and boogie. I had at last learned to dance very well. In those days, though, dancing with someone who also loved to dance was not just a sexual experience; it almost went beyond the sexual. The uncertainties of war meant we danced with a heightened tribal sense of being together. Dancing became a passionate affirmation of life and the desire to go on living.

Derek's great love was classical music and he used to take me to the RAF camp's musical evenings. Lord, how stilted that sounds, and was. Englishmen who loved music would sit around with their girlfriends from town and listen to Beethoven, Bach, Brahms, and various other "greats."

Mum encouraged my attendance, with the thought obviously still in the back of her mind that she had not seen properly to my musical education. I loved Beethoven, but I was ill educated in terms of other music. My soul music had always been the bagpipes. One of our neighbours, an elderly man, used to come out in the spring and pace up and down his backyard, opposite my grandfather Simpson's house, playing the pipes. I would sit on our back steps and listen. I would have followed pipe music to the ends of the earth. The men from the Cameron Highlanders had done just that. To this day, I can't hear the pipes without being profoundly moved. It is my ancestral music. I cannot listen to the "March of the Cameron Men" or the old pibroch, the lament for the dead, "Flowers of the Forest," without crying.

I didn't tell Derek about my penchant for the bagpipes. In love though I was, I was at least smart enough to realize that no Englishman would understand the Scots part of me. I dutifully sat and listened to classical music on the gritty old 78 records at the camp, pretending a warm response. Derek told me, quite modestly, that he was, in fact, a composer. His real name was Benjamin Britten. Knowing absolutely nothing about music, and less than nothing about contemporary composers, it took me a long time to discover that he was no more Benjamin Britten than I was the Queen of Siam. Derek had been back in England for months and his letters had stopped coming (the usual syndrome) when I finally found out. I can recall precisely how hurt I felt, how hurt and betrayed. I still find it hard to understand why anyone would do such a thing.

In July 1944, I turned eighteen. It was obvious that the war was drawing to an end, but I was determined to join up. I sent in my application to the navy, the WRCNS (Women's Royal Canadian Naval Service). I would have been hard pressed to say why I, a prairie person in every bone, wanted to join the navy. It may have been because it was the farthest one could get from a prairie town and therefore, at least in my imagination, mysterious and glamorous. I finally received a reply. They were not accepting recruits at the moment, but they would be taking on more soon and would let me know. Mum was distraught. She was determined to send me to university. In fact, I wanted to go, but my country was calling, and so was life, experience, and adventure. I don't suppose that trio would have called quite so loudly if I hadn't known that women were not sent into the actual battle areas. Since I was of an age to join up, Mum could only worry. She had just finished panicking about a seventeen-year-old daughter who might at any moment declare her intention to wed an RAF man ten years her senior. Now this. Mum and I used to quote poetry to each other while we did the dishes, taking turns line by line, but with all these tensions, Browning's "My Last Duchess" no longer tripped from our lips as we performed our after-dinner tasks.

The telephones of our town were regally presided over at the telephone exchange by a splendid lady who, although she had a name and family, was always known as Central. When I was a little kid, I used to think her name really was Central. May and June and Ruby and Pearl were names. Why not Central? Central knew all of us and usually knew where we were at any particular moment. If you were expecting a call and had to go out, you simply told Central where you would be and she would redirect the call. One afternoon, I was at Mona's place. Mum was out, my brother was out, my grandfather was deaf, and even if he hadn't been, there was no way he would have treated a long-distance call, unless it was from one of his sons or daughters, as anything except the most outrageous infringement upon the privacy of his home. The WRCNS had phoned me. Central didn't know where I was. I hadn't told her my every move. I thought the navy would write to me. Nobody in our family ever phoned long-distance, except to communicate disaster. So I missed the call. Several days later, I received a letter from the navy informing me they had phoned, had been willing to take me on, but now did not need any more people and advised me to go ahead with other plans.

Had I thought about it longer, I would have realized that I'd have hated life in the forces. I had steadfastly, all my life, refused to join organizations. I was never a Brownie or a Girl Guide. I had belonged to the CGIT (Canadian Girls In Training) for two months. Dressed in middies and navy-blue pleated skirts, we met in the Presbyterian church hall once a week until I asked myself, In training for what? When I got the news from the navy, I felt, to tell the truth, immensely relieved. I applied for a Manitoba scholarship, which was granted both on academic standards and on financial need, and sent off an application to United College, an affiliate of the University of Manitoba. To my astonishment, I received the scholarship and was accepted by United College. Since Grade Twelve in Manitoba counted as the first year of an arts degree, I could get my BA in a three-year course. The doors to the world were opening. Mona was going to the University of Manitoba. As we contemplated our futures, we both felt a touching combination of bravado and fear.

That last summer before I left home was spent partly at the lake with Mona and some other friends. We stayed for several weeks in my family's cottage, unsupervised for the first time, responsible for ourselves, for our meals and our morals. No doubt our parents worried. My Mum's guideline had become, "All you can do is love them and leave them." All – that was everything. That was trust. Mum and I had argued, we had fought. All the same, in matters that really were important, she loved and trusted me unconditionally, however much she worried. It's a tribute to her that I ultimately found I was bringing up my own children along the same general principles, and that at every stage of my children's lives, I felt I understood my Mum more, and felt closer to her.

United College, now the University of Winnipeg, had a long tradition (long in Canadian terms anyway) of liberal arts and the kind of social conscience closely associated, in the prairies, with the Methodist and Presbyterian churches and, ultimately, with the United Church of Canada, in which I myself was brought up. From such a tradition had come many of the early reformers in the prairies, founders of the Social Democratic Party, the CCF, people such as J.S. Woodsworth, Stanley Knowles, Tommy Douglas, and many others. I had a very privileged education. Although the library was absurdly small and unsophisticated by today's standards, classes were also small, perhaps twenty or thirty students, sometimes fewer. We got to know one another very quickly and we got to know our teachers personally. We had the good fortune to be taught by people such as Arthur Phelps, surely one of the greatest teachers of English literature in our country, and A.R.M. Lower who, even then, was one of our most distinguished historians.

Small though United College may have been in relation to the University of Manitoba, it was an awful lot bigger than the Neepawa Collegiate. It was not the same as going to school with the kids you'd grown up with. Many of the Winnipeg students had known one another in high school. Old friends fell into one another's arms the first day of classes. I did not know a living soul. Neither, however, did any of the other small-town and country kids. Those of us who stayed in residence quickly formed an unspoken but strongly felt alliance. We knew, with unerring accuracy, the hierarchy of the prairies. Kids from the farms were lowest on the scale; kids from the very small towns, whistle stops, were next; kids from slightly larger towns were next; kids from small cities, like Brandon, were next; the city kids (and Winnipeg was the only proper city) ranked as overlords. Given the agricultural nature of the province and its economy, the order presumably should have been reversed, but that never occurred to most of us until much later on.

United College was a pleasant, grey-stone building with several towers that gave it the appearance of a castle. Sparling Hall, the women's residence, was situated just behind the college, and the men's residence was on the top floor of the main building, close enough for the boys to engage in such pleasant activities as dropping brown-paper water-bombs from the fire escape onto strolling damsels. Since residence was not particularly quiet, some of us, with a sense of great daring, used to study at night in the empty college classrooms on the floor below the men's residence. On one occasion, standing on the fire escape, I dramatically orated a few appropriate lines from Shelley only to receive a water-bomb treatment from the occupants of the floor above. It cured me of public oratory.

The food was wartime fare – lots of healthy stews featuring large chunks of turnip. Although we complained bitterly, we actually did pretty well. (I have since discovered that it's a universal trait of resident students to complain about the food.) If we felt we couldn't stand the cooking any longer, we'd repair to a nearby hamburger joint called the Salisbury House, where we spent an inordinate amount of our slender allowances.

I had had my own room all my life and was apprehensive about having a roommate. Luckily Helen and I got along extremely well and ended up rooming together for the two years we were in residence. We did a large mural for our tiny refuge, depicting dinosaurs and jungles and working up, as I recall, to Adam and Eve. The room contained two single cots, a small table, two straight chairs, one big dresser with drawers for each of us, and a clothes cupboard of somewhat less than giant proportions. The cramped conditions never worried us much. Neither of us came from well-to-do families. Like those of most girls in Sparling Hall, my wardrobe consisted of two sweaters, two skirts, two blouses, one good dress, one pair of sensible shoes, and one pair of high heels. It was fashionable to wear pleated wool skirts and long, droopy sweaters called Sloppy Joes. Brown-and-white saddle shoes, carefully scuffed to make them appear old, finished off the ensemble. A few girls had half a dozen angora sweaters and a set of artificial pearls. Our souls yearned for these possessions. In self-defence, we developed a type of reverse snobbery. We felt superior because we were poor. I later subscribed to a similar philosophy in my north Winnipeg days, roughly summed up as, "Filthy capitalists, they can't be happy," which of course was rubbish. Those girls in their angora sweaters were as happy as larks and furthermore, they averaged more dates.

The relationship between the sexes was much the same as in high school, except that now we were going out with boys our own age. The war was clearly coming to an end and young men were no longer needed in large numbers in the armed forces. It would be another year before the veterans began to return and enrol in droves in the universities, mostly in such faculties as science, medicine, and engineering, seeking security after their experiences first of the Depression and then of war. Otherwise, it was the same old story. You hoped and prayed that some guy, however gauche or buck-toothed, would ask you to one of the dances or to a film. The prettiest girls, who were frequently also smart enough to play dumb, got the most dates. I had several friends who were much more glamorous than I. Pat and Madge were not only stunningly beautiful, they were also intelligent. It must have upset them at times to be valued, as they were, primarily for their physical beauty. They had to cope with things that I didn't know about. Life was not necessarily easier for them, although at the time I used to imagine it was.

Sororities were a big deal at university. I was asked to join one, or rather I was invited to attend the "freshie" tea, a social gathering at which, apparently, one either did or did not pass muster. I turned down the invitation. I can't remember what reason I gave. My true reasons were mixed. In many ways my Scots-Irish independence, plus my strong egalitarian beliefs, didn't permit me even to contemplate joining such an elite. This was very high-minded of me, but of course I had other reasons. I couldn't afford it, for one. I was also afraid I'd be weighed in the tea balance and found wanting. Anyway, from my observation of the afternoon teas given by the Neepawa ladies of my mother's generation, I was fairly sure that wasn't how I wanted to spend my time. I told myself that sorority girls were vain and dim-witted and rich. I didn't bother finding out whether any of that was true. My principles, although relatively laudable, were also a crude mask for my own uncertainties.

In other ways, my uncertainty simply had to be overcome. College was quite literally a brave new world, and I didn't intend it to elude my grasp if I could help it. I summoned courage and timidly asked Professor Arthur Phelps how a person got to join the English Club. This, I had discovered early on, was an informal association of people interested in English literature. It met at the Phelps' house every month. Members delivered papers on some aspect of literature; discussion of the paper then took place. I didn't know that membership in the English Club was by invitation only and that second-year students seldom, if ever, were asked to join. It is a measure of Arthur Phelps's great kindness that he did not put me off until the next year. Eyes twinkling in his gnome-like face, he asked me to come along for the next meeting. I did, and found to my puzzlement that all the others were at least one or two years older than myself. They were enormously kind, though, and didn't scorn to listen when this upstart kid expressed a view. I attended English Club regularly after that. It was one of my happiest and most rewarding college experiences. Many of the people who attended that club became professors of English, literary critics, and writers. One, who became executive vice-president of the Toronto-Dominion Bank, told me when I met him thirty years later what had happened that first time I went to the club.

"Phelps announced to us," Alan Hockin said, "'There is a second-year student coming to English Club this time and, I think, hereafter. You are expected to show courtesy and no surprise at her presence in your midst.'"

They got the message. God bless Arthur Phelps. I wish he had lived long enough for me to thank him. Phelps knew many writers and critics, men like Morley Callaghan, Frederick Philip Grove, and William Arthur Deacon. The most famous story about the English Club concerned a young woman who had prepared a paper on Morley Callaghan's fiction, only to find that Callaghan himself was there on the evening of the meeting. Gamely, she proceeded. It must have taken a lot of courage, but, on the other hand, it afforded an opportunity, rare in those days, for a group of students to realize writers are human beings.

I had wonderful teachers of English at United College: as well as Arthur Phelps there were Meredith Thompson, Doris Peterson, and especially Robert Halstead. He and his wife Anne became valued friends. Malcolm Ross taught me a course on Milton and seventeenth-century thought at the University of Manitoba, a course that profoundly affected my life. Malcolm was an early mentor of mine, as he was of Adele Wiseman, and he has remained a friend. I am one of the many writers and academics who owe Malcolm Ross a debt of gratitude for his encouragement. Long after I'd graduated, he published, as editor of *Queen's Quarterly,* my first real story (real in the sense that it deserved to be published in a worthwhile journal), but only after he had rightly turned down several others, saying in letters, "You can and will do better than this."

It had been my ambition almost as soon as I arrived at United to publish some of my writing in the University of Manitoba student paper, *The Manitoban,* which was distributed to all the affiliated colleges. I was mainly writing poetry, not because my talent particularly lay in that direction but for the same reason that many undergraduates interested in writing tackle poetry or vignettes rather than longer prose: I didn't have enough time to concentrate on prose. Poetry isn't easier to write than prose, but many young writers think it is, and it's less daunting to undertake at that age than, say, a novel. As a short, intense form, it often appeals to young writers as being more in accord with youthfully intense, and usually intensely subjective, feelings.

Initially, I submitted several poems under the pseudonym of Steven Lancaster. I suffered severe suspense each week as I rushed to grab a copy of *The Manitoban* and retreated to my room. And yes, one day a poem of mine appeared. Astonishment. Wonder. Ecstasy. Fast followed by the awful fear that I would hear, from the lips of a friend or someone whose opinion I valued, the comment "Did you see that poem by Steven Lancaster? Piece of garbage." No such comment came. I breathed again. No favourable comments came either. Still, I felt I was on my way.

By the next year, I had gained enough confidence to submit poems under my own name. I even went over to the *Manitoban* office on Broadway on several occasions, where various among us would offer to do odd jobs for the privilege of hanging around the ink-smelling rooms filled with the senior students who made up the paper's staff. The writer Jack Ludwig was then editor. I viewed him, with his leonine countenance and rich, booming laugh, more or less from afar. Years later, when we had both published several novels, I met him for the first time in England. The same rugged, handsome face, the same warm laughter, only now we met as colleagues. When I was a young student, however, I was trying to get up my nerve for nearly everything. It was the fashion for aspiring poets to nip over to the *Manitoban* office, sit down at a typewriter, and dash off a poem on the spur of the moment, which was then offered and frequently accepted in that week's issue of the paper. I worked every spare moment in my room for a couple of weeks, composing, rewriting, and shaping a poem, fortunately now lost to history. I then tripped merrily over to *The Manitoban* and proceeded to type out this poem from memory. One of the staff read it, gave me a slightly surprised glance, and said, "Gee, that's not bad." It was sent to be typeset at once. I always used to wonder afterwards if the other purveyors of instant poetry used the same technique.

Tony's was the name of the United College coffee shop. Tony's is still, as far as I know, the name of the University of Winnipeg coffee shop, although it is a different and much larger and more sophisticated establishment these days. Tony himself died some years ago. The name is a mark of the affection and gratitude so many United students felt towards him throughout his many years there. He was a short, stocky, always smiling man, and he ran that coffee shop as though it were his own home, which, in a sense, it was. In the days before student counselling, any student with a problem could unburden himself or herself to Tony and be certain of a sympathetic listener. If you were broke, he would let you have a coffee and a doughnut on credit, though it was a point of honour to pay him back as soon as humanly possible. We would sit there for hours after classes or in the evening, talking interminably. Those of us who were writing would show one another our poems and stories. Mostly, however, our two favourite topics of discussion were religion and politics. I suppose every generation asks itself the same questions. The nature of good and evil. Does God exist? If not, how did the universe come into being or has it always existed? Why were there so many brands of Christianity and such wide differences of belief among them? Where did the other great monotheisms stand in the eternal scheme of things? I was beginning to find out about Judaism, but at that juncture I knew literally nothing about Islam, for example, or any of the world's polytheisms.

When politics came up, it wasn't usually in the form of party politics or an analysis of local governments. We tended to discuss political thought in a wider sense, thought about society, social justice and injustice, ethical and moral attitudes to one's own society. All of us knew exactly where we stood on one form of totalitarianism, namely fascism. It was, and remains, a social and moral evil, destructive and death-oriented, an elite of a dictator and his cohorts suppressing all human rights of the rest of the population, ruling by fear and violence. The totalitarianism of the left was by no means apparent. Russia, our ally, was fighting for its life, with an unsurpassed courage. The Russian people had sustained greater losses than any other people. Most of us who were left wing, however, myself included, leaned towards the reformist outlooks of people like J.S. Woodsworth and Tommy Douglas. Whatever our different views, we knew one thing. The war was coming to an end. A new and better and more just social order had to emerge. We would make sure that it did. The world could and would be a better place. Poverty could be eliminated. People could be free in a free and peaceful world. We were not mouthing clichés. These things mattered. We ourselves had not suffered physically in the war, but we knew men who had been killed. Many among us were Jews who had lost all, or many, of their European relatives. We knew of the horror, the terrible and unspeakable waste of war, and we passionately believed that things could be improved, that human beings could take intelligent and compassionate charge of their own lives.

Forty years on, I could weep for how naïve we were in so many ways. Yet the death of hope is the death of the will and perhaps of the spirit. I continue to believe, all evidence to the contrary, that it is not too late to save our only home, the planet earth, and that it is not too late, even at this very late date, to learn to live on and with the earth, in harmony with all creatures. Part of that belief is social belief, part of it is religious faith. Even after all the failures

–the wars, the pollution, the radioactive waste, the real possibility of nuclear reactors melting down, the slaughter of whales and dolphins–even after all these atrocities, I believe that we cannot and must not give up.

I never look back at my younger self and smile wryly, thinking how curiously simple-minded we were. We were naïve and idealistic, but we were on the right track. We cared, and we must continue to care. Each generation must believe it can change the world for the better, whatever the odds are against us. We desperately need God's grace alongside a strong sense of our human responsibilities, however short of that ideal we may fall as individuals and as a society. These basic tenets of my own social and religious faith were, I am sure, formed largely in my childhood and were added to and consolidated during my years at United College. Over the years, they have acquired more complexity. They have been doubted and questioned. But although I did not know when I was young what form my writing would take, it is no coincidence, I believe, that two of the major threads running throughout all my work have been, in some form or another, religious and socio-political themes, or that one of my main concerns has been to show the uniqueness, the value, and the reality of the human individual.

May 8, 1945, was VE-Day. Germany surrendered; the European war was over. Our celebrations were enthusiastic, naturally, but muted, somehow apprehensive. The war in the Far East went on; American and Australian troops were suffering heavy losses. Still, the war in Europe had ended after six years. Hitler was dead and so was Nazism, or so we imagined. It must have been only those who had lost sons in battle or whole families in the death camps who truly knew that day what the real cost had been.

On August 6, the first atomic bomb was dropped on Hiroshima, and a few days later, on August 9, another on Nagasaki. Harry S. Truman, President of the United States, a nice, kind, family man, took on the responsibility for having those bombs dropped, those bombs that killed men, women, and children in their thousands and thousands, blowing them apart, etching their shadows on stones. We didn't realize the survivors would have to bear such damage within their bodies and their genes, that their children would be born dreadfully deformed, death within their blood and bones. No, we didn't realize at all what the long, long, far-reaching effects of nuclear war would be. None of us could conceive of the buildup of nuclear arms that has been taking place for so many years, at such dreadful hazard to all life on earth.

Yet we did know, somehow, that the world would never be the same again. I was nineteen years old. My life was opening out before me, but when we all went back to college in the fall of that year, we talked about it interminably. There was a sense of terrible insecurity. We had all read T.S. Eliot's lines, "This is the way the world ends / Not with a bang but a whimper." Now we had the feeling that the world might very well end with a bang. We were the first generation in the whole world to know that humankind had the power to destroy itself, all other creatures, and the planet on which we lived. Many of us have struggled against the awful, the unconscionable, nuclear arms race. We have not been prevented from going on, marrying, having our children, doing our life's work. Yet that shadow has, for us, always been there and will always be there.

I had been at college several years when Mum decided to sell the Simpson house. She knew I wouldn't be living at home again and the Big House was too big just for herself and Bob and Grandfather. Grandfather was beginning to sink into his last years of irritable, furious senility. Mum thought it would be easier to cope in the Little House and besides, she needed the money, although real-estate prices were low. She was helping me through university and the three of them were living on very little. Oddly enough, reluctant though I had been to move to the Big House, I felt sad that it had to be sold. It had become my place. What had once been my grandmother Simpson's bedroom had for years been my room, my refuge, where I had spent so many hours sitting at the white enamel table in the bay window, writing, but I was old enough to accept that I had to let it go. I never again saw the inside of the house, although years later, on brief visits, I looked at it from the outside, but it will always be part of my emotional luggage.

In the Little House, my brother inherited my old attic room. It remained his until he, too, grew up and left home. Grandfather had the back bedroom that had once been my brother's. As the boy grew into young manhood, so the old man relapsed into a sour second childhood. I was spared those years and I was too self-absorbed to want to look closely at what Mum went through when Grandfather, in his last years, would rant and rave, going out into the night streets of the town looking for his long-dead wife.

I meanwhile was entering my adult, hopeful life. I graduated from United College in the spring of 1947. I won a prize for poetry, unlikely as that now sounds, and had the highest marks in English in the university that year, although in all other subjects I had either mediocre or fairly abysmal marks. Obviously I had a one-track talent. Mum was enormously pleased at my marks in English literature. She had been a teacher; marks meant something. I no longer believe that marks, in the narrow scholastic sense, mean as much as I thought they did. I had the ability to write a good exam paper in English not only because I cared passionately about the material, but also because I had the gift of the gab in that one subject only. In other subjects, my writing stuttered. The only exam I ever failed in my entire life was a second-year course on the French Revolution, which I had actually found fascinating. What scuppered me, however, was that the paper was one of the first multiple-choice exams. My own children used to call them "multiple guess." If you know nothing about the subject, you still stand, with gambling odds, about a 25-per-cent chance of passing. I had a sense of the French Revolution, but I certainly couldn't answer questions with a tick.

At the time I graduated, I was also in love, seriously and deeply and, for the first time, realistically. I met Jack Laurence when both of us were living in an old rooming-house on Roslyn Road. I was in my final year at university. I and my friend Mary, a year older than I, had rented a large room together, an elegant place with old wood panelling and high ceilings. This may sound silly, but one day I came into the house and on the stairs stood a young man. I thought his face not only was handsome but also had qualities of understanding. I said to myself, "That's the man I'd like to marry."

I was twenty-one and Jack was thirty-one, an engineering student at the University of Manitoba. He had been in the RAF and then in the RCAF throughout the war, leaving Canada just before the war began. With the sparse savings he had from being an apprentice printer in Edson, Alberta, he'd bought a one-way boat ticket to England and had joined the air force, reasoning that the Depression in the Canadian prairies would never allow him to do anything and he had to arrange his escape. He went through the Second World War as a sergeant and mechanic in the RAF, finally being seconded to the RCAF towards the end of the war. He served some years in Burma, where he was called "Driver" Laurence for the way in which he drove himself – and those under his orders – to extremes of work and perseverance. Through a series of bureaucratic bunglings, so common in wartime, he never received a commission, although he was recommended on numerous occasions. Much later, he became a distinguished irrigation engineer who spent much of his professional life working in under-developed Third World countries.

We were not to know in 1947 that we both would have vocations that would ultimately set our lives on different courses. What we knew then was that we were in love and intended to marry. Mum must have thought I was rather young to get married, as indeed I was, but she took it in her stride. Jack and I were married in the United Church in Neepawa on September 13, 1947. This was the first time I had met his father and his mother, a woman who was to become so beloved to me, and I was terribly nervous. I so much wanted Jack's mother to like me and from the moment I met her, I knew I had found a kindred spirit.

Mum and her friends held the wedding reception in the Little House. A few of my college friends came to Neepawa from Winnipeg, but it was a small and simple gathering. Sandwiches, cookies, and different varieties of cake, plus the wedding cake, which Mum had made and iced herself, with tea and coffee. Mum was not a teetotaller, but she knew the community in which she had spent most of her life. For a reception of roughly thirty people, she'd bought one bottle of sherry. The toast to the bride was drunk with a thimbleful of sherry for each guest, apart from the minister, who drank his toast with a delicate wineglass full of water.

We had considered being married in a civil ceremony, but had rejected that idea. A friend of Jack's, who had been a United Church minister but had left to become a counsellor, talked to us when we asked him about the meaning of being married. He spoke of the words "before God and this congregation," a commitment made within a community to the future, to each other, and to life. Although our lives eventually would take us in different directions, our commitment was real and meant and honourable.

There is a picture of me as a bride, taken in the Little House. I'm standing in front of a table covered by a Chinese lace and linen tablecloth. My hair, usually done up in a French roll, is long and loose. I am twenty-one and, although I don't realize it at the time, I'm quite beautiful. I look incredibly happy. Mum and I had bought my wedding dress, even though fabric for sewing was more available after the war. It was made of white satin, and I thought it very glamorous. (When Jack and I moved to Somaliland, I wrote to Mum and asked her to have the dress dyed blue so I could wear it as an evening dress. Months later it arrived, but by then I was pregnant and couldn't wear it.) Before the wedding, Mum had asked me what china pattern I would like. In fact, I couldn't have cared less, but to make her happy, I said, more or less at random, "Spode, in the Gainsborough pattern." We received one Spode dinner plate and one Spode cup and saucer, and that was as far as we ever got in collecting a dinner service. One of Mum's presents to me had been the old silver teapot brought to Canada in the mid-1800s by my great-grandmother Wemyss, a marvellous pot-bellied affair sitting on a silver frame that held a small spirit lamp underneath to keep the tea warm. "You can clean it now," Mum had said with a small laugh.

Mum hadn't been too forthcoming at telling me about sex. Like so many of her generation, she was embarrassed. I learned more than the generation before me, however. My mother-in-law once told me that she had had absolutely no idea about any of the facts of life before she married. Mum didn't leave me quite so much in the dark. I had been told most of the basics, but Mum wanted me to know about birth control without actually having to tell me. It was a subject that was never talked about except secretly, among women. All the doctors were male and highly unsympathetic to young married women who did not want children right away.

Mum did her best. She passed on the advice not of the local doctor, but of his wife, who had told her the name of a birth control cream I could buy without a prescription. In the first year of our marriage, I got up my courage to ask a doctor in Winnipeg for a diaphragm. He looked at me sharply and said, "Why don't you want children?" I was twenty-one. I wanted children very much, but we simply couldn't afford to have a child yet. I never told my husband of my rage and bewilderment about the whole matter of birth control, but I do wish I could have discussed it more with Mum. I couldn't. Her uncertainty about how to talk about sex led her to make a joke out of it. Just before I was married, she and one of her friends gave me a story. It was called "Here We Are," by Dorothy Parker, about a young couple on their honeymoon who are very embarrassed about sex. I didn't know if Mum thought this amusing, but I was upset and offended, although I never told her so. In the following years, I came to see that what I'd always suspected was true: sex is never as much of a difficulty in marriage as, for example, money, methods of child-rearing, and birth control itself.

Jack and I moved into an apartment on Burrows Avenue in Winnipeg, opposite the Wisemans' house. Adele Wiseman and I had become firm friends and I wrote to her and her family just after I was married. I had gone to visit my Mum for a week. The letter is dated merely: "Neepawa, Monday (blue)." It's an amusing example of some of my youthful feelings, but it horrifies me to read my narrow-minded sentiments regarding Neepawa.

Dear Adele, Mary, Abe, Moe, et al: Stranded. Neepawa, as usual, is very much like itself. Nausea, real not mental, as usual, has set in. The uncomfortable accompaniment of great mental stress and strain. However, your voyageur is making valiant attempts to control the digestive system, and so far I haven't thrown up on anyone's oriental rugs. I'm writing to you because, if I don't, I shall explode. Mentally, that is. Jack is at St. Norbert [he was working as a surveyor] and I forgot to tell him to go to the post office there, for mail, and I'm sure he wouldn't think of it. So I don't think there's any point in writing to him. If you see him, however, tell him from me that he's the most wonderful guy in the world, and when I see him on Saturday, I'll fall on his neck and weep. I know it's ridiculous to be writing to you all so soon, especially as I'll be seeing you in a week, and I'm sorry if this epistle appears a trifle disjointed, but my need is great, believe me. We are all going to the lake tomorrow, about twenty people. Gay fun. Who should we ask? *A* isn't speaking to *B* right now, you know. Oh yes they are. I saw them say hello on the street. Well, *A* has never liked *B*, but they get along very well together. Okay, settled. Both *A* and *B* will come. But what about *C*, who is really such a bore? Oh, we have to ask her, well, you know, we just can't leave her out, and by the way, I heard the most dreadful thing, girls, about *C*'s daughter. It seems she was in a cafe one night and she. . . . No, she didn't. My dear, she certainly did. I wouldn't dream of telling her mother, of course. Tra la la, the flowers that bloom in the spring. And, of course, there's the story of the poor little Polish D.P. girl that the minister's wife met on a bus. She wanted to take medical training. What's that? No money? Ah, but my dear, such wonderful spirit, so determined, poor child. Her family, she said, was taken to Russia. . . . I'm probably being very unkind, but perhaps you will forgive me. I miss you all very much. We'll see you on Monday night, eh? Regards to you all, and to Mr. and Mrs. Wiseman.

Peggy, alias Prairie Flower.

I made the occasional visit to Neepawa, but Jack and I did not see much of Mum after our marriage. He was working to finish his degree in engineering and I had been hired by a Communist newspaper, *The Westerner*. At first I didn't realize it was a Communist paper (I guess I must have been a naïve kid) and when I discovered its political affiliations, I was surprised but not alarmed. I was then, and have remained, a Christian Social Democrat. I stuck with *The Westerner* until they had to fire me for lack of funds. Mitch, the editor, and I had many long arguments. I once wrote a very negative review for a book of poems by Joe Wallace, a Communist and a Catholic. He had been imprisoned for some years during the Second World War and appears in the late William Repka's *Dangerous Patriots,* a book on Communist Canadians imprisoned during the war. I thought Joe Wallace's poems were awful. I still think they're not very good, although they may be worth more than I knew at twenty-one. I recall Mitch telling me, "You can't write that kind of review about Joe's poems. He's a hero of the Left." I said, "They're not good poems, Mitch. That's all I care about." Obviously, I knew nothing about the writing of the Left. Obviously, Mitch knew nothing about the writing of any other sphere. But I learned a lot at that paper. I learned that the people whom I knew and worked with for about six months were very idealistic. They cared about the sufferings of people everywhere. Those old-time Communists in the forties in Winnipeg were not proposing violent revolution. They were proclaiming a need for social justice in terms of our land, and I discovered that many of their views were close to mine.

When *The Westerner* folded, I got a job with the burgeoning *Winnipeg Citizen,* the only co-operative daily ever to come into existence in Canada. It lasted a year. I wrote a radio column, did book reviews, and covered the labour beat, about which, at twenty-one, I knew absolutely nothing. Jack and I were living in an apartment in Anne and Bill Ross's house. Bill was an organizer for the Communist party and Anne was a nurse but wasn't herself a Communist. Because of our friendship and physical proximity, I, too, was apparently thought to be a Communist and was summoned by the managing editor, who told me this interesting fact about myself. I resigned on the spot. Years later, when a history was being written about the *Winnipeg*

Citizen, the old-time Liberal editor was asked whether he thought Margaret Laurence was a Communist. He replied, "Well, I don't know." For the record, no, I wasn't. If I had been, though, it would not have been a disgrace to be among their number. In fact it would have been an honour to be counted with people like Bill Tuomi, a Finn from Alberta, who as managing editor of *The Westerner* frequently didn't take a salary because the paper had no money, even though I was always paid mine.

After I left the *Citizen,* I worked at the YWCA as registrar. Twice a year we had massive registrations, when mums and daughters would sign up for swimming and gym classes, and I was supposed to organize all this. The scene was chaotic, and at the end of the day, the books never balanced. I used to want to put up the bucks we were missing or put into some common fund the money that was over, but things are never so simple.

While I was there, the Japanese Canadians were released from the camps and the Y formed a Teen Club for the younger ones. I'm not sure if this was the right thing to do. Possibly if the Y had tried to get those young and newly released people into a teen club with other teenagers who hadn't shared their experience, the Nisei would have stayed away in droves. I do know that the Y was one of the few places that at least tried to do something.

North Winnipeg in the 1940s decided a lot of my life. Mum didn't know much about what was happening to me. She was in Neepawa, coping with her ancient and difficult father and bringing up her young son. I was out there dancing on the earth. She worried about Jack and me, of course, especially when I once told her that we might go to Bulgaria to help build a railway, but our lives had grown increasingly separate. Jack and I went to England in 1949, and then to Somaliland in 1950. I only saw Mum four more times in the next eight years, but I wrote letters to her every week, for all those years. How patient and pained she must have been. How little I knew, and how much I know and care now, now that it's too late.

Mum managed to visit us in England in 1952, when Jack's and my daughter, Jocelyn, was born, despite the fact that grandfather Simpson was still stomping around and she had to find a housekeeper to look after him. She came to our flat in Hampstead, intending to stay for several weeks after the child was born, but our daughter was born two weeks later than predicted. In the weeks before she was born, Mum and I had some good times together, and some sad times. I was twenty-six and totally taken up with having a baby. I was ecstatic. I also knew that I would go on and write books. I had the energetic optimism of the young. I thought I could do everything. Mum knew, as I did not, that there would be a price. That year Mum was sixty-two. She seemed so old to me, although I perceive her differently now that I am sixty myself. Mum hated growing old. I don't like it much either, but I wonder if I hate it as much as she did. One day in London, just before Jocelyn was born, I was fussing with my hair. Mum, whose hair had been grey for years, said to me fairly angrily, "A lady gets dressed and makes up her appearance and then forgets about it." I felt a bit hurt, but I later saw that what she was trying to say was about herself, not about me at all.

When Mum went back to Canada, she had to look after the old man for another eight months, until his death on April 29, 1953, one month before his ninety-seventh birthday. Bob was twenty, working in Neepawa and soon to move to B.C. I was in Africa. After his death, she sold the last of our places, the Little House, and moved to Victoria, B.C., to be with her sister Ruby. In the spring of 1954, Jack and I and Jocelyn, who was then a year and a half old, went on leave to Canada. We crossed the country from Montreal to Vancouver by rail, and took the ferry to Victoria. Jack's parents lived there, too, so we divided our time between their house and Mum and Aunt Ruby's place. That was a wonderful leave. Jocelyn was talking non-stop, totally captivating her two grandmothers. We had waited to have her christened in Victoria for the sake of the grandparents, and my brother, who was working near Victoria, was able to be at Jocelyn's christening as her godfather.

Mum and I didn't have much time to talk by ourselves, but she wanted to hear all about what I was writing. I showed her a story set in West Africa, "The Drummer of All the World," which was finally published in *Queen's Quarterly* in 1956. I was relieved to see her living in Victoria, where the winters were not as severe as Manitoba's and where at last she was free of the old man. Yet there was a weariness in her. I sensed that she missed having her own home. All those harrowing years with Grandfather had also taken their toll. She was tired. No longer did she hate the thought of growing old. She felt old. It wasn't easy to have her daughter living so far away, although the saving grace was that her son lived relatively close by, but leaving her that spring, I felt enormously sad.

The next time I saw her was just after our son, David, was born in August 1955. He was born on the Gold Coast – what was soon to become Ghana – and Mum and Aunt Ruby came to London for part of our leave when he was only three months old and our daughter was three years. That was not one of the easiest times of my life. Affordable flats were hard to come by and we needed one quickly. Jack spent several days of weary and solitary looking, while I stayed with the children and Mum and Aunt Ruby in their expensive service flat, trying to keep Jocelyn entertained and David from yelling, simultaneously talking to Mum and my aunt, who had unfortunately slipped and broken her wrist several days after their arrival.

We finally all moved into a flat in Knightsbridge, only a block away from Harrod's, and we did our grocery shopping in those famed food halls. In fact, plain groceries were no more costly at Harrod's than anywhere else, and we did not, needless to say, go in for the more exotic items. Our flat was on the third floor so I had to drag the baby's carriage up and down two flights of stairs every day. The occupant of the floor below was, we presumed, a prostitute, who arrived home with an impressive variety of men and didn't appreciate my leaving the pram on the landing outside her door. She persistently moved it upstairs until I took the hint.

The flat was dark, dusty, gloomy, and, when we first arrived, filthy. I scoured, scrubbed, and almost literally threw Dettol around the place. David never adjusted to the time difference between West Africa and England, with the result that he awakened for his morning feeding at about 4 a.m. I would totter out of bed in the freezing dark, feed and settle the baby, and make myself a cup of instant coffee and a piece of toast to fend off the November chill. The flat was supposed to have central heating, but it didn't work. We used electric bar heaters, which meant our electricity bill was enormous. After my lonely repast, I would go back to bed, rise again at 8:30 with everyone else, and have a second breakfast. I gained pounds. Jocelyn, at three, toppled over on a frail little chair and hurt herself. I felt guilty for not having eyes in the back of my head. Aunt Ruby, who had been a nurse, couldn't understand why I kept the window slightly open in the children's room. She frequently told me that if the cold didn't kill them, the fog certainly would. Mum, who never gave unasked advice on how to raise my children, nonetheless didn't request that her elder sister refrain from doing so either. She twittered unhappily, torn between us. Jack bore all this with patience, but it was clear that this was far from his idea of a rejuvenating leave in a cool climate. Even Jocelyn moped, missing her friends back in Africa. No warm sandy beaches in London. Only David, being so young, was happy and continued to thrive, despite my aunt's gloomy prognostications.

Mum was there for David's christening, a private ceremony in a nearby Anglican church, and was thrilled to be able to buy a christening cake for her grandson at Harrod's. My joy on this occasion could not even be banished by the moment when my adored son burped up what looked like two cups of milk on the shoulder of the minister's splendid purple robe.

The time came for Mum and Aunt Ruby to return to Canada. We were staying on in London for another couple of months. Whatever the difficulties of a grotty flat in a London winter, the visit had been worth it for her, just to see me again, to see how her granddaughter had changed in the year and a half since we'd been to Victoria, and to see her grandson for the first time. Just before the taxi arrived, I gave Mum a long letter I had written to her and asked her not to open it until they got aboard the ship. It was odd that I felt so strongly moved to write that letter. I had no premonitions. I simply wanted to tell her (and for me, this was more possible on the page than in speech) how much I loved her, how much she meant to me, and how much her encouragement of my writing had strengthened me, even though I had had nothing published professionally. I also wanted to tell her that she could not have been more my mother if she had actually borne me.

I've always been glad I wrote that letter. When I next saw her, she was dying. Just before Christmas in 1956, Jack received a telegram from Aunt Ruby. She had sent it to him so he could give me the message and help me cope with it. Mum was dying of inoperable cancer of the pancreas. The doctors had, I learned later, tried to operate but realized when they did so that it was hopeless. They hadn't told her the operation hadn't been a success. It was the wrong strategy. Of course she knew, but she handled the knowledge, as she had always handled her problems, by herself.

I left Ghana with the two children early in January 1957. Jocelyn was four and a half and David was one and a half. Jack's tour of duty wouldn't be completed for several more months so he couldn't go with me, but we had already

112

21. My brother, Bob, and Mum.

22. Myself, age 17.

*34. Myself, Jocelyn, David, and Jack,
in Victoria, B.C., 1959.*

*35. David (age 6), Jocelyn (age 9), with their dad and
Granddad Laurence, Vancouver.*

decided we would go back to Canada at the end of this tour. We both felt a need to return to our own land after having been away for nearly nine years. Jack told me later how affected he had been, after saying goodbye at the Accra airport, by the sight of me walking across the tarmac to the plane, carrying one child while the other gamely trotted by my side.

We flew first to London, stopping over with Adele Wiseman, who was living there. Then a flight to Montreal, where we also stayed for a day with friends, and another flight to Vancouver. My childhood friend Mona met us at the Vancouver airport and a few days later took us to catch the small plane to Victoria. Aunt Ruby met us there. I'll never forget the relief with which she greeted me. "Here you are," she said. "You're young and strong. You'll take over. You'll manage things." Her voice was confident. I was suddenly petrified. I felt like my life had changed irrevocably. The fun was over. I was thirty-one.

Mum was home from hospital, weak, needing large doses of painkillers, but able to be up for part of the day, although she spent most of her living-room hours lying on the chesterfield. The next three months were among the most difficult and anguished of my life. Somehow I had to keep my children busy and happy and quiet, while not alarming them about their grandmother's illness. I desperately wanted to spend as much time with Mum as I could. Aunt Ruby was worried and tense, which made her touchy and easily upset by the slightest thing. I often felt like blowing up at her, but knew I absolutely must not. There was a lot of John Simpson in us all, his impatience, his quick anger, but also his endurance and strength. Under those circumstances, no one behaves like a saint. Inevitably there were times when Aunt Ruby and I did snap at each other, but we used to try to do it in whispers so Mum wouldn't hear.

One bone of contention was that Aunt Ruby had, she thought, arranged our accommodation perfectly. Hers was a small, one-floor house, with only two bedrooms, her own and Mum's. There was one finished room in the basement that belonged to my brother. The children were to sleep there and I was to sleep on a folding bed in Aunt Ruby's room. Contemplating this arrangement, my first thought was that I couldn't have my kids in the basement when I was so relatively far away. I would also have no privacy. Lights out when Aunt Ruby chose. No place to work late at night on the novel I had already completed in the second draft, or privacy to write letters to Jack and friends. Without privacy, I knew I would break down entirely.

It's strange how supposed trivialities can take on gigantic proportions. As Mum recovered from the surgery, she became able to go out for short periods, several afternoons a week. One afternoon shortly after our arrival, when she and Aunt Ruby were at a friend's for tea, I took action. Regarded with glee and astonishment by my prancing and excited young, I constructed a bedroom for myself in the basement, right beside theirs. Their bedroom had walls and a door and was furnished with a rug, a single bed, my brother's bookshelves, the old Wemyss desk that belonged to Bob, and a crib Aunt Ruby had borrowed for David. My room was somewhat different. The basement was a jumble of old trunks, cast-off furniture, clotheslines, and assorted junk. I wrestled the fold-up bed and mattress out of Aunt Ruby's room and down to the basement. I dragged two trunks and spaced them at the end of the bed. I found an old door and placed it with one end on each trunk; I had a desk. I rigged up a discarded lamp from the ceiling light with an extra socket. I strung up clotheslines across the open sides of my room and slung blankets from them to act as walls. I had my own space before Mum and Aunt Ruby returned.

When they got home, my aunt was furious. She not only couldn't conceive of a decent bedroom in the basement, she couldn't understand my need for privacy or my need to be

114

close to my children. Under great strain, she lashed out at me. I became angry myself. "You don't understand, you just don't! You've never had children. I'm not going to have them sleeping away down there if I'm not near them. And I'm not a child! I can't sleep in your bedroom!"

Mum, of course, was terribly distressed, but if anyone was a tower of strength during those months, it was Mum herself. Aunt Ruby was, as she always had been, efficient and capable. Every day, despite our occasional disagreements, I marvelled at her determined cheerfulness, at the way in which she concealed her own grief. I could see, more than I ever had before, the qualities that had made Ruby Simpson such a fine nurse and administrator. When personal emotions threatened, she became all practicality, concentrating on the details of everyday life: meals, medication, the evening glass of sherry, news of neighbours and friends. She was magnificent. As for me, I tried my best. What held me together was that I had to follow Aunt Ruby's lead for Mum's sake and for the sake of my children. My brother, who was working in Nanaimo, came home as often as he could. He was a great help and support to me when he was there. Another thing that saved me was taking the kids for visits to Jack's parents. I could hardly believe the strength his mother gave me.

Mum knew she was dying. I have often wondered since if she would have liked to talk about it. I decided at the time that if she wanted to, she herself would bring up the subject. I didn't feel I could. Undoubtedly I was frightened. But there are ways of communicating other than words. She was quietly affectionate towards us all. She took a delight in the children, even when their chirpy, sometimes angry voices disturbed her. David was too young to understand what was happening, although he did seem to know when it was okay to yell and when it wasn't. It should have been all right for a little kid to make a noise any time, though, and I worried about this. Jocelyn knew her grandmother was very ill. She would often present Mum with drawings, or bring her a bird feather we found on one of our walks, or tell her a story just composed by herself, or just sit beside Mum as she lay on the chesterfield, sharing one of the Little Golden Books we had brought with us.

I never did end up discussing death with Mum. The closest we came was one day when I was sitting with her in her bedroom. She suddenly told me that she'd always admired a verse by Walter Savage Landor, and she quoted it:

I strove with none, for none was worth my strife
Nature I loved, and next to nature, art
I warmed both hands before the fire of life
It sinks, and I am ready to depart.

It was a verse I knew by heart, too. Its title is "On His Seventy-fifth Birthday." Mum was in her sixty-eighth year. After she said the lines, I couldn't speak. I couldn't help the tears. They came to my eyes in the way they do when one is moved, by literature and by great love. I reached out for her hand and we sat in silence for a while. Then she changed the subject.

I think she wanted it that way. No long discussions of what was to come, soon, for her. In the most amazing way, she was trying to comfort me, comfort all of us. I don't know what she said to Ruby or her other sister Vem, who came over from the Okanagan to be with her, or to Bob, her son. I only know what she said to me. Naturally, she thought of a poem. I remembered the times we had done the dishes in the Big House, taking turns at quoting the lines from poems to see who could get the farthest.

I thought, too, of our shared love for writing. I was anxious, but very hesitant, about showing her the second and, as I mistakenly thought, final draft of the novel I had written in Ghana, *This Side Jordan*. I finally brought the typescript up from my basement study-bedroom, a room for which I had developed a very great affection, much as I had long ago for my play-house. I had been writing it for nearly

116

two years. I gave it to her and asked her to read it, as she had read so much of my writing for so long. My aunt Ruby also asked if she could read it. Somewhat startled, I agreed. I didn't think my aunt would like it and she didn't. When Aunt Ruby read it, her only comment was very restrained: "Dear, I think it's rather *gross*." I felt such a surge of family affection for her, I nearly burst out laughing.

Mum read the manuscript differently. I don't think I, as a writer, can convey in words how I felt when, after some days, we talked about the novel. Despite the fact that by then, she was usually not able to concentrate properly for more than short periods of time, I sat beside her bed and she went through the manuscript, section by section. We were back, suddenly, to her critic-teacher, lover-of-literature self, and I, to my young self. It was her final gift to me. It was as though the illness, for some hours, fell away. She analyzed my novel with the same perception and fairness, the same hard, reliable honesty she had always had. She told me she thought I had given a moving portrayal of West African society and the dilemma of Africans torn between the world of their ancestors and the new world of western education, meanwhile hating colonialism and determined to gain independence. She had no trouble in perceiving the themes, but she thought I had over-purpled the prose in some of the African chapters and had been less than sympathetic in the European chapters. She understood I was against colonialism and she didn't take issue with that. She just felt I had put my heart and soul into a portrayal of the African characters and had, unconsciously or deliberately, made stereotypes of the whites. For a novel, that was not good enough.

We didn't talk for an hour, as planned. We probably talked for three, me dashing out to get the kids fed and put to bed, the kids somehow understanding that something important was going on. Aunt Ruby, too, was puzzled, but knew the session mattered, in some mysterious way, so very much to both Mum and me.

Mum was right. Not completely right, but mainly right in her assessment of the manuscript. In fact, the publishers to whom I first submitted the novel didn't accept it, but gave me a long criticism, a compilation of their readers' reports. In essence, they said the same things as Mum. Ultimately, I rewrote half the novel, every other chapter, the ones dealing with the Europeans. I said to Mum that day, "Maybe it will be published eventually. It's dedicated to you." I think she knew that day would come, and it did. *This Side Jordan* was finally published in 1960, three years after she died.

When Jack came back from Africa, the children and I went over to Vancouver, where we would live for the next five years. We rented an apartment in North Van and Jack got a job with an engineering firm. For a while, things were relatively calm. Mum wasn't getting worse and I hoped that the illness was in a long remission. She was well enough to visit us briefly in North Vancouver for a few days. While she was there, she insisted on going out to the nearby supermarket with me. I didn't realize, until we had begun shopping, what a mistake it had been to agree. I looked at Mum. She was struggling hard to keep up, but it was apparent she was in pain and exhausted. A few months later, my aunt phoned to tell me Mum was in hospital again. I took the children and went to Victoria.

She was never to leave that hospital. They had begun to give her morphine and her mind would sometimes drift a small way away. She told me with an ironic smile that the nurses always stood by until she had swallowed her nightly sleeping pill. "They're afraid I'll save them up," she said. She wanted to know how we were getting on. I told her I'd got a job marking English essays, as an outside marker, for the University of British Columbia. "It's pennies from heaven," I said, and immediately regretted the cliché. She knew we needed money and that, when she died, Bob and I would inherit such money as she had. I had no idea what her estate was and didn't care, as long as she had enough money for her lifetime. When she died, her estate came to $4,000, and I realized how she must have worried, those last years, at having such slender resources.

She asked to see Jocelyn and David. The nurses tied her white hair with a blue ribbon, put on her lacy nightgown and a new soft, woollen jacket, installed her in a wheel-chair, and brought her down to the lobby in the hospital, where Aunt Ruby and I were waiting with the children. The kids were very quiet, but they both said hello to Granny. By this time I had told them that she was dying, trying to explain it as best I could. After a few moments, the nurses took her back to her room, but not before she had looked carefully at the children, storing up a picture of them in her memory, memory that was soon to be lost.

Yet the strong Simpson heart went on. I went back to Vancouver once again. Then, in September, not long after my previous visit, Aunt Ruby phoned. Mum was in the final stages of her illness. Bob was working in a bank in Nanaimo. He got several weeks off and drove to Victoria. I found someone to look after the kids and travelled over myself. Bob and I stayed at Aunt Ruby's for several weeks. I had Bob's old room and he slept on the chesterfield. I lay there, praying that Mum would die soon. It is a strange feeling to pray for the death of someone you love so deeply. Every day, Bob and I went to the hospital together. It was the most terrible time of our lives. But my brother, seven years younger than I, was suddenly the one who was enormously strong, who propped me up and got both of us through that ordeal. My brother, who was not a very ver-bal person, was sometimes able to speak when I could not. When Mum's mind had gone far away, when she said to us, speaking of old and dear friends she'd known long ago in Calgary, "Can we have Jen and Sadie for a picnic?" his voice, very steady, said, "Sure we can. Of course we will. I don't see why not."

My brother and I had never been closer, or more suppor-tive of each other, than we were when our Mum was dying.

By this time, her skin had turned very dark, almost an olive black, apparently something that can happen with terminal cancer. It was not frightening. There was even a strange beauty about it. In her last days, though, when her mind wandered away, she never for one minute forgot her children. She always knew it was Bob and me there. She lost almost everything else, but she never lost her children's names.

Our other aunt, Vem, Mum's youngest sister, was staying on at Aunt Ruby's, too. They were devastated, but I think in a different way from Bob and myself. They had been children together, they had grown up together with the same mother and father. That is a special anguish. But for Bob and me, at twenty-four and thirty-one, it was difficult to think of life without her, even though we were both quite independent. After our daily visit to the hospital, we used to go to a quiet bar and have a drink together and talk. That closeness helped both of us a lot.

Mum's death went on and on. Bob had his job in Nanaimo. I had a husband and two small children in Vancouver. When people say, "Life must go on," they don't necessarily know at what price. Her sisters were there when she finally achieved her death. Her children were not. I wish in some ways that we had been with her, but I have a feeling that if her mind had been present, she wouldn't have wanted that. I have the feeling that, when I die, I won't need my children to be there at the last moment. Everything that needs to be either has been said or will never be said. The mutual love of a lifetime doesn't need to be restated. It is there. I've never liked people seeing me off at airports. Mum never liked people seeing her off on trips either. No one can tell about that last voyage – the one truly solitary one, but in a sense, not solitary at all – in which the baggage of an entire lifetime is finally lightened, perhaps in both senses of the word.

Margaret Simpson Wemyss died on September 25, 1957, in Victoria, B.C., in her sixty-eighth year.

It's been many years now. Yet I still think, "So long, Mum. May your spirit still dance on the earth, in stillness and in the lives of your inheritors. I will always miss you, but I will always celebrate you."

IV
ELSIE

My mother-in-law was one of my mothers. I'm privileged to say that, as are her other daughters- and sons-in-law. This memoir of my mother-in-law will be short, because I was not one of her own children. In one way, I wondered if I had the right to write about her at all. I think I do, though, because I cared about her so much, and she about me. She was not only my mother-in-law; she was my friend. I write about her out of family legends and my own memories. I don't want to intrude into her children's or grandchildren's or great-grandchildren's lives. I am extremely aware of the privacy of families. What I want to express are my own feelings about that remarkable woman, a woman who gave me such loving strength over so many years. Almost immediately I called her Mother, and I continued to do so throughout our friendship. I had never called anyone Mother before. She remained one of my mothers until her death. Her story became part of mine. She was what is now called a role model. I realized only partly at the time what great determination she passed on to me through all my writing and childbearing life. I owe her a debt of loving gratitude.

Elsie Fry, the youngest child of a Church of England minister, was born on April 26, 1893, in Waterfield, Sussex. She had two sisters, Beatrice and Bessie, and two brothers. Her brothers decided to emigrate to Canada; her elder sister, Beatrice, became a missionary in India; her sister Bess became an artist.

When she was eighteen, Elsie went to pre-revolutionary Russia and worked in Moscow as a governess for a Jewish family. While she was there, she wrote a novel under the pen name of Christine Field. The novel, titled *Half A Gypsy*, concerned a young Englishwoman who went to Russia as a rebellious young person – half a gypsy – taught as a governess, and ultimately met and married a young man who turned out to be an English titled gentleman. It was a romance, a fantasy, but its backdrop of Moscow society in the days preceding the Revolution and the First World War was authentic enough.

Elsie completed her novel while in Moscow and submitted it to an English publisher, Andrew Melrose, Ltd., in 1912. She was nineteen. She had supplied her Moscow address, but heard nothing. Eventually she returned to England. Her father died and her mother decided to take her daughters and join her two sons in Canada. Elsie, her sister Bessie, and their mother all left England, and in the emotional and physical turmoil of that decisive move, all thoughts of the novel must have gone from her mind.

She had no idea that the novel had been published in 1916 until about a year later, when the book finally found its way to her, presumably through friends or relatives in England. The note printed at the front of the novel tells the strange story:

> Publisher's note. The Ms of this story of an English governess in Russia was sent to us some time before the war, by "Christine Field," c / o F.E. Fry, Malaya, Bronnaya, Moscow House 28. Since then, attempts made to get into communication with the author at this address have been unsuccessful. And notwithstanding the kindness of the press in giving wide publicity to the fact that Mr. Melrose was anxious to publish, the author remains undiscovered. Meantime, Mr. W.L. Courtney, editor of the Fortnightly Review, Mr. C.K. Shorter, editor of the Sphere, and Miss Smith-Dampier, the well-known novelist, have kindly agreed to look after the author's interests. A publishing proposal has been drawn up and approved by all

three, and we hope that the publication of the novel will lead to the discovery of the author, thus launched on a literary career in an unusual fashion. Andrew Melrose, Ltd., 3 York Street, Covent Garden. September, 1916.

Elsie, her mother, and her sister ended up in South Fort George, B.C., where Elsie met John Laurence, a Highland Scot from the Shetland Isles. John Laurence may not have been well educated in middle-class terms, but he had the pride and sense of honour of the Highlanders. John and Elsie married on August 28, 1915. John had joined the army before they were married. He went away to war leaving his young wife pregnant with their first child, John Fergus Laurence, my future husband and the father of my children. He was born on August 6, 1916.

The next few years for Elsie must have been difficult, despite the support she received from her mother. She worked in the Land Titles Office, looked after her young son, and wrote without knowing that her first novel had been published.

John Laurence came home when the war ended in 1918. My father-in-law once told me about a time during the First World War when the horses were dying, mired in the mud. A young officer (John Laurence, like my father, was never an officer) was raked over the coals, blamed for what no one could be blamed for. "He was just a kid," my father-in-law said to me, eyes even then unbelieving. "Just a kid!" He wept. He had been just a kid, too, like my father, like so many of them.

When John returned, the family moved to Edson, Alberta, where he got a job as a CNR lineman. Six more children followed. The Depression came and the prairie drought of the thirties. Then the Second World War in which two of Elsie's sons participated – Jack as a mechanic in the RAF, Robert as a bomber pilot in the RCAF. Elsie kept writing, on and off. She had stories published in magazines such as *Chatelaine* and some of her poetry was published in Ryerson Chapbooks. Her writing had to be, in a practical sense, secondary to her husband and children. She and John Laurence were from a generation where a woman's primary role was as a homemaker, not a writer. Nonetheless, if her writing was an activity that could only occupy the corners of her life, she was a woman with a vocation, a vocation she had known about since she was an eighteen-year-old girl in Moscow.

She was also a woman who not only wanted her own children, but needed them. Jack was the first of her children to get married, when Elsie herself was fifty-four. I was terribly nervous about meeting her, but when I finally did, we embarked on a close relationship that lasted until her death. Through our correspondence, and whenever we met, we would talk interminably about the two things that mattered most to both of us, children and writing. She was always tactful and kind. She once read one of my West African stories and commented, "People do seem to punctuate fairly oddly these days." It turned out she didn't want to hurt my feelings, but she couldn't ignore the fact that I had used the semicolon incorrectly.

She also told me she thought I was a good mother. That meant an enormous amount to me. I was so uncertain by then about my triple role as wife, mother, and writer. My sense of being torn apart, in those five years in Vancouver, was severe. It reached its peak when my first novel was published in 1960. Jack and I separated in 1962, he to pursue his own vocation as an irrigation engineer in East Pakistan. I took the children to England.

It was a wrenching time for both of us. Our families – my aunts, Jack's brothers and sisters – were understandably somewhat hostile towards me. I, a woman and a mother, was the one who insisted that I had to do my own work at the price of my marriage. My aunts thought I was acting very badly. I had no real support from my family, or my husband's family, for several years, except for one person.

My mother-in-law was probably the only person in either family who truly understood what I was experiencing and who gave me her total support and love. She knew how much I cared about Jack and our children, but she, and she alone, knew too how much I had to follow, with doubt and with guilt, but with certainty, the vocation that had been given me. She told me in a letter that at the end of the First World War, when Jack was two and her husband had just returned from the war, she seriously considered taking her young child and leaving her husband so she could concentrate on her writing. She stayed, of course. Her decision was very much a product of her background, a background that demanded she choose what she felt to be the most difficult and morally right course. She bore her children and lived to rejoice greatly in them, and in her grandchildren, and even her great-grandchildren. She never ceased to give thanks for the survival of her husband and two of her sons in the two wars, and she never ceased to hate war. But she must have wondered sometimes why it couldn't be possible both to have children and to write books.

The writing she did was perceptive and delicate, staunch in faith, honouring the human spirit and the Holy Spirit. Her second novel, *Bright Wings,* was published in 1964, almost fifty years after her first, the same year that my novel *The Stone Angel* was published. She and I had a very different idiom, of course. Our writing almost came out of different cultures, but she could understand *The Stone Angel* just as I understood *Bright Wings.* It is a novel that has never had the acknowledgment it deserves. It was published, in a sense, too late, out of a pattern that had not been fashionable for some time. Although it has its didactic moments, it is basically a novel written out of a passionate ecumenical faith, akin to Gwethalyn Graham's novel *Earth and High Heaven.* It is, in the end, an honourable statement of faith and compassion.

I wish my mother-in-law's life had allowed her to write more. She was a talented and courageous woman, growing up in a society that, for the most part, didn't care to know about talented and courageous women unless they were from upper-class, wealthy families and their talents could be nurtured by private means. She didn't have those advantages. Virginia Woolf said, "A woman must have money and a room of her own if she is to write fiction." Woolf always had both, and in her husband, Leonard Woolf, she also had someone who looked after her devotedly. Virginia Woolf is a writer whose perceptions helped shape my view of life, as did her brand of feminism, but by the time I was in my late twenties, I began to feel that her writing lacked something I needed. That something was a sense of physical reality. Her characters were beautifully, ironically drawn, but what was lacking was ordinariness, dirt, earth, blood, yelling, a few messy kids. Woolf's novels, so immaculate and fastidious in the use of words, are also immaculate and fastidious in ways that most people's lives are not. She says a great deal, but there is a profound way in which she doesn't speak to my own life.

But Woolf had the freedom to write. Elsie Fry Laurence, who wanted to have children and to write, could not. She did what all Canadian women writers at that time, and most now, have done: raise the kids, do the housework, be a wife, try to be an understanding comrade if possible, and do your writing in short spaces of spare time, usually early in the morning or late at night. Almost all the Canadian women writers of my generation, and indeed of a generation younger, have married and borne children. Many of us have had to bring up those children, for the most part, by ourselves. Some men of my children's generation have begun to take a more active role in child-rearing and housework, but it's usually a woman who ends up doing the cooking, the cleaning, the mending of clothes, and the mending of hearts. Although these areas are no longer thought of as exclusively women's responsibilities, my sense of it is that the division of domestic labour is still not as equitable as I had hoped it would be.

Elsie was in fact a pioneer in the area of Canadian women's writing, in the area of women writers' needs, although I don't think she ever realized quite the effect her efforts had on the generations to come. I know it, and so do her children and grandchildren. Jack always thought his mother's writing was comparable to Katherine Mansfield's. That's true, but Mansfield was both more protected and much more damaged. She was somehow never quite able to take on her own life. Elsie did take on her own life, with faith, integrity, and caring.

When Granddad Laurence died in 1967, Gran remained in the house in Victoria by herself. She was alone, but never completely. Her children and grandchildren visited her constantly. In one of her last letters to me, she wrote that as all one's senses decline, one is very grateful for a continuing sense of humour. That comment, that wisdom, was typical of her. I was able to tell her, as I had told my Mum, how much she meant to me, but in Gran's case, I did it not with one letter but over many years. On her part, she always started her letters to me "Dearest Margaret." She told me many times how much she cared about me, and I was able to say the same thing to her. In fact, I don't know how I could have survived as well as I did without her support and love. I remember the late Ethel Wilson telling me when I was a young writer in Vancouver, "Only God can be fair to more than one person at a time." I loved and respected Ethel Wilson, but in that respect, she was wrong. My mother-in-law, with God's help, no doubt, did manage to be fair to more than one person at a time.

Elsie Fry Laurence died on March 4, 1982, at the age of eighty-seven. She had lived in her own home until very shortly before her death. When I leave life, if I am half as much loved as Elsie Fry Laurence was and continues to be, I will consider myself, as I think she was, blessed among women.

Mother, my mother-in-law, my mother in heart, beyond any law, my friend, may your spirit continue to proclaim itself in the dance of life that goes on in us, your children, your grandchildren, your great-grandchildren. Dance on, Elsie, dance on, and you will live on, in all of us. I have learned from you, and will always, in all ways. May God bless you. May you know how grateful I am to you.

V
MARGARET

When my children were young, I used to tell them their birth stories in ways they could understand. Their own entries into life fascinated them. I've told these stories to women friends, as they have told me the stories of their own children's births. Women often talk of birth, though it continues to be considered, for the most part, an unsuitable and indeed boring subject for conversation in mixed company. Women don't really *converse* on this subject, however. It isn't the stuff of idle chatter. It is the core of our lives.

I had, in thinking of this memoir, a lot of doubt on the matter of writing about my children. I have always refused to talk about them in interviews. Their lives belong to themselves, not to me, much less to the media. I finally decided, however, that their births are an integral part of my story as well as theirs, and that I was justified in writing about them as children solely in terms of our situation when I was writing each of my books.

The fact is that being a woman writer and a mother is very different from being a male writer and a father. This difference may be diminishing. I hope so. I approve of both parents sharing not only the work but the many rewards of daily child-rearing. This was not common in my generation, nor in any preceding ones, but I should add, with gratitude, that in the early years of my children's lives, I didn't have to earn a living. Young mothers today may share parenting more fully, but they also have to contribute to the family income. I am qualified to speak only as a woman writer. I am aware of the dilemmas experienced by women who have had to work at outside jobs, as well as being mothers and wives. Their work, often ill-paid and boring, has involved more difficulties and required more sheer guts than I've ever had to have. Women writers with children are fortunate in some ways. Among women with vocations, women who have felt that sense of dedication and passionate interest in being doctors, lawyers, scholars, or teachers, only writers (and, occasionally, visual artists) can do their work at home.

Despite being at home, however, with all the benefits to the nuclear family that might imply, women writers have high divorce rates. The reasons are not obscure. Faced with the daily demands of their own work, the daily needs of their children and their husbands, and the ever-present pressures of a household – the cooking, the shopping, the cleaning, and so on – a woman writer often feels what I believe is termed role conflict. How can you do everything, be everything, at once? So many women writers have, for too much of their professional lives, put themselves and their work last, as women in all areas have been socially conditioned to do over centuries. The best, most poignant description and analysis of such situations are found in Tillie Olsen's heart-rending book, *Silences*. Many married women writers with children have found this multiplicity of roles ultimately insupportable, and have either stopped writing or left the marriage, almost always taking their children along with them on the unknown and perilous path. Stay or go. The choices are unambiguous.

In Canada, women who were writers as well as wives and mothers have an honourable tradition. Nellie McClung has long been a heroine of mine. Catharine Parr Traill, another heroine, was writer, wife, and botanist, although I have a feeling, looking at books of hers such as *The Backwoods of Canada* and *The Canadian Settlers Guide*, that Catharine's determined faith, not only in God but in the new country, precluded her ever recording how awful, what a shock, it must have been. Her sister Susanna Moodie was somewhat more forthcoming in *Roughing It in the Bush,* but she was also more self-pitying, a quality Catharine never permitted herself.

I always wanted both: children and the chance to write. And I had both, though at a price. I wrote to Adele Wiseman just before and just after Jack's and my daughter Jocelyn was born.

> 16 Belsize Lane,
> London, NW 3, England,
> 18 August, '52.

Dear Adele,

I wonder if you ever received the air letter I wrote you some time ago. I should have written again before now, and hope you'll forgive me. I seem to have found it so hard to settle down to anything, even letter writing. We're getting a bit worried about you, as we thought you'd be arriving in England soon, and it has just occurred to us that you may not have received my letter. The whole problem with me is that the wretched baby hasn't arrived yet, although nearly a week overdue. I know this isn't unusual with first babies, but it is rather maddening all the same. Especially as I'm about twice the size I was when we saw you, and I can't seem to focus my mind on anything much except wondering when this kid is going to arrive. It weighs about a ton, or so it feels, and I wish the little so-and-so would decide to get itself born. My Mum is here. We've managed to get out quite a bit, despite my condition, and have shown a lot of London to her. It's been nice to have her here. The whole thing is, when you come to England, we would like you to stay with us here and, in any event, we want to meet you at the station. Please let us know when you're coming. I do hope you're all right and that everything is okay as regards your passage back home, etc. Please excuse this short and inadequate letter. As I said

137

before, my mind is sort of vacant these days, preoccupied as it were. If this baby doesn't arrive soon, I think I shall have to take up riding, or gym classes, or something. Please write soon and let us know when you're coming to England. It'll be good to see you again. I hope you're coming soon.

Love, Peggy.

Elizabeth Garrett Anderson
Maternity Hospital,
Belsize Park, London NW 3
England,
6 Sept. '52.

Dear Adele:

Well, the great event has happened at last, after what seemed interminable waiting. The baby was born on August 28. She is a lovely little girl, and not so little either. She was 9 lbs, 4½ ozs. at birth. Despite my confidence that it would be an easy birth, unfortunately it wasn't, partly because the baby was just too big for me. I was in labour for 36 hours, which was rather unfortunate, since by the time she came to be born, I was too tired to manage her by myself. Finally, they had to give me an anesthetic and finish the delivery with forceps. Her shoulders were terribly broad, and they cracked her collarbone when they were delivering her. However, this isn't as horrible as it sounds, and is quite common in forceps deliveries. It heals awfully quickly in new babies, and hers is quite healed already. She moves the arm quite naturally, and it gives her no pain any more. The doctor says that there will be no after effects, thank goodness. I never thought I'd be such a doting mother, but quite honestly, she is such a lovely child. She is so sturdy and well built, and has none of that puckered, newborn look. I suppose because she was two weeks late in arriving. She has masses of dark hair. I think her eyes will be blue-grey, like Jack's. Despite the fact that Jack wanted a boy, I think he is quite pleased with her and says she is really quite good-looking, which is high praise indeed. We are calling her Barbara Jocelyn. I'm so keen for you to see her. Thanks for your last letter. We'll be so glad to see you again. If you let us know the exact time and place of arrival, we'd like to meet you. I'll be out of hospital on Sept. 10, and I'll certainly be glad to get home, although the hospital here is extremely nice. I feel quite well again, which is a great blessing. Must go. Please excuse the poor effort of a letter, but I'm no good without my typewriter.

Love, Peg.

My young self sounds quite different from the way I feel now, but I couldn't entirely express my feelings. I was so guarded, so conventional. I wrote that Jack wanted a boy, but was "quite pleased with her." Men were supposed to want sons and so, of course, they responded that way. From my current perspective, I realize that Jack probably wasn't as concerned about having a son as I then imagined. He was likely more concerned about me, about whether I would survive what he imagined, like most men, to be a terrifying ordeal. My thoughts were for the child. His thoughts and concerns, shut out of the childbearing process as he was, were for me.

Most of my first pregnancy took place while we were in Somaliland. A friend in England had sent me Dr. Grantly Dick-Read's book on natural childbirth and I had done the exercises as much as I could. I believe in those theories and still do, but they didn't entirely work for me, partly because our daughter was a very large baby and partly

139

because I had had no real help or instruction, although the doctors in London at the Elizabeth Garrett Anderson Hospital gave me every support when I told them I wanted to attempt natural childbirth. The entire staff were women, and I can clearly recall when my child's head was born and her shoulders got stuck, the doctor saying to me, "Mrs. Laurence, the spirit is willing, but the flesh is weak." I gave them my permission to give me an anaesthetic and deliver my baby with forceps from the shoulders. I didn't hold her for two days and wasn't told until some time after the birth that her collarbone had been broken. I later heard that, before I ever held her or nursed her, they had taken her out of the hospital twice to have her collarbone x-rayed.

I don't know the exact time my daughter was born because, of course, I was out like a light. I remember waking up from the anaesthetic, though. A nurse was nearby and I asked the question that I guess every mother asks, which is never "Is it a girl or a boy?" The question is always "Is my baby all right?" The nurse said, "Yes, Mrs. Laurence, you have a lovely daughter. She's just fine." My next words have always amused me. Groggy as I was, I asked, "Did I have to be cut? Have I got stitches?" The nurse said, "Yes, you've got a few stitches," and I said, "Oh my God, I won't be able to sleep with my husband for months." I must have sounded so appalled the nurse simply laughed. "Take lots of salt baths," she said. "You'll be okay."

Finally, they brought Jocelyn to me. This was a moment of revelation. I had always wanted to bear a child with the man I loved. Now she was here, so beautiful, so much herself, and I didn't know what to do. I had no idea how to look after her. I had Dr. Spock's book, but that wasn't going to solve every daily problem. And yet, and yet, holding this miracle in my arms, seeing her quiet contented breathing, her latching onto my breast for nourishment, taught me something I had never begun to guess at. Our children are indeed our hostages to fortune. It is the only

140

time that we realize we love somebody more than we love ourselves, more than we love our beloved mates, our parents, our friends. Adele and I have said over the years, about our children, my daughter, my son, and her daughter, "We pray a lot," and we do. Some people have wondered why I have become so voluble in my protests against the nuclear arms race. It is because, by an extension of the imagination, all children are mine. All the children, beloved by their mothers and fathers, belong to all of us.

When our daughter was two months old, she nearly died. We were living in our flat in Hampstead, preparing to go back to West Africa. Jocelyn had just had her injections for smallpox and yellow fever. We took her home and put her to bed. Suddenly her small body went into convulsions. I can't remember ever having been so frightened. We had no idea what was wrong. We called around and were told to take her to the Lawn Road Fever Hospital in Hampstead. I could only think that if my child died, I wouldn't want to live.

Jocelyn was admitted to hospital, but she wasn't diagnosed. I kept asking to see the doctor, who kept refusing to see me. Apparently he was annoyed because I had refused to stop breast-feeding my child during her illness. I was only twenty-six years old and not very knowledgeable, but I did know that if a very young baby is ill, it isn't advisable to change the feeding or substitute bottles for breast-feeding, so I remained firm. The nurses were wonderfully sympathetic. The doctor wished I would go away.

I walked nearly two miles, four times a day, to feed our daughter. Jack was heroic. When I got back to our flat, I cried until I had to go to the hospital again. It was dreadful for him. I cried constantly. He must have nearly floated out of the flat on a tide of my tears.

I finally got an audience with the doctor, a young man who looked at me as though I were a kind of lesser species and who told me that probably the child had a tendency to convulsions, which she might or might not get over by the

141

time she was sixteen, or else she had spinal meningitis, which at that time I believed to be inevitably fatal. The fact was that he didn't know what was wrong so he tossed out those two facile and brutal answers.

Jocelyn remained in the Lawn Road Fever Hospital for more than a week. Her convulsions finally ceased and she actually came out of hospital blossoming, having gained nearly two pounds. It turned out that she'd been given her yellow fever and smallpox shots too close together and in the wrong order. I discovered this three years later when I took our son to the Hospital for Tropical Diseases in London to have *his* shots when he was two months old. I mentioned what had happened to our daughter. The doctor said, "Mrs. Laurence, please write down everything you remember about the experience. You're lucky that your daughter was a large, healthy baby, because some babies who were smaller and more vulnerable died from the same thing." So little did we know when Jocelyn was a baby, however, that after she was discharged from hospital, we thought the smallpox vaccination hadn't taken and immediately had her re-vaccinated.

We were about to embark on the next stage of our adventures, which took place on the Gold Coast (later to become Ghana). For the first year Jack was second-in-command of building the new port of Tema. When we arrived in Accra, we stayed with Jack's boss and his wife for three weeks. They were an older couple who had never had children, and unfortunately our kid was doing a lot of yelling, since her smallpox vaccination made her extremely uncomfortable. I walked the floor with her, hoping she wouldn't disturb the boss and his wife too much, while Jack tried to accustom himself to the new job.

One of my responsibilities was to buy things for our new house. The Public Works Department provided furniture, but I had to find curtains, china, all the accoutrements of a household, at the same time not wanting to leave

142

my baby for a second. I didn't have the self-confidence to say, "Somebody else has got to go." I did what was expected of me, and Jocelyn was cared for by several African servants. I began to realize that, as I had been in Somalia, I was going to have to be a memsahib, a concept I hated and despised.

At last we moved into our own house in Accra. It was an architect-designed house that had no screens in a land replete with bugs. The living room and dining room had louvers, as did the bedrooms. You took your choice. Either you opened the windows and took the chance of thieves, or you closed the windows and opened the lower-level louvers, inviting in scorpions and snakes. Occasionally we'd leave the dining-room doors open and bats would flit in. I was petrified of bats, and would stand turned to stone as Jack, understandably annoyed, yelled, "How the hell do you expect me to get this damn bat out unless you help me?" Oh, true. It was a lovely house to look at, but unpractical to a degree. When we went to bed, we chose to close the louvers in the bedrooms and open the windows, preferring the chance of marauders to the chance of snakes and scorpions.

There were also other dangers farther from home. When Jocelyn was about six months old, she nearly drowned. We had taken her to a beach near Tema. I was holding her in my arms, she naked and slippery as a little eel, when I did something that no one should ever do. In fact, I even knew better myself. I turned my back on the ocean, on the South Atlantic with its enormous breakers. You couldn't swim there. The sea was very shallow close to shore, but the breakers came rolling in, high and strong. I wasn't far from shore but a giant breaker came in and swept me off my feet. I clutched my daughter desperately; if I had loosened my grip on her for a second, she would have been gone forever. Breakers came in and swept out. Jack ran down and instantly hauled both of us onto the beach. He saved our lives that day, but I can still have nightmares about what could have happened.

Although we had these few tense moments, for the most part in Accra, and later when we moved out to Tema, a small fishing village that was to become the central port of the country, we had a lot of good times. We were young, we were in love, we had a beautiful child, and we had a lot of pure enjoyment in life itself. I was writing, but I didn't talk about it much. I wrote to Adele, however, when I was twenty-eight and pregnant with my second child. The novel I refer to was never finished; it simply didn't work out.

c/o Chief Engineer,
Port of Tema,
P.O. Box 1, Tema,
Gold Coast, West Africa,
12 March, '55.

Dear Adele:

First of all, are you all right? Did you receive my last letter? I'm beginning to get worried. We don't seem to have heard from you for a long time. If you're okay, please don't take this as a reproach. I can't talk about not writing letters, as apart from that one letter to you, the only people I've written to for months are my mother and Jack's. I'm trying to get up enough stamina now to tackle the dozens of letters I owe. I hope you're alright, and also the rest of the family. I can't remember what I said in my last letter, but I think I mentioned we'd be going on a leave in November. It is now changed to the middle of December. Lovely time to go on leave from a hot country, but there is a chance that my Mum and Aunt may be going to England to see us on our leave and, if so, I may go early, say beginning of Nov. to be with them. We now plan to spend two months of our leave in London and the other month, if we can find a heated flat, in Rome. Any chance of your being there? How is your novel? Have you sent it to a publisher yet? I hope so. Mine is just over half finished. I want to get it done by the time the baby is born but don't know if I will manage it. Still, even if it is nearly done, it won't be impossible to complete it afterwards, but I must get a lot more done before July. I'm doing my own housework now, which means I have much less time than I had before. However, the story is moving on at its usual snail's pace, so one of these years it ought to be completed. Sometimes I feel quite sure it is all a stupendous waste of time, but even if it is, I must finish it now. It is impossible for me to judge the essential thing. Is it interesting? Jack also feels he can't judge this, as he knows the whole background story so well. He says he can criticize the writing and style, but not answer that basic question, as he is too close to the setting of the story and the types of people involved. I wish you could read it and tell me honestly. Don't get me wrong. This is not the only reason I hope you'll be in London when we're there. I've been very well. This pregnancy seems less eventful than the last, possibly because it has not taken up so much of my thoughts this time. I guess the novelty wears off, but last time I could hardly think of anything else, and I don't think that was a good thing. I'm not yet five months and am already the size of a house. I thought if I did my own housework, I wouldn't get so enormous, but I guess I just have a tendency that way. Jack and Jocelyn are both very well. Jocelyn is really getting her parents well organized. By the time she is 18, we won't dare go out without her permission. Today at lunch she told us we could both have one of her candies, "if you eat a good lunch." She has become very independent. She often says, haughtily, when called, "Don't bother me, I'm a busy woman." Today someone gave her some cashew nuts and she told me, "I'm eating my ground nuts." I told her they were called cashews but she replied, with great poise, having never seen cashews before, "I generally call them ground nuts." She told me the other day, "When our new baby is born, it can sleep in my room, and if it cries, I'll pick it up and put it on the potty and give it a drink of water, then I'll pop it straight back into bed." Obviously she feels she's not going to tolerate any nonsense. She is very social now and really loves playing with the other kids here. Of course they still have their battles and sometimes, when it is my morning to look after them, I feel I'll go round the bend before the morning is over. The other day, after playing with the others, Jocelyn brought out the simple philosophy born of hard experience, "If somebody bites somebody, then they get smacked on their bottom, hard. But if somebody didn't mean to do something, we mustn't get cross." Every time I back the car out of the garage, I seem to knock over our lovely tall bougainvillea bush. I've never broken it yet, but it's taking an awful beating. The other day Jocelyn was backing up her bike in the house, and she rammed it into the sideboard. "Oh dear," she shrieked in mock horror, "I've knocked down the bougainvillea again." She and Jack thought this a wonderful joke. From now on, I suppose, she will never allow any of my mishaps to be forgotten. Must go. I hope you're okay and not working too hard. Please write soon. Love from us all. Peg.

P.S. The police have just come with a warrant to search our cook's quarters for hashish. Never a dull moment.

When I became pregnant, I had gone to the local doctor in Tema and asked him to do a pregnancy test. Our regular doctor was on leave, which was just as well, since he was an alcoholic and I didn't intend him to deliver my baby. Temporarily taking his place was a nice young African doctor who no doubt thought I was just as neurotic as he imagined all European women to be. In those days, a pregnancy test was carried out by injecting the urine of a presumably pregnant women into a female frog. If the frog laid an egg, the woman was pregnant. In my case, no egg. The young doctor was very sympathetic and asked me if I was upset to learn I wasn't pregnant. I said, "No, it doesn't upset me, but I sure hate feeling pregnant if I'm not." He said, "Well, sometimes European women in the tropics do – um – they can develop neurotic symptoms." I could see his point about neurotic white women, but nine months later I would have loved him to see my son in my arms so I could say, "Here's my little neurosis."

I opted to have my child in the Accra hospital, some twenty miles from where we lived. One of the few doctors there, who not only attended births but looked after nearly everything else, was a young Polish man. The hospital was, of course, class- and race-conscious. It was for Europeans, African civil servants, African professional people, and the families of East Indian merchants. When the doctor examined me at three months and confirmed my pregnancy, he said, "I won't be attending the birth unless something goes wrong. I can be reached quickly, but you are a healthy young woman, this is your second child, and there should be no problem. A highly qualified midwife will be there."

I went into hospital twice with false labour. I was terribly embarrassed – my second child and I couldn't even tell whether I was in labour. Jack, driving me in each time, was worried about me, of course. I wasn't worried about myself in the slightest, but I was getting pretty annoyed at the fact that this child just wasn't arriving. He did arrive, two weeks late, just as Jocelyn had. I was determined to have my child by natural childbirth, although I had doubts about being able to do it by myself. Then along came Salome, a large African nurse / midwife. She sat beside me throughout my labour and held my hand. She had had a number of her own children whom she told me about. She would listen to the fetal heart with a small, trumpet-like thing and say, "There's my boy. He's so active he has to be a boy." A white nursing sister came around when breakfast was served and commanded me to eat. Salome, standing by, looked sympathetic but could say nothing. I said, "I'm in labour, I can't eat right now." She said icily, "Eat your breakfast." I got angry. I said, "Okay, but I'll throw it up." While she stood over me, I ate it and immediately threw it all up.

The Accra hospital was a good place to have a baby, though. Generally, the atmosphere was friendly and relaxed. My labour was a short one. I was taken to the delivery room about two hours before the birth. Leg straps were obligatory and I submitted without a thought, not knowing that flat-on-the-back, legs raised, is actually the most uncomfortable position for birthing. The breathing methods worked wonderfully. I believe Dr. Grantly Dick-Read said that in many natural births, women feel no pain, but when they do, it is never more than they can bear. I certainly didn't achieve the "no pain" category, but birth is not an obstacle race or a competition. The last two hours of my labour did hurt, but I was in control. I felt calm and confident. Salome and her young nursing assistant were beside me, encouraging me. I knew things were going well. Salome had shown me how to use a gas and air nozzle beside my hand if I felt the pains were too severe, but I was too busy to think of gadgets. Labour is aptly named.

When the final stage started, I suddenly could feel the child pushing into life. Ten minutes and there he was. Salome said calmly, "A fine boy." She placed him on my belly to make up for all the weight that was no longer inside me and to alleviate any cramps from this abrupt change. Because he was still curled up, they placed him with his back towards me, so what I saw was his tiny backside, his shoulders and the back of his head. I saw my son at the moment of his birth, before the cord was severed. I felt as though I were looking over God's shoulder at the moment of the creation of life. I was witnessing a miracle. When I think of women like Margaret Thatcher, the belligerent and awful prime minister of England, who herself has two children, or the late Indira Gandhi, also a mother, I wonder what fallacies of reasoning I must have to believe that if men could give birth, the predominantly male governments of the world might not take life so lightly.

The cord was tied and cut. Salome took him to a nearby table and said, "A little mucus in his throat. It will be all right." The mucus was sucked out while I waited in momentary terror. Then the first cry, the first giving of voice by a new human being, coming into a totally unknown life, after the life in the womb. How is it that a baby can take such a deep breath and yell so strongly? For the first and only time, Salome and I had a disagreement. "We'll bring him to you after we've cleaned him up," she said. I was restrained by the leg straps, but I was alert and strong. "No," I cried, "I want to see him right now. What if you get him mixed up with somebody else's baby? I want to see his face. Bring him over or I'll get up off this table and go to him myself."

One rationalization for my outburst was that in the Accra hospital, newborns were not given name tags, nor were their footprints or handprints taken. On the other hand, since I was probably the only European (that is, white) mother in the ward, the chances of getting my kid mixed up with someone else's were not great. Sweet reason, however, does not govern these circumstances. Salome laughed and brought the child to me so I could hold him and see his face. I laughed too. He looked so much like me as a baby that I could have picked him out of a nursery of a hundred babies with no problem.

Jack didn't arrive right away and I was worried and concerned. He turned up at four o'clock that afternoon, the beginning of visiting hours. He looked terribly upset.

"What's happening?" he said. I couldn't believe it. "Don't you know?" "Know what?" Jack said. "We have a son," I said. It turned out that he had kept on phoning the hospital but had never been able to find anyone who knew anything about me. He hadn't known our son had been born.

They brought the baby to us, and Jack and I chose his names – Robert David Wemyss Laurence. Robert was the name of my father, my brother, and one of Jack's brothers. David was the name of one of his brothers and a name in my family also. Wemyss, of course, was my family name. Jack grinned and said, "Well, he's got three names – maybe he'll be a colonial governor." "No," I yelled, and we both laughed. "Well," Jack said, "maybe the first man on the moon." "Not my kid!" I said, and we laughed again, in joy and relief.

I wrote to Adele just after David was born.

The Ridge Hospital, Accra,
Aug. 12, '55.

Dear Adele:
Well, at last the baby has arrived. Our son David was born August 9, he was 8 lbs, 12 ozs. and is a dear little boy, very tough looking already. He looks quite like Jocelyn when she was born, but without her angelic look. This one looks unmistakably masculine. He has a very pugnacious look and will probably prove to be a little demon. We were very pleased that it was a boy, nice to have one of each. I am very well, had an easy labour, only 8 hours in all, and only 2 hours really bad, and the birth was very quick. The second stage of labour lasted only ten minutes – two pushes and there he was – I could hardly believe it. I feel fit enough to go home right now, but will have to stay another week. Perhaps just as well, as I might not feel quite so well once I get home and have both kids to cope with. It took David a long time to decide to be born. I had

150

bouts of false labour, off and on, for three weeks before, and actually came into hospital twice before the event, and went home again when the pains went off. It was maddening as well as ridiculous. The second time I came into hospital was a terrible, or rather hectic night. We had had a spitting cobra in the garage that evening, and Jack with several African policemen, etc., was trying to get at it while I was pacing the kitchen floor, having contractions and worrying myself sick at the thought of Jack blinded for life. Spitting cobras aim for the eyes and have dead accuracy up to seven feet. However, it was alright in the end. A strange old man from the northern territories of the Gold Coast, a real bushwallah, finally drew the cobra out by some mysterious means, and the whole bunch of men fell on it with machetes and killed it. Jocelyn is fine, quite pleased about the baby but, of course, a bit resentful that she can't see him yet and that I'm not home yet. Jack says she's quite cheerful but clings to him a lot, and needs a lot of reassurance. I hope she'll take to David once we've got him home. Jack says her attitude so far is an odd mixture of pride and interest in David, plus obvious jealousy, but I expect she'll be okay in time. David, incidentally, was delivered by an African midwife, a vast woman named Salome. She was really wonderful. Must go. Do write soon. I hope you are all well, and that your novel is nearly finished. Will you be in London between Oct. and Jan., when we're there? I certainly hope so. Love from us all, Peg.

I stayed in hospital for nearly a week. I soon became aware that at night the maternity ward was very under-staffed. The one young and sprightly African nurse on duty had to be extremely athletic, racing from room to room as the requests arose. We quickly established an understanding. I could hear my kid's voice; when he cried, I would get up and creep into the nursery, change his diaper, and quieten him down. The night nurse would exchange greetings with me and the other mothers who were tiptoeing into the nursery to see to their babies: African, East Indian, Syrian mothers, and me.

Finally, there came the wonderful day when Jack and I took David home, and his three-year-old sister saw her new brother for the first time. I began writing the first draft of my first completed novel shortly after. I looked after the children myself, but I had a great deal of help with domestic chores. I accepted this with enormous guilt. I didn't want to be privileged. I rejected the label of memsahib and yet Shira, the wife of Grey, our cook, washed my children's diapers and clothes while Grey planned and made the meals. This helped me more than I can say in terms of my writing, but I still felt ambivalent. How could I justify it? I couldn't, but I accepted it, not only because it was the line of least resistance but also because I badly needed that time to do my writing.

I began writing again when David was just over a month old. The kids had to be in bed and asleep before I could begin. This was my own rule; no one imposed it on me, least of all Jack, who was always patient and understanding about what he conceived of not as his wife's vocation but as a kind of work she was interested in doing. If you haven't published a thing except one story in *Queen's Quarterly* and a small book of translations from Somali poetry, you can't really claim to be a professional writer, or so I felt. I worked three nights a week, from about 10:30, or whenever Jack went to sleep, until two in the morning. Those late-night hours when I wrote the first draft of *This Side Jordan* were exhilarating. I scribbled on and on, as though a voice were telling me what to write down. It was the easiest novel I ever wrote because I knew absolutely nothing about writing a novel. The pages poured out.

Meanwhile I was, as usual, concealing my work from the community in which we lived. It was uncomfortable enough that most of the British couples from my husband's firm knew that I didn't agree with them politically. They used to say, "Independence will never come. If it does, they'll be asking for us back in five minutes." I believed the opposite, which did not make me popular. I saw around me a collection of well-meaning human dinosaurs, old colonialists who couldn't recognize that their time was over in Africa and who, I suspect, were terrified to go back to their own countries. They had advantages in Africa that none of them would ever have had in England, among them power, power given to people who were, some of them, mediocre, who wouldn't have got very far in Britain, but who imagined themselves to be totally necessary to Africa. They couldn't see or accept that they had become, historically, totally redundant, and that their years of privilege and arrogance were swiftly coming to an end.

There were times when old colonials walked out of a cocktail party on account of remarks I had made. I *was* tactless. I was tactless, though, because I believed profoundly in what I was saying. We had only a couple of African friends, one of whom taught at Achimsta College, which became the University of Ghana. I learned a great deal from Ofosu. One thing he taught me was that even if I were an anti-colonialist, I need not expect any communication with Africans at that point in history. I learned what it is to be a white liberal. Yet Ofosu and I kept in touch for many years after Jack and I left Ghana, and historical circumstances can change. I have since written one rather amateurish book of literary criticism on contemporary Nigerian writing, *Long Drums and Cannons,* and have met, on several occasions, the Nigerian novelist Chinua Achebe. Knowing that, in our different ways, Achebe and I have been trying to do much the same sort of thing all our writing lives, I recognized that communication could be possible.

In January 1957, when Mum was dying, I came back to Canada with my two young children, stopping off first in

153

England to stay with Adele. That was one of our most memorable visits. Adele's novel *The Sacrifice* had been published the year before, and she had her incredible reviews to show me. She was twenty-nine and I was thirty-one. She also had some experience to pass on. She told me, "You think that when the book is published, that will be the best thing, that will be wonderful. The truth is that the joy is in the doing." It's true; for writers, the joy is in the doing. We had an almost all-night session. However, as Adele read the first draft of *This Side Jordan* and I read the reviews of *The Sacrifice*, we were temporarily interrupted by a crisis. I had foolishly put a disposable diaper down the toilet and it had plugged up the works. Adele phoned a Canadian friend who came by and did wonders with a coat-hanger. While he worked, Adele announced firmly, "We will not be put off by this event," and we kept on reading.

Jack came back to Canada, we settled in West Vancouver, and my mother died. I had submitted the novel to an American publisher and had got it back with some honest and helpful comments. I took the manuscript with me when the kids and I went up to northern B.C. for the summer to join Jack, who was in charge of dismantling the old Peace River bridge. We rented a house in a part of Fort St. John where the houses were so new they had no boundaries, hedges, or fences. David was almost three, and Jocelyn almost six. It reminded me in many ways of Africa. The local wives, who were friendly people, used to have morning and afternoon Kool-Aid parties. I would avoid them by concealing myself in the bedroom for an hour or two in order to rewrite the novel. I had told Jocelyn about this ploy, but she proved honourably incapable of telling even a gracious lie. One day I heard her saying to a neighbour, "My mother is writing a book but she doesn't know if anybody will publish it." I was reminded of this scene a year or so later, when David, listening to Jack and me at the dinner table talking about some book by a male writer, laughed and laughed and said, "You mean *men* write books?"

I sent the manuscript of *This Side Jordan* to McClelland and Stewart in Toronto. Jack McClelland read it and wrote back that he would like to publish it if an American or English firm would also pick it up. Macmillan in England and St. Martin's Press in America agreed to publish it, and the book came out in 1960.

I wrote most of the stories in *The Tomorrow Tamer* when we were living in Vancouver. I had read a book called *Prospero and Caliban: The Psychology of Colonization* by Dr. Dominique O. Mannoni, a French psychologist. That book was a revelation. Mannoni said things about colonialism and the people who had been colonialized that struck me deeply. I felt I had been doing some of the same work in *This Side Jordan*, but here was somebody who was explaining why those things had taken place. I wrote what I think is my best short story, "The Voices of Adamo," after I read Mannoni's book. Some of the stories I was writing were published in magazines like the *Saturday Evening Post.* This was wonderful. Not only was it publication, it was money. What angered me, however, was that many magazines felt they had a perfect right not only to change my title, which the *Saturday Evening Post* did with both stories of mine they published, but also to edit, delete, even take out whole column-inches without my permission. I was young and didn't have any clout. I certainly didn't think I could protest.

This Side Jordan received the Beta Sigma Phi first novel award, and I went to Toronto to collect it. The day the news arrived that not only had I won this award but it had $1,000 attached to it, I had just begun writing another novel. I was sitting in our house in Vancouver and I suddenly began to write. An old woman had come into my mind. I suppose she had been there for a while, but all at once she became insistent. That novel became *The Stone Angel.* I had decided that I couldn't write any more out of

Africa, and that what I most wanted was to return to my own people, my own land. I have often been asked if the character Hagar is based on anyone I knew. No, she is not, but she is so deeply a part of my Scots prairie background that I imagine there must have been a number of similar women in the place where I grew up. Writing the first draft of that novel was a wonderful release. To my amazement, idiomatic expressions I hadn't thought about for years came back to me, as did visual memories of the town and the valley and the hill. Manawaka is not Neepawa, but many of the descriptions of places, the houses, the cemetery on the hill, are based on my memory of the town that was my world when I was learning the sight of my own eyes. The novel poured forth. It was as if the old woman was actually there, telling me her life story, and it was my responsibility to put it down as faithfully as I could.

There were a number of technical problems that I solved as best I could, sometimes imperfectly. I had to record Hagar's life in time present, and encompass her long past in a series of dramatic memories. People don't recall their pasts chronologically, as I was well aware, but random reminiscences in the life of a ninety-year-old person would have made the novel confusing. I tried to get around the chronological memory problem by having each one of her memory sequences triggered by an event in her present. The fact that the story demanded to be written in the first person posed another problem. The way in which the writing was welling up often meant that Hagar's descriptions of places and events and her inner feelings were emerging in a kind of poetic, even rhythmic prose, whereas her speech to others was brusque, down-to-earth, testy, and cranky. Was this disparity of styles too great? I decided I couldn't help it. That was the way the story was coming out. I rationalized that even the most inchoate person must have dramatically strong responses to places and people and events, even if those responses are not verbalized. It was my business to translate those feelings into words that might best convey her feelings.

I was still working in the evenings when the children were asleep. David was five and hadn't started school. Writing became easier when both kids were in school because I could work for at least a few hours during the day. We had bought a small summer cottage at Point Roberts, just across the American border, and were in the process of fixing it up, Jack doing most of the fixing while I looked after the children. It was fairly primitive, with no plumbing and only partial dividers between the rooms. I recall many weekends when I scribbled by the light of a candle in the kitchen while the others slept. I realized the novel would need a lot of revising, but my first goal was to get the story down, as though Hagar might stop talking if I didn't write quickly enough.

My biggest frustration, as usual, was lack of time. When the writing was demanding to be put down on the page, it was difficult to have to leave it in order to make meals, look after the kids, and try to be a sympathetic and loving wife. There were times when I didn't succeed and felt like I was attempting an impossible juggling act.

Finally, the first handwritten draft was finished. I typed it out, revising a lot as I did so, as I've always done. The novel meant more to me than anyone else knew, and I was frightened. I thought if it was rejected by a publisher, it would be more than I could bear. I had so many self-doubts that I put the manuscript away for a whole year while I got out all my old diaries from Somaliland and wrote *The Prophet's Camel Bell*. This account of our experiences in East Africa was dedicated to Jack, for it was our common story. I think I half-realized that it was also my farewell to him. Jack got a job in East Pakistan, in irrigation, and I made the traumatic and anguished decision that I couldn't go with him, that I had to take the children and go to London, England, where I imagined, wrongly as it turned out, there would be a literary community that would receive me with open arms and I would at last have the company of other writers, members of my tribe.

I suppose I should say something about Jack and myself. We both had a strong sense of our own vocations but they led us into different areas. It was hard for him, when I had one novel published and another book, *The Prophet's Camel Bell,* accepted, to understand that this was my vocation and I had to do it. It was hard for me, too. When I wrote the first draft of *The Stone Angel,* Jack wanted to read it. I didn't want him to. I think I knew his response would be pivotal in our marriage. I didn't want anybody except a publisher to read it. I allowed him to read it in the end and he didn't like it much, but for me it was the most important book I had written, a book on which I had to stake the rest of my life. Strange reason for breaking up a marriage: a novel. I had to go with the old lady, I really did, but at the same time I felt terrible about hurting him.

Jack went to Pakistan in the fall of 1962 and I went to England with our children, who were then ten and seven. I felt guilty and worried sick about what the separation might do to them. I was also very much aware that within a year I would have to be self-supporting, although Jack would give me an allowance to help support the kids. I couldn't take a job outside the home, however, because of my children, and in any event, I wasn't qualified to be anything except a typist.

I can never be that frightened again. I had literally never been on my own before. I had married almost as soon as I left university. Now I was on my own with two young children. In fact, it was the children who kept me going. You can't collapse into despair or give way to anxiety if you have children. I found strengths I never knew I possessed, strengths that had probably been given to me by all my mothers.

Mona, my oldest friend, drove us to the Vancouver airport, supportive as always. We were to stop off in Winnipeg to see Adele, who was back living in her parents' home on Burrows Avenue, and then go on to Toronto where we would get the plane to London. I was so tense I kept having horrible cramps in my legs and feet. When I learned at the airport that our luggage was fifteen pounds overweight (we had sent a trunk on ahead by boat), it was the last straw. I had been trying to keep calm and cheerful for the sake of the kids, and to treat this trip as the great adventure that, heaven knows, it was, although not quite in the sense I pretended. I don't suppose Jocelyn and David were fooled for an instant, but they gamely played along. The man at the airport must have taken pity on my stricken face. "Well, okay, lady," he said, "I'll let you through, but you better get rid of those extra fifteen pounds at Winnipeg." "Yes, yes," I said. I would have promised anything.

We stayed several days at the Wisemans'. It was tremendously reassuring to talk with Adele, who realized, as Mona had done, what a state of panic I was in. Adele's mother, who was like another mother to me, helped me get rid of our excess baggage. Into a big cardboard box went David's Meccano set, several cherished books of Jocelyn's, old tennis shoes, and the only copy in existence of the manuscript of *The Stone Angel*. I took the box to the post office and posted it, sea mail, to friends in London.

How could I have done such a thing? As soon as it was posted, I immediately thought, "My God, what have I done? My only copy!" That parcel took three months to arrive in London. During those months, I was in agony every single day, imagining it gone forever. This was the novel for which I had separated from my husband and embarked on who knew what, uprooting and dragging along my two children, and I almost seemed to be trying to lose it. Guilt and fear can do strange things to the mind and the body. I questioned my right to write, even though I knew I had to do it. I had just wanted everything – husband, children, work. Was this too much? Of course it wasn't, but the puritan conscience can be a fearsome thing and when, in a woman, it is combined with the need to create in a society that questions this need or ignores it, the results are self-inflicted wounds scarring the heart.

Mercifully *The Stone Angel* did turn up. Meanwhile, a friend, Nancy Collier, helped me find a place to live in Hampstead, the one area of London I knew well. Our flat was fairly unprepossessing. It was on Heath Hurst Road, on the top two floors of one of those big Victorian red-brick terrace houses close to Keats Grove, where stood the tree under which the poet is said to have written "Ode to a Nightingale." I certainly didn't take the flat for its literary associations. It was affordable and it was large enough that each of the kids had a bedroom, tiny and cramped though they were. There was no private stairway, but we had a small kitchen, a living room, and a largish bedroom all on the third floor, with the children's bedrooms on the fourth. We shared the second-floor bathroom with a Scots couple who lived on that floor. Despite my Scots-Canadian background, it was enough to put me off the Scots for life. They used to have loud arguments that filtered upstairs, along with the pervading and repellent smell of the kippers they cooked for breakfast. Perhaps because of the kippers, they were also fresh-air fiends. In the coldest winter weather, they would throw open the window in our shared bathroom, rendering the temperature sub-arctic. The bath water was heated by an old gas geyser; you fed the pennies in according to how much hot water you required or how many pennies you happened to have. The kids and I used to joke about whether to have a six-penny or a twelve-penny bath, but the bathtub was so cold, you had to spend about six pennies merely to warm up the tub with water before you actually began filling it. There were times when my children thought I was cruel to insist on a bath three times a week.

The children adjusted, of course, as kids do, and quickly got used to their new school. We lived in that flat from September 1962 to December 1963. We didn't have much money, even though Jack was sending us a cheque each month that covered the rent and some of our food expenses. I had phoned Alan Maclean of Macmillan's once we were settled and asked him if he could see his way clear to paying me the £100 advance for *The Prophet's Camel Bell* that Macmillan's owed me. Alan, who was to become a close friend, instantly agreed. I told Alan when we met that there were a number of Canadian stories, perhaps even a novel, that I wanted to write. I also told him about *The Stone Angel*. He advised me to finish rewriting the novel before I did anything else. When the manuscript finally arrived, I began to rewrite it, and it wasn't long before it was in its final form.

That winter was a severe one in England. My aunts wrote constantly to ask, "Are you sure you should be there with the children?" Cold and fog and snow. It was not a terribly pleasant time, particularly since the English are totally unprepared for large quantities of snow. People were skiing down Hampstead High Street. The electricity kept going off, and it took me a while to discover that if you lit the gas oven and opened the oven door, you could at least be warm in the kitchen. Jocelyn, at ten and a half, was about to write the notorious Eleven-Plus exam, which would determine her level of schooling and thus her whole educational future, a concept I found appalling. I tried to help her with her mathematics, but I had about as much talent in mathematics as I now have in computer science, namely none. We soldiered on. David came home from school justifiably bewildered, saying he'd been marked wrong on a test question and he didn't think he was wrong. The question had been, "What does B.C. mean?" My son had put down "British Columbia." For my part, I was rewriting *The Stone Angel* and typing out the stories in *The Tomorrow Tamer*, sometimes with hands nearly freezing, in between walking the kids to and from school because I was terrified they might get lost in the fog.

Despite our difficulties, we managed to have lots of fun. Every weekend, we used to take small tours. I was determined to show London to the children so we tramped through the museums, we mastered the Tube, we walked up and down the millions of stairs at the Tower of London. In the Tower of London museum, I remember David, then eight, looking at a miniature cannon designed to fire miniature cannonballs. My son, impressed, said, "Gee, what a lucky kid." The miniature cannon had belonged to King Charles I.

One cold day, I went down to the local tobacco and newspaper shop to get a packet of cigarettes and buy the *Hampstead and Highgate Express.* I took the paper home, opened it, and was stunned by what I saw. Sylvia Plath, the poet, who had been living in Primrose Grove in Hampstead with her two young children, separated from her husband, the poet Ted Hughes, had killed herself.

I read it but could hardly believe it. She had attempted to kill herself several times before. This time, however, she had prepared breakfast for her children, set the table, done all the dutiful things, but when her children got up, they found the gas oven on and their mother dead. I was living in the same area, also in a crummy flat, also separated from my husband and also with two young children. I had often felt depressed. I had spent many evenings sitting around, doing a kind of self-analysis – what had gone wrong with my marriage? But I knew in that instant, looking at the newspaper, that I was not within a million country miles of taking my own life. No thanks to me, and no blame to Sylvia Plath. I had been given, as a child, as a teenager, so much strength by my mothers. Plath's fate may have been indicated years ago. I had never met Sylvia Plath, but I could only mourn for her and for her children. I later read *The Savage God,* a book about suicide by the poet A. Alvarez. He himself had apparently been tempted to

162

commit suicide but had consciously rejected it. He had known Sylvia Plath, and his opinion seemed to be that a large reason for her incurable depression was her situation: the dingy flat, her solitude, the two children. I knew when I read his book that he was quite wrong. Her situation had little to do with her death. I had once jokingly said to Alan Maclean that I might write my autobiography – I was then thirty-six – and call it *A Broken Reed*. When I read about Sylvia Plath's suicide, however, I realized that, joking aside, I was definitely not a broken reed.

That winter finally ended and in 1963, *The Prophet's Camel Bell* was published by McClelland and Stewart in Canada and Macmillan in England, as was *The Tomorrow Tamer*, my collection of West African stories. *The Stone Angel* had been accepted by both McClelland and Stewart and Macmillan. I had had a great deal of difficulty with the title of the book, which I had originally called *Hagar*. Neither M&S nor Macmillan liked the title. I didn't like it much myself. In the middle of a series of weird exchanges about the title, my agent, John Cushman, phoned from New York to tell me the momentous news that Alfred Knopf had taken on three of my books: *The Prophet's Camel Bell*, *The Tomorrow Tamer*, and the novel that was to become *The Stone Angel*. This was truly a breakthrough. I remember John's voice saying from New York, "Listen, honey, this is going to change your life. This is big news." It certainly was. Alfred Knopf himself made the decision to publish all three of the books on the same day. This had rarely, if ever, been done, but it helped draw attention to my writing.

Meanwhile, we were going through tribulations over the title of the novel. Macmillan, unfortunately, had already printed a dust jacket with the title *Hagar*, but they were far from happy. Knopf and McClelland and Stewart frankly hated the title. All three publishers kept sending me suggestions. All were awful. *Old Lady Shipley* was one. I read the Psalms again, hoping I would find a title there. Finally, early in 1964, the struggle over the novel's title was resolved when I picked up the manuscript, not having looked at it for months, and the title stared out at me in the first sentence of the book itself: "Above the town on the hill brow, the stone angel used to stand." I called my agent and all three publishers and said, "I've got it."

The three books were published in 1964 in New York. *The Prophet's Camel Bell* and *The Tomorrow Tamer* had already been published in Canada and England, but *The Stone Angel* came out in those countries in the same year. Knopf's taking on those books was not only a stroke of good fortune, it was one that I owed to a great extent both to my agent, John Cushman, and to Jack McClelland, who had personally talked to Alfred Knopf and urged him to read the books. Throughout our years together as writer and publisher, Jack McClelland and I have had our differences of opinion, but ours has been a long and rewarding association. He remains one of the most skilled readers I have ever met. It may be long after the fact, but it's good to be able to acknowledge publicly what a deep debt of gratitude I owe to him.

My fantasy about the literary scene in London proved to be just that. How wonderful it would be, I thought, to get to know other writers, but this simply didn't happen. I did get to know Alexander Baron and his wife, Dolores, who were extraordinarily kind to me, and the novelist Jean Stubbs. The year we were in London, Mordecai and Florence Richler were there too, and they were friendly in the brusque, understated style that Mordecai has always had. One person, however, who was supportive of me in those early years in England was Rache Lovat Dickson, a Canadian, a distinguished writer, and at that time a director of Macmillan's. He had yet to write his best biographies, of Grey Owl, H.G. Wells, and Radclyffe Hall. He had known many famous writers, but nonetheless, he had time to be generous to a young Canadian like myself.

164

Rache gave me a sense of my own worth as a writer. He may not know how many writers he has saved and brought on. I am one among them. He is also one of the best biographers we have and one of the best publishers in our century. I owe him a deep debt of gratitude.

Rache introduced me to the Canadian Universities Society. I was program director, or whatever it was called, for a year. One speaker we arranged was Stephen Vizinczey. He had published his first novel himself, *In Praise of Older Women*, and was regarded as an *enfant terrible*. The dinner began. The dinner finished. He wasn't there. I was frantic. When he turned up at last, he said, "I had to write an article." I said, "When was your deadline, for heaven's sake?" He airily said, "Oh, I have not submitted it anywhere yet." I was so angry I don't recall anything of his speech.

When Alan Maclean had read the manuscript of *The Stone Angel*, he phoned me up and said, "This book is going to make a difference to you, probably for the rest of your life." I didn't believe him, but dear and good Christian gentleman that he was and is, he has been proven right. I simply hoped that the novel wouldn't get too many bad reviews. That book meant an enormous amount to me. It was the novel into which I had invested my life, my heart, and my spirit. It was the novel that had finally made me feel it was necessary to leave my marriage. I never expected the novel to justify what I had done. I just hoped that it would stay in print for a year or so. Twenty-two years later, as I write this in 1986, the old lady is still helping me. I'm told that it has in fact sold more copies in the New Canadian Library edition than any other of their titles. It is in print in paperback editions in Canada, the States, and England. It has been translated into French, Norwegian, and Swedish, and is being translated into Danish, Dutch, and Italian. It has been used in geriatrics courses in Canadian hospitals to teach young nurses about the reality of old people. I must have received, over the years, thousands of letters from readers and from students, letters that have been a mainstay of my life.

When the book came out, I recall one English reviewer commenting, "This is the most telling argument for euthanasia I have ever read," which amused me greatly. It was interesting that the novel was reviewed in England as a study of an old person and in America as the story of a strong pioneer woman – but in Canada, Hagar was, and still is, seen as everybody's grandmother or great-grand-mother.

While my children were growing up and I was doing most of my writing, my main problem was not loneliness, although that was certainly an element of my life. My chief difficulty, however, was in splitting my heart and my time between my children and my work. When the crunch came, of course, the children were always infinitely more important. I could never work when one of the kids was sick. Real people are more important than writing. Life is always more important than Art. This may be a major dif-ference between women writers who are mothers and men writers who are fathers. I certainly don't mean this as a dia-tribe against male writers, but many women writers have known the pain of being asked to choose between their children and their writing. For us, there is no choice. Chil-dren come first. I don't believe, on the other hand, that this has made women's writing less powerful, less broad in scope. In fact, I believe the reverse is true. If I hadn't had my children, I wouldn't have written more and better, I would have written less and worse. I suppose many male writers and artists who are married with children take for granted a mother for those children who is not herself a writer or an artist and who is always there, not only to look after the children but to look after the comfort of the man himself. There are exceptions to this, I know, but unfortu-nately not as many as most women would like to see.

The day that changed my life and the lives of my children immeasurably for the better came in the late fall of 1963. Alan Maclean invited us to go along with him to Buckinghamshire, to see his family's old country house in Penn. When Alan was a boy, he and his family had spent their summers at the house, and Lady Maclean had chosen to spend her final days there. After her death, Alan had rented it to various American families at the military base in nearby High Wycombe. Alan drove us out to Penn and we roamed around the house and garden while Alan arranged for repairs on the place, which had been empty for some time. It's a cliché, but Jocelyn, David, and I immediately fell in love with it. On the way back to London, Alan said to me, "It just occurred to me, Margaret. Would you like to rent Elm Cottage for a while?" He knew that we weren't happy in our London flat, which had never felt like a home for us. He wanted to make it possible for me to work and raise my kids in a place that we really felt was ours. "Just think about it for a while," Alan said. "There's no rush." I stayed awake all night and phoned Alan at seven the next morning. I think I woke him up. He was quite surprised and a bit grumpy, as well he might have been. "I've made up my mind," I said. "I want to rent Elm Cottage." We moved three months later. Thus began the next decade of our lives.

Those years in Elm Cottage were the years in which my children grew up. That house remains in their minds, and in mine, as their childhood home. It was also the house in which I wrote six books, the most productive years of my life. The day we arrived, however, the weather was wintry and cold, and the house was a wreck. Mould grew out of the walls, much of the furniture was old and feeble, and the American military tenants had apparently not caught on to the use of ashtrays. Every one of the ten wooden mantelpieces was covered in deep cigarette burns. The moving van unloaded our few possessions: a trunk, my books, our clothes, David's Meccano set. We didn't have much. After the van took off, leaving our stuff dumped in the middle of the kitchen, everything we owned looked like a pile of garbage. I wondered what on earth I'd done. Jocelyn and David had picked out their bedrooms, Jocelyn's the one that for years had been Alan's own when he was a child. That first night I think they were excited and possibly a little scared. I was petrified.

The few months after we moved in were exciting times. Restoring Elm Cottage as a home was an adventure. We had rented the house furnished, but the arrangement of furniture didn't suit us, and some of the furniture had been too mutilated by previous tenants to keep. We used to have "moving parties" when myself and the two kids would take the furniture and heave it from one room to another. After we had accomplished the evening's work, we'd have supper and then drink cocoa made in a blue pottery jug while I read aloud from *Treasure Island* and other books. Those were months of great closeness among the three of us, with a shared sense of real achievement. One of our major projects was to buy a roll of linoleum to put on the stairs and the upstairs hall. David had brought some of his tools with him from Canada, including a pair of tin snips. Jocelyn held the lino flat while David hacked away at it and I tacked it down. That lino stayed on the floor until we could finally afford to buy carpet.

For the first year, we rented the large bedroom at the back of the house to a couple of women teachers, since that bedroom had the advantage of having a sink. The next year we rented the same bedroom, then restored to some extent, to a young married couple. I fixed up a semi-kitchen for them downstairs in the back hall and slightly refurbished what we called the old living room, reupholstering the furniture myself in an amateurish and sloppy way. There were very few places to rent in that area, and the couple had very little money, otherwise they certainly wouldn't have taken what we had to offer. After they left, we rented the same space to a young woman married to a sailor who would be away for a year. Those tenants were part of our lives for the first three years in Elm Cottage. My children absolutely hated even the idea and I didn't like it much either. I was reminded of my own childhood and the man from Miramichi.

I used to think about Mum a lot and I grew to understand more about her and how her life must have been. The other person I thought about was a person I had never met, Alan's mother, Lady Maclean. When we moved into the house, Alan lent us a portrait of his mother, painted when she was young. She wore a white dress and had long fair hair which gave her the look of a pensive Alice in Wonderland. That portrait became in a sense the spirit of the house. We hung it in the downstairs hall where we could see it every time we went upstairs or into the kitchen or into my study. For years, when the kids were asleep and I had been working, I used to open the study door and look out at the portrait. I used to talk to her and she always smiled back. Before she died, his mother had told Alan she would like the house to be lived in by a family with children. I used to call her The Lady. I used to say to her, "Lady, life is pretty rough from time to time, but just keep on wishing us well because this home of yours has become our home." My daughter thought she actually saw that child once, the good spirit of the house, and perhaps she did. I never saw The Lady except in her portrait, but she gave me a certain kind of strength. I think it would have pleased her to know that.

Our mornings began at quarter to seven when I would make breakfast for the kids, an English cooked breakfast of bacon and eggs, fried tomatoes, toast, and tea. After they left for school at quarter to eight, I would have two or three cups of coffee and then start my day's work. I rapidly learned to put off domestic jobs, even though my conditioning ran completely against this. I'd been brought up in a society in which jobs such as washing the dishes, making the beds, and scrubbing the floors were valuable work for

169

women; writing was not. What helped me change my priorities was that my writing, as well as being my vocation, had become a source of income. One tends to think a lot less about making peanut butter cookies under those circumstances. I learned every conceivable short-cut in making meals and managing a house, and I learned to write in the morning, when I had a maximum of mental and physical energy. I would stop writing a few hours before the children arrived home from school, not only to make dinner and do the domestic stuff but also to be mentally and emotionally out of the fictional world and back in the world of my life. Heaven knows I was not Supermum. There were many times when I felt frazzled and worried by domestic crises, of which there were plenty, repairs to the house and so on. But there were good moments, too. My kids observed Mother's Day, for example. They used to bring me touching breakfasts in bed: burnt toast, slopped-over coffee, with little flags stuck in each offering of food, labelling each item as "Toast" or "Jam." Eventually they understood that breakfast in bed was something I endured lovingly for their sakes.

Loneliness was an almost constant part of my life, but I had always been a lonely person. The presence of my children meant that, in the deepest sense, loneliness could never be a real threat. I severely missed having a mate, however, someone to talk things over with and to share worries with, but there were also times when I would have settled merely for a sexual relationship. I had one or two sexual liaisons, of such a brief span that they really don't deserve the term affairs, and I quickly realized that casual sex was not for me. It was a foregone conclusion, in my mind, that I would never take a man to Elm Cottage. My children were more important than any sexual relationship could ever be. Anyway, living out in the wilds of Buckinghamshire, where was I going to meet anyone? I used to wonder if I had deliberately isolated myself so that a relationship with a man would be all but impossible. I certainly felt it as a deprivation for a long time. The fact that a woman has children and is a devoted artist in no way lessens her sexual and adult emotional needs. However, my priorities were clear: the kids and the work, the work and the kids. I once told Alan Maclean that I'd always thought if I were ever on my own, I would spend all my spare time thinking about sex, and it had turned out that I spent all my spare time worrying about money. This was flippant and not quite true. I suppose it expressed some of the bravado I had to maintain. When I heard tales of the sexual escapades of some of my male writer colleagues, and of the girl groupies who allegedly fell at their feet and into their beds, what I felt was not any sense of moral judgment. I felt envy, even though I realized that a bunch of young groupies was by no means what I wanted myself. Still, male writers seem to have a kind of glamour attached to them while the reverse is usually true of female writers. Far from having an aura of glamour, we are positively threatening. And if we happen to have a couple of children, we simply become invisible as women.

The village of Penn in 1964 was not a quaint tourist spot; it was a place lived in by so-called tradespeople who had been there for generations and by a number of old and wealthy families and an even greater number of wealthy newcomers who had moved there because it was within commuting distance of London. We, of course, belonged to none of these categories. Because Elm Cottage had been rented to a number of American military families who had not done well by the house, we used to make it clear to everyone that *we* were Canadians. It held the nasty implication, of course, that all Americans were vandals and all Canadians sweetly reasonable citizens. I have to say it worked, and I'm ashamed to admit I used it constantly. My excuse at the time was that my kids had to live and be educated there and I wasn't about to have them regarded as North American gypsies. (Yes, this was unfair to gypsies as well. The liberal conscience and the Christian outlook

171

often become profoundly tired when it comes time to reconcile them with the well-being of one's own children, a thought I have often unhappily pondered.) In fact, we never could be accepted as villagers – an entire lifetime in the village would scarcely have sufficed – but we were regarded in a friendly way, and for that I was grateful.

The shops were clustered around the village green, where a fair was held in the spring. At the edge of the green was the village pond, said to have been a witches' ducking pond several hundred years ago. Those hapless women, usually living alone, often healers and midwives whom malicious rumour designated as witches, were strapped to a chair, ducked into the pond, and held under water for a considerable length of time. If they survived, they were innocent. I imagine none survived. The shops were few, but varied. There was, most importantly, Woodbridge's, a small family business where I took my order book once a week and groceries, fresh vegetables, and bread would be delivered the following day. Penn had a post office, which also housed a sweet-shop and a ladies' ready-to-wear section; a second-hand furniture shop; an artificial flower shop that specialized in arrangements for pubs and hotels; a second-hand book shop, the upper floor of which contained rare and antique books in glass-fronted shelves; the Red Lion pub; and the butcher's shop, whose sign proclaimed it to have been established in the late 1700s.

Some of the houses were very old. Opposite Elm Cottage, on Beacon Hill, was a house called The Beacon, lived in by the so-called local squire and his lady. It was a vast, rambling, red-brick edifice, surrounded by a high brick wall. At nights I used to look out my bedroom window and see its impressive, solid, Victorian shape looming against the grey sky, and I used to wonder how on earth we had found this strange refuge here in this unlikely place.

On the grounds of The Beacon there was a small brick and flint cottage, typical Buckinghamshire architecture, where Mr. and Mrs. Charlett lived. He was head gardener at The Beacon, and his wife became our friend and helper. The Charletts had known Alan Maclean and his brothers and sisters when they were youngsters in the house, and they had a special attachment to Elm Cottage. Our hot water was heated with a coal boiler, and it was Mrs. Charlett who, in our first weeks in Elm Cottage, was pleadingly summoned by one of the children first thing in the morning because I couldn't get the damned boiler to burn. I learned from her, with a speed born of sheer despairing need, how to get pieces of coal alight with judiciously screwed-up newspapers. From Mr. Charlett I learned how to prune the beautiful roses, some of them nearly a century old, that grew in the rose bed just outside our kitchen windows. I have never been a gardener, but I did look after the roses and even planted ten more bushes that miraculously survived.

The house stood on two-thirds of an acre. At the side, overlooked by the kitchen window, was a huge lawn with two giant beech trees at one end and a venerable elm after which the house had been named. A mulberry tree grew near the front gate. It produced quantities of red-purple berries that were impossible to pick off the high and somewhat fragile branches; all we could do was to shake the boughs and gather up the semi-squashed fruit from the grass. The children's bedrooms faced out onto this tree, and the wall underneath their windows was covered by wisteria, so old and gnarled it was virtually a tree. The back garden had once supported vegetables, but it had grown wild and untouched, full of nettles, grass, and dock-leaves. It was a fine place for young children. They built a tree-house in one of the old apple trees, trees that, although untended, always yielded enough fruit to last us until well after Christmas. At one point, David and his pals built a fort out there from packing cases and dug a secret tunnel as an approach, covered over with planks and turf. I was briefly in New York one summer for the publication of a book, and I used to look out the window of my borrowed apartment while I had my breakfast. Across the road was a small playground: slides, a teeter-totter, all metal on a concrete ground. Not a tree, not a blade of grass. I thought of my own children with their English jungle to play in. I thought of my son coming into the kitchen after working on his tunnel with a couple of friends, covered with earth and mud, healthily filthy, triumphant, and I realized how privileged we were.

We acquired two cats when they were small kittens, first Calico and then Topaz. I based the characters of Topaz and Calico in *Jason's Quest* on our cats. Calico was an outdoor cat, dignified, a true lady. Topaz was a frivolous and affectionate slob who preferred to remain indoors. They were with us for years. Those cats helped to make the place home for us, but I think in a sense it was home from the moment we moved in. Its appearance altered over the years, as we came to afford decent carpeting and curtains of good material, rather than the patched-up jobs I had originally sewn on an antique and exceedingly temperamental sewing machine I bought in a second-hand shop for the equivalent of about five dollars. We replaced many pieces of furniture, things I bought in the second-hand furniture shop at the far end of the village, but the character of the house never changed. We always tried to be true to the house itself and I think we succeeded. A previous tenant had covered the red stone tile floors in the downstairs hall and kitchen with flecked red linoleum, presumably because it was easier to look after. When we moved in, the lino was buckling and chipped and coming loose. The kids and I decided to take them up and restore the old red stone tiles, not realizing what a major job this would be. We were on our hands and knees for what seemed like weeks, wielding chisels and scrapers and sugar soap, a nauseating yellow mixture containing, I suspect, neither sugar nor soap, which was spread on the floor to loosen the lino glue.

As more of my books were published and then went into paperback editions, I felt an indescribable relief to know that we had some financial reserves. I used to worry about trying to over-compensate, trying to be two parents when in fact one person can only be one parent. I was determined that my children weren't going to be deprived of anything if I could help it. The outings we took in those days, though, were actually done because they gave us all pleasure. One of our favourite trips was to London for two specific purposes. "Okay, guys, we're not rich, but today we feel rich" was my slogan when caught up in a mood of either ebullience or a need for reassurance. I would give them each a pound, twenty whole shillings over and above their modest weekly allowance, but there was one condition. They could put the pound in their post office savings accounts if they wanted to, but they never did. The pound was to be spent on books. These days, a pound sterling won't buy you much, but in those days a pound, judiciously spent, could get you Arthur Ransome's *Swallows and Amazons* in hardcover, for example, plus one or two Puffin or Pelican children's paperbacks put out by Penguin Books. In this way, my kids acquired *The Railway Children, Emil and the Detectives, The Borrowers, Stig of the Dump,* and many more. Some of them were books they had read in the school library but wanted to own, others I tentatively suggested. Some they had simply heard of and others attracted them by the jacket description. I read those books too, and learned a great deal about the children's books that had not been available, or even written, when I was young.

Laden down with our treasure, we would proceed to the second part of the ritual – tea at Fortnum and Mason's. Casually we would wander through the food department of that legendary store, where you could buy costly baskets of exquisite delicacies to send to convalescent friends or poor relatives in far-flung places such as Canada, where decent pâté was presumably unknown. Like Harrod's and Liberty's, Fortnum and Mason's was a source of unending delight. The quiet, classy ostentation struck me as a wonderful entertainment. For a moment, I could put aside my social conscience, my bred-in-the-bone anger, and simply marvel that anyone could take such things seriously.

I can only skim over the surface of our time in Elm Cottage. Those years saw so many changes, so much work on my part, so much growing up of my children and of myself. I think of the friends who came out to Elm Cottage through the years, writers from Canada, a few writers in Britain, many sons and daughters of friends, nieces and nephews, young writers I had met on one of my many trips to Canada. I can't even begin to mention them all, those friends who propped me up in times of need and whom, in fact, I myself propped up as well.

I began writing *The Fire Dwellers* before *A Jest of God,* but I destroyed about a hundred pages of that manuscript when I realized there were two novels in my head and I had begun the wrong one. The novels concerned two sisters, Rachel and Stacey, and took place within the same span of one summer. The books were self-contained but interrelated. Each sister envied the other for what each imagined was an easier life than her own. Rachel at thirty-four, an unmarried schoolteacher looking after her supposedly frail mother, and Stacey, thirty-nine, mother of four children, struggling to communicate with her nonverbal husband. When I discovered that Rachel's story had to be told first, it was a revelation. Stacey's story would come later. I remember sitting down in my study in Elm Cottage one morning, the kids safely off to school, opening a notebook and beginning, as I always have, as though taking down dictation.

During that time, I twice took the children to the Highlands of Scotland, to the Black Isle of Ross-Shire. I later used some of the descriptions of that place in *The Diviners*. On our first visit, we stayed with the Scots novelist Jane Duncan, in her house in a village called Jemimaville. I later took David and a friend of his to the Black Isle. I and the two boys, who must have been about eleven at the time,

36. *Elm Cottage, Buckinghamshire, England, c.1967.*

37. *Myself, London, 1963.*

38. *My study in Elm Cottage.*

52. In my study, c.1984. Photo by Doug Boult.

went to Culloden, where the last battle of the Highland clans took place, and where the clans were broken forever. My own family, the Wemysses, had come from the Lowlands, from Fifeshire, but the Laurences were Highlanders from the Shetland Isles, a sept of the Clan McLaren. I always said that a trip with me might not be historically accurate, but it certainly was dramatic. The boys and I walked around Culloden while I explained to David that some of his ancestors lay in the clan graves, for the Clan McLaren was raised in 1745, when Bonnie Prince Charlie tried to come back from France with a spectacular lack of success. Having read John Prebble's fine books on Highland history, I in fact knew quite a bit about Culloden. One thing that had always touched me almost unbearably was that, in the heat of the battle, some of the Highlanders threw away their muskets without ever having fired them and attacked the redcoats with the magical sword of their ancestors, the claymore.

That evening, in the lounge of the hotel in Cromarty, I was having my after-dinner coffee. The boys were in another room looking at TV. There was only one other person in the lounge. She introduced herself to me. Her name was Miss Campbell and she too was a writer. She was in Ross-Shire researching a children's book. Miss Campbell belonged to the clan who had fought with the British and against the rest of the Highlanders. At Culloden there is a small, rather pathetic sign, saying, "To the Campbell graves." They are buried apart, away from the others. The feelings about that ancient battle still run strong, so strong that Miss Campbell and I, these two nearly middle-aged women writers, sat for several hours re-fighting the Battle of Culloden.

In the summer of 1966, *A Jest of God* was published. I arranged for our neighbours, Mr. and Mrs. Charlett, to stay with the children while I went to Canada for a month to do some publicity. My publishers, notably Jack McClelland himself, maintained that these appearances – TV, radio, interviews with the newspapers, and all that hoopla – sold books. I wasn't convinced. I found public appearances excruciatingly difficult. I realized later that McClelland was right. Publicity does sell books. Some writers even enjoy it, but I'm not among that number. I've done hundreds of interviews of one kind or another, but I still get extremely nervous. My voice is reliable and never shakes, which is lucky, but *I* tend to shake. Once I get going, though, I'm usually all right, and at least I know now that I'm not going to faint on stage. In 1966, however, I still hadn't done many interviews. I was also anxious about leaving the children. I trusted Mr. and Mrs. Charlett, of course, and I wrote to the kids constantly and phoned several times. Nevertheless, I missed them horribly. The whole month was an ordeal.

The trip began in nightmare fashion and continued that way, with small breaks for humour. McClelland and Stewart had very decently rented an apartment for me in a block of apartments on Avenue Road in Toronto. I couldn't have afforded a hotel and I don't like them in any event. Since the plane landed first in Montreal, we had to go through Customs there. I dutifully went to collect my baggage: one large suitcase containing an entirely new wardrobe, bought for the summer tour. My suitcase wasn't there. To say I was distraught would be putting it mildly. I was hysterical. The officials told me to calm down. Undoubtedly the suitcase would turn up in Toronto. The suitcase did not turn up in Toronto. A kindly man from McClelland and Stewart met me at the airport, totally unprepared for a woman who was babbling about a lost suitcase. All I had was the blue-and-white linen dress I was wearing and a flight bag that contained my tickets, traveller's cheques, my few cosmetics, and a paperback. Desperate inquiries at the airport resulted in a message to call Air Canada the next day. It turned out to be many next days.

I was taken to the apartment and the representative from my publishers, by now perspiring freely, thankfully left me. I was finally alone in an apartment in which McClelland and Stewart had graciously left a large bunch of flowers and a bottle of whisky. I fell into bed in my underwear and thought, "Sufficient unto the day are the troubles thereof." The next day was Sunday. I had forgotten that I'd need some Canadian cash and of course nothing was open. Flowers and whisky are swell, but not on a Sunday morning when you have no money, no food, no coffee, and only the clothes you arrived in. It was a low point. I desperately regretted having left England. I tried to raise the apartment superintendent and, after some considerable time, he tumbled out, looking justifiably angry. By that time, I regret to say, I was thinking of Canada, my home and native land, as a foreign country and myself like the biblical Ruth, "in tears amid the alien corn." The super told me I couldn't cash a traveller's cheque on a Sunday, but given the fact that the rent had been paid in advance by my publishers, he lent me five bucks. I sashayed down Avenue Road, walking miles, or so it seemed, until I finally found a café and had breakfast. I have seldom felt so lonely and so out of place.

On Monday, I phoned Air Canada several times, but with no results. I even went down to their central office. No record of a lost suitcase, "but we will take all the particulars, madam." I cashed some traveller's cheques, stocked the apartment with food, and made contact with Jack McClelland who arrived with Elizabeth, his wife, to take me out for dinner. Most important of all, I phoned my old friends Chris and John Marshall. John had been the best man at my wedding and I had worked with Chris at the YWCA in Winnipeg. In 1966, Chris was executive director of the Metro Toronto YWCA. My call to her was a cry from the heart, to which she instantly responded. I had remembered that I had five hundred dollars in an account at the Royal

Bank in Toronto. "Chris," I whimpered, "it's me. My suitcase got lost. I have no clothes. I have to do all this publicity stuff and I have *no clothes*! I have some money. Help! I don't know where to shop."

Chris arrived early the next morning. We went out that day and got a whole new wardrobe. In 1966, five hundred dollars got me, among other things, a lovely gold lamé cocktail dress, three summer dresses suitable for almost any occasion, a light wool suit of blue and grey, two pairs of dressy sandals, several handbags, nightgowns, a full complement of underwear, and a suitcase. I must say I enjoyed it. I have never before, and have never since, sauntered out and bought a complete wardrobe in one day. Chris said, "I've never had so much fun spending someone else's money." So I was outfitted, and if not exactly ready to go, at least I looked decent and even slightly elegant.

I have rarely had launch parties for my books, partly because I don't enjoy parties and partly because when most of my books came out, I wasn't in Canada. For *A Jest of God*, however, there was a party held at Jack McClelland's house in Toronto. A TV crew was there, making a feature on McClelland, as well as a huge throng of people, so the house was filled with scorching TV lights, cameras, and camera cables over which people tended to trip. I was amazed. How had I ever found myself in this bizarre situation? I certainly didn't know then what I subsequently learned about the whole literary scene in what I came to call the V.M., the Vile Metropolis. I didn't know how the strategies worked. I didn't know the ground rules. I was a babe in the literary woods, or perhaps I had come from the woods into this place that I found, and still find, bewildering. I should add, though, that I wasn't in any way intimidated. A reviewer who had slashed *A Jest of God* came up to me at the party, wanting my approval for the damning review. I had, thank God, the presence of mind to say, "I am not a spiritual masochist. Write what you like about my books, but don't expect me to approve when you pan one of them."

While I was in Toronto, I received a phone call from my long-time agent and dear friend, John Cushman. He told me that *Holiday* magazine, a very glossy American travel publication, wanted me to do two articles on Egypt. Their first choice had been Lawrence Durrell. I had been their next. I wasn't, of course, about to turn this offer down. A few days later, I got a call from Alan Maclean in England. He was going to get married, and he and his fiancée, Robin Empson, wanted to settle in the south of England. I was absolutely delighted. I had known Robin for some time. She was the daughter of a diplomat and the niece of the poet and critic William Empson. Her family connections, like Alan's, were never very important to me, however; I loved Robin because she was such a warm, spirited, generous person. Alan told me, along with this good news, that he had to sell Elm Cottage to buy a house in Sussex. "Do you want it, Margaret?" he asked anxiously. "Of course I do," I said, "but I don't have any money. Could you possibly wait until I get back to England?" He said he would. I thought that perhaps, just perhaps, a miracle might happen, but I didn't really have that much hope.

Meanwhile, *A Jest of God* had been reviewed in *Life* magazine. I had only been back in England for about a week when John Cushman phoned from New York to say that Paul Newman and Joanne Woodward wanted an option on the book. Woodward's agent had seen the review of the novel in *Life* and had thought it might be something Woodward would like to do. So there I was. I suddenly had enough money to make a down payment and get a mortgage on Elm Cottage.

One would think that arranging a mortgage would be easy, but not so. It was enormously difficult. I had two strikes against me. I was a woman and I was a writer. Both, according to the financial institutions, were highly unreliable. I was told I would have to have my husband (we were not yet divorced) co-sign the mortgage if I hoped to get it. I refused. Finally – and this still enrages me – the mortgage went through thanks to the old boys' network. Alan Maclean called his own bank manager to say that I was indeed a good financial risk and that Macmillan had faith in me. I was extraordinarily grateful to Alan, of course, but at the same time resentful that a professional woman with two children was considered an unacceptable risk. One of the happiest days of my life was when I eventually wrote the cheque that paid off the rest of the mortgage. Frankly, I was proud of myself. At the same time, I recognized I wasn't typical, as a writer and certainly not as a woman, as far as my financial independence was concerned. I have been very fortunate. Yes, I did work hard, but so do a lot of women who are nonetheless unable to establish financial independence because of the structure of our society.

We departed for Egypt about six months after I got back from Canada, in December 1966. I had made a few conditions. *Holiday* magazine would pay for my airfare and two first-class hotel rooms. I would pay for my children's airfare and their food. In return, I agreed to write two articles, one on the Suez Canal and the other on the Valley of the Kings. Agreed expenses would be paid, but the final fee would depend on acceptance of the articles. I was to get a third of the total price if the articles were turned down.

I had been in touch with the United Arab Republic Tourist Bureau in London before we left. No one hears much about the U.A.R. now, but at the time, Nasser saw himself as the leader of Pan-Arab Africa and the Near East, just as Nkrumah of Ghana once envisaged himself as the leader of a Pan-African alliance. Since I was going to write two articles for an important American travel magazine, the U.A.R. Tourist Bureau was kindness itself. They assigned us a guide for the trip, a young man named Hanafy Bashir who was attached to the tourist bureau in

Cairo. He helped us negotiate the maze of travel arrangements inside Egypt and did it admirably and enthusiastically. To this day I remain grateful to him and often wonder whether he survived the subsequent wars.

I had read voluminously beforehand. It was impossible to transform myself instantly into an informed person when it came to the vast span of time and complexity of Egyptian history, but I struggled along, making notes on the dynasties. I conceived my job to be that of personal observation, with at least a minuscule amount of background reading, bringing as sharp an eye as I could to the present and connecting it to the very long-ago past.

Back in England, I worked hard to get the articles in shape and meet the deadline. It has always been my absurd pride never to have missed a deadline. The articles were accepted and *Holiday* paid me. I was in the bathtub one evening, more or less whistling a merry tune and thinking how well things were going, when Jocelyn came pounding up the stairs and knocked on the bathroom door. "Mum! Egypt and Israel are at war."

The moment of truth is sometimes humiliating. My first thought was not for the young Israelis and the young Egyptians set to killing one another. My first thought was, "Thank God I got paid." A few minutes later I collected myself enough to see how awful my initial reaction had been. It was then that I thought of Hanafy Bashir and his Israeli counterparts, and of my own children who had been, thus far, spared war. We think first of our own – how can we help it? I had read the English-language newspapers while we'd been in Egypt and had even met with the editor of one of them, but I hadn't seen the crisis coming at all. I was suddenly grateful for the luck that took us out of Egypt before that war.

The two articles were never published in *Holiday* – it would be a while before Egypt was again a place for tourists – but they were included years later in a book of essays called *Heart of a Stranger*, published in Canada.

They're not bad pieces, but they don't cover even a fraction of what happened to us. During the trip we went out to Ismailia, where we were allowed to board a British oil tanker and go on to Port Said. I wrote about it in "Captain Pilot Shawkat and Kipling's Ghost," but I didn't mention, for example, that my son was allowed into the engine room of the tanker while Jocelyn and I were not, thanks to the superstition that maintains women are bad luck in the engine room. I had been allowed on the bridge, though, when the Egyptian pilot guided the big tanker through the Bitter Lakes to Port Said itself. Along the final portions of the canal, the captain always yields his command to the pilot, who knows the complexities of the course. These big ships, however, can't afford to stop in the harbour. The pilot disembarks into a motor launch and the ship carries on. We discovered, as we approached Port Said, that the ship wouldn't stop for us either. Much to my terror, we had to get off the same way.

The tanker was going at a tremendous speed. It was growing dark. When we entered the harbour, two sailors lowered a rope ladder to meet the motor launch that was running alongside the tanker. We had to climb down the rope ladder and jump from it into the motor launch. David went first, then Jocelyn, then me, the small motorboat trying to keep pace with the speed of the tanker. We had to time it exactly. I knew that if my kids missed that jump and fell into the water, they would instantly be sucked under the tanker and that would be that. When all of us were finally safe in the launch, I trembled with relief and with the horrible thoughts of what might have happened. As I shook, David said brightly, "Gee, that was great, Mum. I wish we could do it again."

We got back in January 1967, and I continued to work on a survey I was writing of contemporary Nigerian literature. I had met a number of young Nigerian writers, including Wole Soyinka and the poet Christopher Okigbo, through mutual friends in London, and had begun to read other works by Nigerians. I found it exciting that African writers were producing what I thought I and many Canadian writers were producing: a truly non-colonial literature. *Long Drums and Cannons* was never intended to be a deep analysis. It was, rather, a survey and an interpretation, from the viewpoint of a reasonably skilled reader who stood outside the culture and who hoped to make these works better known and more accessible. The title was taken from one of Chris Okigbo's poems, "Heaven's Gate":

> I have visited the prodigal
> in palm grove
> long drums and cannons
> the spirit in the ascent.

The book was published by Macmillan in England in 1968, and a year later by Praeger in America. By the time it came out, however, Nigeria was in the throes of a civil war that split the country and caused unbelievable suffering. Wole Soyinka went to jail and Chris Okigbo was killed. The lines from his poem seemed cruelly ironic.

Our lives went on in by now accustomed ways: we tried to keep Elm Cottage warm in cold weather by an assortment of heat sources (coal, gas, wood, and electricity); the kids continued school with its attendant problems; there were weekend visitors, and Canadian visitors who often stayed several weeks and whose company was much valued; and in the spring and summer, we sat out on the big lawn beside the rhododendron bush, the apple trees, and the hedge of climbing roses. I was working hard, trying, once again, to get into *The Fire Dwellers,* but I'd found my way blocked. I was still too close to the first attempt, even though all the pages I had previously written had gone up in smoke in a backyard bonfire.

I was informed, to my astonishment and delight, that *A Jest of God* had won the Governor General's Award for

185

fiction in English for 1966. The awards were given in the spring. I asked Mrs. Charlett to stay with the kids while I went to Canada. The Governor General's Award carried with it a cheque for $2,000, a huge sum to me then. Even though I felt guilty about leaving the children, I reasoned that we would be two thousand Canadian dollars richer.

I stopped off en route to see Adele in Montreal. We had our usual talks far into the night. An irony, fully appreciated by both of us, was that when Adele had received the Governor General's Award for *The Sacrifice*, nearly ten years earlier, the award had been a pretty bronze medal – no cheque and no special leather-bound edition of the book with marbled endpapers. Adele's mother, who made not only inspired dolls but wonderful tapestry-like pictures using cloth, buttons, sequins, and whatever came to hand, had, in a burst of humour totally typical of her, incorporated Adele's medal into a wall hanging. "It might as well be used for something," she said.

Adele had begun work on her amazing novel *Crackpot*, and I read a few chapters. Our work methods are very different. She writes and rewrites a chapter before moving on to the next. The whole intricate structure, although it can change, moved by the characters themselves, is held firmly in her mind throughout this long creative process. I tend to start at the beginning and work through to the end of the first draft, hardly daring to look back, "lest," as I always say, "like Lot's wife, I am turned into a pillar of salt." I knew, reading the few completed chapters of *Crackpot*, that it would be a very remarkable novel, one of the best not just in Canadian literature but in contemporary literature anywhere.

It was on that visit that I first met Sinclair Ross, whom Adele knew and who was within a few years of retirement from the Royal Bank, where he worked in the public relations department. He was reluctant to meet anyone, but he probably agreed to see me because, like Adele, I was a prairie person. We went out to a Greek restaurant, the three of us, and I told Ross what his writing had meant to me. I think he found it hard to believe. We discussed a possible selected collection of his stories, something that did happen later with the New Canadian Library edition of *A Lamp at Noon*. I wrote the introduction and the whole project was supported and arranged by Malcolm Ross, the general editor, whose idea the NCL had been and to whom so many of us owe so much.

I moved on to Ottawa and booked into the hotel arranged for me. The ceremony, at Government House, was both impressive and funny. The winner of the Governor General's Award for poetry in English that year was Margaret Atwood, for *The Circle Game*. I met her for the first time that day, in what was euphemistically called the Ladies' Powder Room at Government House. She told me she had been slightly nervous about meeting me. Me! I was forty-one and Margaret was all of twenty-eight. "Honey," I said, "*I'm* nervous about meeting everybody. Do we have to curtsy or what?" If memory serves, we were then joined in that sumptuous ladies' room, with its marble-topped counters and elegant appurtenances, by Claire Martin, who had won the French fiction award for her book *In an Iron Glove*. I hadn't read it because it had not yet been translated into English. (Some years later I was extremely honoured when she translated *The Stone Angel* into French for Pierre and Michelle Tisseyre's publishing house in Quebec.) That day in the ladies' room at Government House, Margaret Atwood, Claire Martin, and I decided that we wouldn't curtsy to the Queen's representative because none of us had the faintest notion of how to do so. We needn't have worried – the curtsy had been eliminated.

At the banquet that evening we received the all-important cheques. I never eat much at these formal affairs, particularly if I have to participate. My ideal formal dinner consists not of five courses but of a roll and cheese and a glass of milk. After such occasions, I'd love a double scotch and a huge steak, but by then the food and drink have disappeared. It was during that dinner, though, that I met the poet Al Purdy. He discussed a collection of essays he was putting together related to Canadian independence, to be published by Mel Hurtig in Edmonton. Al asked me if I would contribute something to it. I promised I would, and subsequently wrote "Open Letter to the Mother of Joe Bass," which was published in 1968 in Purdy's collection *The New Romans* and republished in *Heart of a Stranger* in 1976.

My talk with Al that night led to a long friendship and an exchange of letters, mainly about what we were writing and how it was going. He and his wife Eurithe later came to England after they had been in Greece, where Eurithe had become ill. I recommended a doctor in London, who told Eurithe she had to have an operation. I went to visit them in their bedsitter in Earl's Court. It was a small, depressing room. I told them, "This won't do. You're coming to my house," and they did. They lived in the back bedroom for about a month. We had some great talks about Canadian writing in the days that followed. Al used to go to the local second-hand bookshop, where he found quantities of rare Canadian books, buying them for next to nothing since they weren't known or valued in England. He made a strong impression at the local post office since nobody, in their experience, had ever mailed off so many parcels in one month.

After I got back from Canada, I suddenly began to write an animal fantasy. I wrote it quickly, and ultimately had to do a great deal of rewriting, but it was completed and published within two years. I called it *Jason's Quest*. Our lawn had been inhabited by moles for a long time. Each day in spring and summer molehills would appear, about two feet high. David would scoop up the earth and throw it into the bushes or try to stuff it back under the grass. The next morning there would be more mole mountains. One day I felt the grass actually springing under my feet. I was convinced there was an entire city of moles there, but I wasn't

188

about to sacrifice my entire lawn to them. I put up a sign in our local post office: "Are there no mole catchers left in England?" My sign was answered. A mole catcher, complete with explosives and gas, went to work and cleared our lawn of moles. I felt like a murderer. I had already begun writing the first draft of *Jason's Quest*, in which one of the heroes is a mole. Nevertheless, it was a relief to be rid of them. Perhaps it was a penance for me when Sheila Egoff, in *The Republic of Childhood*, her book about Canadian children's fiction, said something to the effect that *Jason's Quest* is the most disappointing book in all of Canadian children's writing.

Not long after I completed the first draft of *Jason's Quest*, I began writing *The Fire Dwellers* again. This time the story moved quickly. It was a relief, because I had feared I would never be able to write it. During the time I was writing that novel, I truly felt I was living two lives, Stacey's and my own. She had four children, I had two. She was certainly not me. I was luckier. I had my own work to do, and she didn't. Nevertheless, we had a fair amount in common. I was so involved with her life, there were times it felt like I actually had six children, two of mine and four of hers.

In the summer of 1968, I met Clara Thomas, a professor at York University in Toronto who taught Canadian literature, and indeed was a pioneer in its teaching. She came to visit me at Elm Cottage. She was writing a small book on my work for McClelland and Stewart and we had written back and forth a few times, but that first visit established a firm and enduring friendship. Later that same summer, Jack returned from Belize, where he had been working. I was beginning to make a little more money from my books and I told him I would like to pay for a holiday in Italy with the kids. I was tired of the persistent rain and dull weather in England and desperately wanted some sunshine. He had visualized a holiday in Ireland, but he yielded to my request. So, trying unsuccessfully to get together as we had several times in the past, we took the children to northern Italy. It rained constantly. Ireland had beautiful sunshine. I was in the last stages of rewriting *The Fire Dwellers* but couldn't work during the holiday. I also realized that Jack and I were not going to get back together. The holiday must have been a strange one for the kids. I was in a state of constant tension and constant diarrhea. I kept gulping down medicine and, in a quite futile way, rewriting parts of *The Fire Dwellers* in my mind. I must have seemed like a kind of superactive zombie, either talking absentmindedly or rushing for the nearest toilet.

In 1969, I decided to accept the position of writer-in-residence at the University of Toronto for the academic year of 1969-70. I was the first woman to have an office at Massey College, a fact that sounds strange now. I was probably also the only person at Massey College who wondered what the hell I was doing leaving my kids for a whole academic year. I justified it by the fact that I needed the money, I needed the clout, or thought I did, and I felt I needed the experience. If I was to leave my children, then seventeen and fourteen, for nearly a year, then I certainly wanted someone both reliable and agreeable to take over the fortress. Clara Thomas put me in touch with Ian and Sandy Cameron. Clara had known them both for some time, Ian as a graduate student of hers at York and Sandy as a don there. I had never met them myself, but I trusted Clara's judgment. We arranged for them to look after Elm Cottage and be around for my kids. In return, I would pay the household expenses and Ian could have that year to complete his master's thesis.

The summer before I began at U of T, the kids and I travelled to Canada together. We went first to Victoria to visit Gran Laurence, who had been living alone since Granddad died. I had to tell my beloved mother-in-law that I was about to be divorced, but I was eager that our visit be for the most part a happy one. I certainly tried my best, but it didn't always work out perfectly. One morning, David and I went to the Victoria Aquarium. On the way home to Gran's, running late for a lunch she was holding for me and in a hurry to catch the departing bus, I ran smack into a power pole with a metal box attached to it and cut my face deeply, next to my right eye. David probably thought I was wounded for life. I mostly worried about blood dripping onto my good beige linen dress. A police car took me and David to the hospital, where the gash was sewn up. My sister-in-law, Muriel, picked us up and I still recall her running every yellow light to get us there on time. We zapped into Gran's place, and much to my relief, the lunch went off as though nothing had happened.

On the final lap of that journey, we stayed for a few days with Adele and her husband Dmitry in Montreal. Their daughter, Tamara, had been born in June. We had had snapshots of the baby but this was the first time we had seen her: a gorgeous child, already showing signs of being the bright, inquiring, and loving person she has become. Dmitry had just got a new job in Toronto, which selfishly made me very glad as it meant they would be living there when I arrived.

I took Jocelyn and David to the airport in Montreal and saw them onto the plane to London, where Ian and Sandy would meet them. I can't remember, either before or afterwards, when it had been so difficult to say goodbye to anyone. I wanted to ditch the university job and get on the plane with them. I thought once again that I must have been totally insane, if not totally irresponsible, to agree to leave my children for a whole academic year. Even the knowledge that I would go back to Elm Cottage at Christmas did nothing to relieve what I felt. I had to wait for an hour for my own plane to Toronto. It was a long hour. I could think of nothing but leaving my kids, worrying about how they'd get along without me and, perhaps more important, how I could possibly get along without them.

We all managed somehow. I wrote to the kids several times a week and I went back in December for almost a month. That wasn't a totally happy occasion, unfortunately, since Jack and I were finally divorced three days before Christmas, but I was there with them for a while. Ian and Sandy, who had become good friends, were marvellously supportive. I had to go down to a court in the south of England for the divorce proceedings, but Alan Maclean had called to say that Macmillan's were sending a car for me. Sandy and I went down together and it was over in a few minutes, but it was still awful. At one point, the judge said to me, "You have one under-age child. Do you look after him in the holidays?" I replied, "He is going to a state school and I look after him all the time." I was so traumatized, I didn't have the energy to be angry. In retrospect, it amused me a little that the judge assumed a woman who presented herself as a professional writer and a man who was a distinguished irrigation engineer *must* have their youngest child in boarding school.

When I had arrived in Toronto in the late summer to take up my post as writer-in-residence, I stayed with Clara and Morley Thomas until I took possession of the house I had rented, sight unseen. It had been recommended to me by a person at the university and belonged to a married couple, both academics, who were on a year's sabbatical. I later realized that I could have rented a small apartment within walking distance of Massey College, but at the time, the thought of looking for somewhere to live in a city I scarcely knew was too much for me to handle. It was a pleasant house, but too large for my needs and full of what I was told was priceless Italian antique furniture. I rented the downstairs study, bedroom, and bathroom and use of the kitchen to a young woman, Eleanor, who was doing publicity work for several publishers. Hers was a cheering presence in the house. We often laughed about our reluctance even to touch the furniture. I never used the living room and very seldom the dining room, much less the good china and crystal. I mostly lived upstairs in the study, which was less intimidating. I don't think I had friends in for dinner more than two or three times during the whole year. On one of the very few occasions when I did stir myself to cook a decent dinner, I invited Jack and Elizabeth McClelland and made a spectacular seafood casserole, only to discover that seafood was totally poisonous to Jack, who had a violent allergy. So much for my role as hostess.

My introduction to Massey College was heartening. I had been regaled by tales of what a male stronghold it was. Robertson Davies, the Master of Massey at that time and whose writing I admired a great deal, was going to be, in my nervous imagination, very daunting. Nothing could have been farther from the truth. He met me at the imposing wrought-iron gates at the entrance to the college and said warmly, "Despite what you may have heard to the contrary, you are welcome here." That warmth of acceptance continued through the entire year on the part of Rob himself and the staff and students.

The term "writer-in-residence" confused many people, who imagined that I actually resided at Massey. I did have an office there, plus, for the first and only time in my life, a secretary. It was a wonderful luxury. I had two books coming out that year and I used to spend Monday mornings with her, clearing up my business mail. She also made appointments for me with would-be writers. The writer-in-residence committee comprised, among others, Phyllis Grosskurth and Dave Godfrey. I met with them just before the term started, as confused as anyone else, and said anxiously, "What am I supposed to do?" They smiled sweetly and said, "Whatever you like." I was only required to give two public lectures on subjects of my choice. The freedom of the job was frightening, but I soon decided that the committee's decision was the right one. It was better for me to organize my own program according to what I considered I could and wanted to do. I had large purple posters printed, informing the university community of my presence, saying I would like to meet young writers, and giving my secretary's phone number. After about a week or so, my schedule was constantly full. What I hadn't bargained for was that people other than students would see the posters. I finally had to tell my secretary to make appointments only for students or individuals connected with the university; I couldn't cope with the members of the general public who came flocking in to see me.

On the three days a week when I held interviews and discussed people's writing with them, I frequently stayed late, after all the office staff had gone home. Early on, I had had one rather scary experience that led me to make an arrangement with a young graduate student, Phil, whose study and living quarters were next door to my office. A middle-aged man came in with a short manuscript and announced, "I want you to tell me how to write." I told him, "I can't really do that." He asked, "What *should* I do?" I said, "Listen to how people talk, if you're going to write fiction." He paused. Then he said, "I don't very often hear people talking." That sentence, and what it implied, chilled me. I realized I knew nothing about most of the people who came to see me. After that, I arranged with Phil that if I dialled his number and said a certain code phrase, he was to come instantly into my office. This cloak-and-dagger stuff was silly, no doubt, but it was a reassurance I needed.

In fact, I only asked for Phil's help once. My office, like all the offices at Massey in the cold weather, was kept far too hot. I could never discover any way to adjust the heat. Fiddling around with the knobs and dials didn't seem to have any effect. Having lived in England, where homes tended to be underheated, I often opened the window just above my desk that faced out into the quad and the large goldfish pond. One afternoon, alone in my office, I had the window open and my back to it while I looked in the filing cabinet. When I turned to my desk, a huge black squirrel was sitting there. I screamed. The squirrel hightailed it out of there in a second, but Phil, gallant protector that he was, came thundering in, prepared to defend my life and / or my virtue.

I saw many students that year. The easiest young writers to deal with were the most talented; they were capable of self-criticism and understood when I myself criticized their work. They also had the best grasp of spelling, punctuation, and grammar. The most difficult were the least talented. I always felt I had no right to think so, but the least talented ones, or so it seemed to me, had absolutely no knowledge of grammar, never mind form, never mind content. I didn't ever aim to stab anybody to the heart, but nor could I tell people their work was terrific when it obviously was not. I've since thought that the job of writer-in-residence would be perfect training for the diplomatic service.

I had recklessly said that I would go out to classes in Canadian literature and have seminar sessions with the students. I didn't realize what I was letting myself in for. I went to dozens. By the end of each week, I was exhausted. Once I was asked to meet after dinner with students in a men's residence, most of whom were in either engineering or medicine. I spoke with a delegation of two young men. "Are you sure they really want to talk about literature?" I asked. "Oh hell, Mrs. Laurence," one of them said, "the guys don't want to talk about *literature* with you. They want to talk about *women*." Thus it was that I came to describe myself as the Ann Landers of Massey College. They were a fine group of young men, but I must say that most of them needed a lot of consciousness-raising. I like to think, however, that there may be a few doctors and engineers out there now who sometimes think of me and of the need for equality of the sexes.

That year my long-time friend Mary Adachi returned to Toronto from a year at the University of Tokyo. Mary had been and still is a close and dear friend. She used to work for several months each year at Canada House, and she was certainly one of the ElmCot tribe. Many were the laughs she and I had had there. Once, Mary had mentioned to a colleague at Canada House that she was going out to our place for the weekend. "Oh, to Margaret Laurence's?" her colleague said. "You must have some stimulating intellectual discussions." In fact most of our stimulating intellectual discussions at Elm Cottage used to focus on how on earth we could control, if not eradicate, the sinister, tough-rooted ground-elder that perpetually threatened to take over the rose garden.

That year in Toronto was an exciting one for me, for both *The Fire Dwellers* and *Jason's Quest* were published. Publication is one thrill that never diminishes. After the long period of struggling to write a book, and rewrite and rewrite and revise it, after the editorial consultations and the horrible task of proofreading, finally one holds the finished book in one's hands. Let the reviews fall where they may. Some will be damning, often for the wrong reasons, while others will be highly praising, sometimes also for the wrong reasons. But no one can unpublish a published book.

The 1969 fall academic term at the University of Toronto was not spent entirely in Toronto. The university was generous in its agreement to let me go elsewhere for a couple of days at a time. I went to McGill to deliver a lecture, and I went to a number of University Women's Clubs. I don't enjoy giving lectures, which I prefer to call talks. I did two talks at U of T itself, sweating blood over writing them and trembling while delivering them. It was then that I learned to sit down at a table when delivering a speech or reading, a lesson that has stood me in good stead ever since.

While I was at U of T I managed to save enough money to buy what I needed: a foothold in Canada – a summer cottage. I wanted to move back permanently as soon as the children had completed secondary school, but in the interim, I needed a house here, something of my own. I finally found the perfect place, a small place on the Otonabee River, just south of Peterborough. A couple of friends and I had gone to look at another cottage there, which I hated, but the real-estate agent told me he had something else that had just come on the market. We went to see a cedar cottage and I knew instantly, as soon as I saw it, that it was meant to be mine. It had been used as a fishing shack and wasn't in terrific shape, but it was basically sound. It had a kitchen, three tiny bedrooms, and a huge front window that faced right onto the river. "I'll have this one, please," I said. My friends gazed at me. Could one really buy a property so precipitously? I did, and I never regretted it.

I acquired my cottage, "the shack" as we came to call it, in the fall of 1969. It quickly proved to be an important part of my life. There had been no running water there, so I found a well-driller who divined a well. I could hardly believe it. He called me in Toronto to tell me he'd found water and I said, "Do you think the well is going to be all right? You didn't have to go more than fifty feet down?" He said with pride, "Lord, woman, you got enough water there for haffa Toronto." It was true. The well never ran dry, even in August when I had lots of visitors. The divining didn't work for me, but when I held the y-shaped willow wand with the well-driller, the point held upwards, I could feel it moving down when we came to the source of the water. That was an unexpected gift that greatly influenced the novel I was about to start writing, *The Diviners*, a novel that was not even completely formed in my mind.

I spent a month at the cottage in the spring of 1970. One of the first neighbours I met was an old man, Jack Villerup. I've written about him in several articles, and the character of Royland, the old man of the river in *The Diviners*, was partly influenced by Jack. He was a retired engineer whose wife had died some years before. When I moved to the shack, he came by and said, "I hope you'll enjoy our river." I did. During my first summer and in subsequent summers after that, he'd sometimes drop over to say, "Would you like to take a breezer up the river?" and I would go out with him in his motorboat.

After the academic year ended, I spent a very unproductive time back in Elm Cottage as far as my writing went. I was glad to be home with the kids, but I spent months in an act of evasion. I was trying to write a novel that I eventually realized wasn't there to be written. I wrote the first paragraph of that non-existent novel day after day, over and over and over. It was to have been an allegorical work, set in a mythical country in West Africa. What I was avoiding was the necessity of coming closer to home, closer to myself.

We had a great many visitors in the fall and winter of 1970. It was a happy time in every way but one: I wasn't working well. In fact, I wasn't working at all, and I found this depressing in the extreme. One good thing did happen, though, in terms of my work. My book of short stories *A Bird in the House,* which I had been working on for some time, was published. Judith Jones at Knopf, my editor of many years, had initially had a major disagreement with me for the first and only time. She thought I should make the collection into a novel. I knew I couldn't. I struggled with the problem and finally phoned John Cushman to tell him I would rather not have the book published at all than make the stories into a novel. John talked to Judith, who hadn't realized my distress, and she, of course, agreed, even though collections of short stories were thought not to sell at all. The cover of this book, which was published in Canada, the U.S., and England, said only "A Bird in the House, by Margaret Laurence." It actually was reviewed in a lot of publications as a novel, much to Judith's and my amusement.

The saving grace during that winter and spring, when I was working to no effect on a novel that was not meant to be, was that not only were there many young Canadians who came to visit but there were also a number of my contemporaries as guests, friends like Alice Frick, who had been a pioneer in CBC Radio. She used to listen patiently while I carried on about my sense of not being able to write, and she encouraged me when I began to talk about the themes I really wanted to deal with. I was probably quite boring that winter, but the support from friends meant a great deal to me.

I've never been able to force a novel. I have always had the sense of something being given to me. You can't sit around and wait until inspiration strikes, but neither can you force into being something that isn't there. Amazingly, the gift was given to me once again. One morning, in the spring of 1971, I woke up with a thought in my mind. I took a notebook out to the lawn and began to write a novel that I knew even then would be called *The Diviners*. It felt as though I had been waiting for it, and it had been waiting for me. I couldn't write it fast enough.

The summer of that year I went back to Canada and lived at the shack, writing constantly. It was the year Jack McClelland got a large loan from the Ontario government. He had a poster printed up for me with a comic take-off of the Ontario coat-of-arms. It stated: "No visitors allowed between Monday and Friday. An important work is going on," and it was signed "J.G. McClelland, servant and publisher." I put it up in the cottage, where it stayed for years.

That same summer, I travelled to Ottawa to be invested as a Companion of the Order of Canada. They had written to me in England in the spring to inform me and I had had to let them know that I couldn't go in May. I had intended to spend the summer in Canada, but I didn't have anyone until the end of June to look after my house and I couldn't afford to go over twice. In my naïveté, I thought they would probably post me the medal. Of course they didn't. Roland Michener, who was still Governor General, graciously arranged for a private investiture. I went with several friends, having first phoned Government House to ask if it would be all right to wear an informal dress. The answer was "No." In my confusion, I phoned Enid Rutland, who, with her husband, Barry, was coming to Ottawa with me. She laughed and said, "Do you really think they're going to turn you out, whatever you wear?"

It was a touching and, in some ways, hilarious event. Before Michener appeared in the drawing room where the investiture was to be held, an aide fastened a hook on my dress so that Michener could avoid grappling with my matronly bosom. That amused me, but in fact I was touched and honoured to wear that pin. I had always thought I had no use for such awards, but this is a Canadian award, and I am proud to have it.

I worked on *The Diviners* during the next two years, in the summer at the shack and, in the intervening months, back at Elm Cottage. The river flowing both ways was, of course, the Otonabee River, and every time I looked up from the page I was writing at the shack, I could see it. One of the most amusing moments while writing that book occurred on a winter day in England. The power was off in the house for some reason, and I sat in my study with two sweaters on, a blanket wrapped around my legs, and a little paraffin stove chunking away nearby. I was freezing, but I was writing a scene that took place on a boiling summer day in Canada. "If I can do this," I thought, "anything is possible."

I finished the first draft in Canada, in the summer of 1972. There was an element of magic about that novel. When I had completed the first draft, I told my friend Jean Cole, who lived in Peterborough and was associated with Trent University. At the time, she was researching a book about her great-great-grandfather, Archibald MacDonald, who as a young man had led the first of the Selkirk settlers on the long march from York Factory to Churchill, and then by boat down to the Red River. I had used, in mythical form, something of that story, when Christie Logan tells Morag Gunn about her ancestors, in order to give her back her past. Although Christie bases his stories about

Piper Gunn on historical fact, I had treated this in a highly fictionalized manner. I thought Jean would be interested since it was a period of history about which she knew far more than I. I mentioned my fictional character, Piper Gunn, and she looked at me in total amazement. "There was a piper," she said, "of course you'd know that." "Of course," I said. "There had to be a piper." "You don't know what his name was?" Jean asked. "No, I don't." "His name," she said, "was Gunn."

Back in England, I realized I had a small problem. I was writing about a character who composed songs, but I was trying to describe the songs without the songs themselves actually existing. I found it unconvincing. I told Ian Cameron, who composed a lot of songs himself, and he suggested I try to write some of my own. I didn't think I could – I'd never been a songwriter. Ian said, "How do you know until you try?" So I did. I had a tune in my mind for the ballad of Jules Tonnerre, so I wrote the words and whistled the tune to Ian. A week or so later, he came back with his guitar and played the song to me. I was so encouraged that I went on and wrote the words for three more songs, with Ian composing the music. The completion of *The Diviners* was, in a sense, a team effort. Ian helped with the songs, my daughter typed out the third draft, and she and a colleague at her office photocopied the manuscript for me, the first photocopies of a book I'd had in my life. I had all kinds of help, help that I needed because writing *The Diviners* was one of the most difficult and exhausting things I've ever done.

My daughter had left home by that time, and in the fall of 1972, I realized that once David graduated from secondary school the following spring, I wanted to move back to Canada. I knew I'd have to sell Elm Cottage eventually, but I didn't want David to have to move out of his home the moment he left school. I arranged to rent the house to Ian and Sandy Cameron for a year, on the condition that David could live there, too, while I took up a one-term job

201

at the University of Western Ontario and a spring term appointment at Trent University in Peterborough. I planned to go back to Elm Cottage then, sell the place, and return to Canada. It didn't work out that way. At the end of 1972, I got a phone call from my accountant. He told me if I left Elm Cottage for a whole year and broke my residency in England, I would have to pay the British government 25 per cent of the selling price of the house. The law was in place to avoid real-estate speculation, but for me, it was a disaster. I thought I had had it all planned so well. I asked my accountant what I should do. He said, "You're going to have to sell Elm Cottage and move back to Canada next summer."

I was terribly worried. I didn't want to leave my son without a home, but neither could I afford to pay that kind of money to the government. I also didn't want to have to sell Elm Cottage to a developer who would undoubtedly tear the house down and build six neo-Georgian monstrosities on the property. I wrote a letter to my neighbour across the road at The Beacon, informing him of my intentions. He was an old Tory, but we had one thing in common: a concern about the increasing sale of houses in that area to developers who cared nothing about them. I told him I would much prefer to sell Elm Cottage to a family, but if I couldn't do it by early spring, I would have to sell the house to whoever wanted to buy it.

I got an invitation to go over for a pre-dinner sherry to The Beacon and, with some apprehension, I went. "If you have to sell Elm Cottage," he said, "would you consider selling it to me?" I can hardly describe my surprise. I hadn't expected this response at all. Apparently one of his sons was working in America but wanted to return to England and might want the house. In the meantime, he planned to rent it.

My business acumen has never been great. On the other hand, as I have realized throughout the years, it hasn't been so bad either. I knew that if I sold the house to my neighbour, I'd get cash for the sale. There would be no question of being pressured into taking back a mortgage. When I moved to Canada, I would need all my assets to buy a house there. Adele has always made affectionate fun of me for boasting about the few occasions when I thought I was being so businesslike and so clever, when in fact I was probably being enormously transparent. This was one of those occasions. I had been reading the *Bucks Free Press* real-estate section for some time, taking close note of the prices for similarly sized houses and properties. I had a sum in mind. A sale to a developer would likely have brought me more, but I had a fair notion of what I could expect from a private buyer.

"I wonder what price you had in mind?" I asked. In my innocence, I thought that if he mentioned a sum several thousand pounds higher than my own estimated figure, I wasn't going to say no. He, however, had evidently been reading the *Bucks Free Press,* too. He named a price. It was identical to my own. I could have quibbled, but I wasn't in any frame of mind to do so. Actually, I was ecstatic. "Done," I said. Never has a house been more amicably or more easily sold.

About a week later, the squire asked me if I would consider selling the house furnished, so he could rent it to a young couple without the bother of furnishing it. The furniture in Elm Cottage was solid and in good shape, but certainly not valuable. Everything was workable, but I would have received virtually nothing for the stuff from second-hand furniture dealers. I was only too happy not to have to think about how to get rid of everything. I set about making an inventory and put down an estimated value, which was quite low. I didn't care. I left off a few things I intended to take with me to Canada: my mahogany desk, a chair made locally in High Wycombe, a few other things. The squire and his wife, towards whom I was feeling more and more friendly with each passing day, proclaimed themselves satisfied, as well they might.

Somewhat later, he came over again. "Would you, by any chance, happen to know of a young married couple who would like to rent the house for a relatively low rent on the understanding that the grounds and house would be properly cared for?"

Ian and Sandy Cameron had a flat in Windsor at the time and their lease was running out. They had originally agreed to rent Elm Cottage, before those arrangements had fallen through. Perhaps, I thought, if they were to rent it, even for a year, David wouldn't have to move out immediately. I got in touch with the Camerons and they were delighted to rent the house. David didn't have to move until he felt he wanted to, which was during that next year, and in fact Ian and Sandy ended up living at Elm Cottage for five more years.

Appropriately enough, I was alone for my last night in our beloved house. Whatever possessions I wanted to take to Canada had been packed up. Ian and Sandy had taken our cats. All I had was my suitcases. That night seemed to me almost like our first night there, years before. I was ready to depart into a new phase of my life, back to my own country, where I not only had to go but deeply wanted to go. I was glad to be alone with the house, so quiet now, a house that had been so noisy through our many years of living there. The portrait that I'd called The Lady was still in the downstairs hall. I said goodbye to her, and thanks to the house. I went through the rooms and just touched them here and there. My study, the bookshelves, the many fireplaces. I would never again see it as our home, but that night, alone in Elm Cottage, I went to bed and slept peacefully. The house, as always, protected me until the very end of our association. It would remain my children's childhood home. It would remain the home to which I owed so much, and where I had done so much of my work. I had loved it, as I have loved all my homes: the Little House and the Big House in Neepawa, the shack, Elm Cottage. I thought that night I would never love a house again as much. I was proven wrong.

Before leaving England, I'd announced that I didn't intend to look for a house in Lakefield, which was where I knew I wanted to settle, until the second half of the academic year, when I would be writer-in-residence at Trent, only a few miles away from the village. Time enough then, I thought. My daughter said, "Mum, I give you two weeks after you get to the shack." I had one month there before I had to go to Western, and two days after I arrived, I called up nearly every real-estate agent in the county. For the next week or so, they would phone to tell me about "this nice little modern bungalow in a new housing development area only four miles away from Lakefield." I kept repeating that I wanted an old house, within walking distance of the shops. August seemed to fly by and I became nervous. I had realized it would be idiotic to wait until I went to Trent to look for a house. Every cent I owned was in a savings account, drawing a tiny amount of interest. Real estate, in the meantime, was climbing. One morning I decided to call a real-estate firm that had an office in Lakefield itself. I listed my exceedingly specific requirements with little hope.

"I want an old, two-storey, brick house," I said, "with three bedrooms and a study. It has to be right in the village. I don't drive. I'm not a gardener, so I don't want a big lot. This is probably impossible, but it would also be marvellous to have a small, self-contained apartment that I could rent to a Trent student who could keep an eye on the place when I'm away."

The voice at the other end of the phone sounded surprised. "Mrs. Laurence, something like that has just come on the market and we haven't yet advertised it. Would you like to see it?" Shades of the cottage. Exactly what the real-estate guy had said to me when I bought the shack. "Yes," I said, "please drive out and pick me up this instant."

There it was, just waiting for me, the very house I had described. Of course, I had the sense to examine such things as the foundations, and I knew I'd have to have an electrician and plumber look the place over. I'd been reading the *Peterborough Examiner* real-estate section as though it contained my hope of heaven and I reckoned that, even if the place had to be totally rewired and replumbed (which it turned out it didn't need), it was still an excellent buy.

The real-estate man from Lakefield drove me back to the shack. I told him I would think about the house. I thought about it for precisely five minutes. I knew that if I hesitated, I would lose this marvel that was obviously meant for me, as I was for it. I phoned his office, asking that he call as soon as he arrived. He did and drove straight back to the shack with an offer to purchase. I signed it and it was accepted by the owners. The whole deal had begun and been signed, sealed, and delivered in a matter of four hours. It was the only house I had looked at. Thirteen years later, I am still awed by my good luck.

That spring, in 1973, The Writers' Union of Canada was starting up. I agreed to be interim chairman until we could hold our first founding conference, discuss and vote on a constitution, and choose a first chairman. I helped to work on a draft constitution, but at the founding conference, all I did was to welcome the members of our tribe who were there, many of them friends and many of whom I had only recently met. I handed the meeting itself over to F.R. Scott, the distinguished poet, constitutional lawyer, and writer, who had generously agreed to help us set up the union. He had gone over the draft constitution with us late into the night before. The half-dozen of us who had worked on it for weeks felt very proud of ourselves. At last we had it all hammered out. Then Frank Scott said drily, "You have forgotten one important thing, my children. You have not said this constitution may be amended."

At the founding meeting, Marian Engel was elected our first chairman. It was a heady time for us, and indeed an extremely important time, for it brought together writers from all over Canada and gave us a sense of true community in this enormous land. Canadian writers have so often felt isolated, separated from one another by vast geographical distances and differences. The union, over the years, has done a great deal to alleviate that sense of isolation. It has also raised important questions about writers' rights and status in our society. The story of the union is not one I can tell here. Indeed, I suspect it is too complex for any one person to tell, but at some point it will have to be chronicled properly. Suffice it to say that it was a landmark in my life, as it was in the lives of so many other Canadian writers.

As the union began, so did my term as writer-in-residence at Western. It was a tremendously busy but fairly lonely time, despite the fact that I had some good friends there, both old and new, and I was received with much warmth and kindness. I had rented a house from a distinguished professor in the English Department and with it, I had inherited a sturdy cleaning woman who loved to polish the hardwood floors. She was also outspoken, a quality I usually admire but which can be difficult to handle at times. I used to wash my hair in the kitchen sink because the one in the bathroom was too small. One day I had to call the plumbers because the sink was blocked. Alas, the cleaning lady was there at the time. Too much of my hair, she insisted, was falling out when I washed it and was blocking the sink. The answer, apparently, was to grate up two large onions and apply this mixture to my hair every time I washed it. After the shampoo, the onions. "No more problems with the hair," she pronounced. Possibly, I thought, no more problems with the hair, but probably no more friends, either.

I missed the kids terribly and called them on a number of occasions. That was the first Christmas I had been away from them, and in some ways it was the loneliest of my life. I stayed with Clara and Morley Thomas in Toronto for a few days and then I went out to Newmarket to be with my aunt and uncle for Christmas. Never was I more glad of family. I went to Adele and Dmitry's for New Year's. Without my friends, and my aunt and uncle, Christmas would have been insupportable.

I left Toronto to spend the winter / spring term of 1974 at Trent. When I arrived, I was told that I should save enough time for my own work. They couldn't afford to pay me much and didn't want to exploit me. Of course, I didn't do a tap of my own writing, but I was grateful for the time I had there. I came to know the university for which, years later, I had the honour to be chancellor, and I grew to respect, admire, and love it as a small liberal arts and science university of the kind I had known when I myself was young.

That term, a young woman from a Canadian magazine came to interview me. She had read an advance copy of *The Diviners,* and I spent several afternoons with her and her tape recorder, trying to explain the difference between autobiography and fiction. Unfortunately, she had already made up her mind. At one point, she said to me, "But you *did* take the obligatory trip to Scotland, the land of your ancestors, didn't you?" "Yes, I did," I replied, "but my ancestors were Lowland Scots, not Highland Scots, as Morag's were." "But you *do,*" she said, "have a grown-up daughter, don't you?" "Oh, yes," I said. "I also have a grown-up son, but actually, neither of them is the illegitimate child of a Manitoba Métis."

When the article came out, she had done exactly what I'd hoped she wouldn't do: she had said *The Diviners* was completely autobiographical. I rank it as a kind of spiritual autobiography. I suppose the one novel I've written that was not thought, by at least some reviewers, to be autobiographical in some sense was *The Stone Angel*. Even the most obtuse of sensibilities could not imagine that I was a ninety-year-old woman. But because I have written so much about women, I have often been told I write autobiographically. I have no objection to writers who do write straight out of their own lives, but apart from *A Bird in the House*, which is loosely based on my family and my childhood, I don't happen to be one of them.

This experience over *The Diviners* led me to recall something that had happened when *The Fire Dwellers* came out. A writer from *Time* magazine wanted to interview me as part of his review of the novel. He couldn't come out to Elm Cottage because he had broken his leg, so I met him in London for lunch. He obviously hated the book. I tried to tell him about fiction, but no, he didn't – or wouldn't – understand. In the end, his review stated, among other criticisms, that *The Fire Dwellers* was autobiographical. Reading this, I found it difficult not to wish that he had broken not his leg but his neck.

While I was at Trent, I spent much of my spare time buying furniture for the Lakefield house. Friends took me out to antique and second-hand furniture shops in the area and I acquired furniture with every corner of the house in mind. It was a great thrill. Another, equal thrill that winter was rediscovering Eaton's catalogue. I spent many evenings going through it, just as I had when I furnished the shack. For a prairie person growing up in the thirties and forties, one universal fantasy had always been to be able to order anything you wanted from the Eaton's or Hudson's Bay Company catalogue. My happiness, my gloating almost, is impossible to describe. I ordered a fridge, stove, washer, dryer, lamps and lampshades, linen and blankets, china, pots and pans, cutlery, the works, and arranged for everything to be stored until I was ready to have them delivered in the spring.

I also had to get the house redecorated. When I went over with the painter-decorator to take measurements, the young high-school teacher and his wife to whom I had rented the house looked at me rather protectively. Then Tom spoke. "Margaret, I don't know if I should tell you this, but this house, about two families ago, um, was a funeral home." I fell about laughing. For a moment they must have thought I was crazy. Then I told them. My own grandfather, on my mother's side, had been an undertaker, and the funeral home came into all my Canadian fiction in one way or another. I thought it was very appropriate. I also thought if any of the long-gone mothers and fathers of the village lingered in the house, their spirits would surely wish me well.

I took possession of the house in the beginning of April and by the end of that month, all the painting and papering was complete. Eaton's arrived on the appointed day with two large trucks. Furniture stores arrived with tables, chests of drawers, beds, chesterfield, and chairs. It was like Christmas a thousand times over. My friend Budge Wilson worked with me all day, trying to get everything into some kind of order. In the evening, I went back to Budge and Alan's house for dinner. It was only then that Budge told me that when we had more or less got everything organized, she had expected me to make some deathless remark. I did not. I looked at the house, my home now, and said, "Oh, wow!"

I picked the day that I would move into the Lakefield house: May 1, 1974. I chose May 1 because I thought it was a propitious day, both politically, for a member of the Old Left, and magically, for a believer in magic. When I arrived, the dishes had been washed and stored in the cupboards, the beds made up, and there was food in the refrigerator. Seldom has anyone moved into a house with such a sense of grace and such help from friends.

The Diviners was also published in May. McClelland and Stewart wanted to have a big launch party, which I was very much against until a woman in the publicity department had an inspiration that not even I could have resisted.

She found a water diviner and got permission to hold the launch on the grounds of the Ontario Science Centre. The diviner found a place where two streams of water met, a marker was buried there, and a divining contest, in which anyone was welcome to take part, was advertised over several local radio stations. Invitations were also sent to members of the media. Seven water diviners from parts of rural Ontario turned up, anxious to demonstrate their skills. For the most part, they didn't know or care that this was an event to launch a book. These diviners all brought their own divining rods, but there were willow wands available for anyone else who wanted to try their hand. All the real diviners got very close to the marker, but only one person in the media – Helen Hutchinson – found she had the gift. By the end of the day, members of the media who had come to scoff were babbling with excitement. The seven water diviners were perfectly calm. To me, it was just one more piece of magic associated with the novel.

I had to do a week's publicity, although it wasn't, thank goodness, a cross-country tour. As usual, I was extremely nervous about the interviews, but managed to get through them nonetheless. One of the last appearances I had to make was to autograph books at the Longhouse Book Shop in Toronto, owned and run by Beth Appeldoorn and Susan Sandler, whom I'd known since they'd started the place. Based on past experience, I wasn't nervous at all. I'd done one book-signing in a bookshop when my first novel was published. I had been in Vancouver and I went to a bookstore in West Vancouver owned by Stephen and Elsa Franklin. It was a memorable afternoon. No one turned up, and I spent about forty bucks on books that I had found while browsing around.

When it came to the book-signing for *The Diviners*, I calmly sallied forth, glad that the week's publicity was nearly over. However, as I approached the Longhouse with Marta Kurc, the publicist from McClelland and Stewart, I was stunned. People were lined up not only in the store but on the sidewalk for about a block. Many of them were carrying piles of my previous novels in both hardcover and paperback. I wanted to run. I wanted to disappear. I could feel myself beginning to shake. Beth and Susan sat me at a table in the front of the shop. My one thought was, "I can't do this, but I have to." If I could have *spoken* with those people, I would have been fine. My voice doesn't shake. But how can you sign dozens, hundreds of books with a hand that is trembling so much you can't even raise a cup of coffee to your mouth?

For the first little while, my signatures in those books were totally illegible. Beth and Susan, aware of my distress, offered coffee, water, anything. Instant action was certainly needed. "Clara Thomas is here," I said. "Get her to come, quickly." Clara appeared beside me a few seconds later. It was one of the many times in my life when I have been saved by a friend. Clara grasped the situation at once. "Here's an aspirin," she said loudly, rummaging in her handbag while muttering into my ear, "It's a tranquillizer." I gulped it down and said to her, "Talk, just talk to me. I don't care a hoot what you say, just talk to me and keep on talking until I'm okay." And she did. Heaven knows what she nobly prattled on about, or how I responded, but it worked. After a while I relaxed, my hand became steady, and I could have gone on signing books for the rest of the day. Since that time, I've done a number of book-signings and have also had to autograph single copies of books, and I've always worried that I will start shaking again. It's never happened, but that day was a frightening and humbling experience. Mind you, I was grateful, too – Longhouse did sell a lot of books.

The reviews, as always, were mixed. Some reviewers slashed me for writing a book that had, in their opinion, a gimmicky structure; some praised me for the innovative format of the novel. Some flailed me for having characters who had appeared in previous novels; some praised me for creating a town in which there was a perceptible continuity through three generations. I don't remember the exact nature of specific book reviews, but I do remember a strange one in the *New York Times Book Review* section, which said, in effect, "This novel takes place on the barren plains of Southern Ontario." The same reviewer referred to Skinner Tonnerre as "a Méti man," obviously assuming that this was the singular form of Métis.

Among the many gifts that novel brought me was a new friendship. Some months after the publication of *The Diviners* a woman phoned me at my house in Lakefield. She told me her name was Alice Williams and she lived at the Curve Lake Reserve near the village. Her mother was an Ojibway and her father a Norwegian. She said she had never called a writer before, but she wanted to let me know that I had got the Métis parts exactly right. I said to her, "You don't really realize what you've just given me. It felt as though those parts were right but I couldn't be sure. Thank you." That began a friendship with Alice and her husband and children that continues to this day. Many wonderful things arose out of the publication of that novel, and a few sad ones, too, but the overwhelming response has been from readers telling me that the book spoke to them. I am grateful for that, because it felt to me like something given.

The following spring, in 1975, I received the Governor General's Award for *The Diviners*. It was a moving ceremony because Jules Léger, the Governor General, had suffered a stroke and had, with great courage and with the support and help of his remarkable wife, struggled his way back into public life. Once again, I felt honoured to receive the award.

The following year, however, *The Diviners* became involved in what, in Peterborough County, we tend to call "the controversy." I don't want to talk about it, I don't even want to think about it, but I must. It will not go away by my ignoring it. It affects not only my books, but the books of all Canadian – and all contemporary – writers, and

I suppose I will never cease to grapple with the issues because I dare not stop, on my own behalf and on behalf of writers everywhere. In 1976, to my total horror and surprise, *The Diviners* was attacked as being pornographic, blasphemous, not fit to be in the school library or to be taught, even at a Grade Thirteen level where students are age seventeen or eighteen and in any other province would be in the first year of university.

I knew, as many other people did, that this novel was and is, to the best of my ability, an honouring of my people. It had felt like a gift of grace to me to be able to write it. I was shocked and hurt by this hostility. The next months were very hard. The letters in the *Peterborough Examiner* were mixed – some supported me, others castigated me. The same people, or their ilk, who attacked me had attacked W.O. Mitchell, Alice Munro, many of our serious writers. Most of the people who wanted my novel banned were fundamentalist Christians who claimed the only book anyone needed to read was the Bible and who took it upon themselves to interpret it. With my sense of being a Christian, or at least an aspiring Christian with an ecumenical outlook, I felt extraordinarily damaged. Although my critics thought they had given the Bible a literal reading, in fact they themselves chose how to interpret any one part. One ironic aspect of their attack on me was that in all my writing there are a great many references to both the Old and the New Testaments. The problem of the people who attacked me, as I see it, is that they are extremely unskilled readers. They may know, superficially, the meaning of each word on a page, but they are incapable of perceiving what is really happening, what is being expressed, and what all the words add up to.

Around the time that the 1976 attack happened, I agreed to be part of a four-woman panel brought together by a women's club in Peterborough. The meeting was held in a United Church hall and the panel sat on stage at a long table covered with drapery that looked rather like a bedspread with a fringe. The inevitable question came, and I was prepared to deal with it. "Mrs. Laurence, why did you find it necessary to use all those four-letter words in *The Diviners*?" I replied, truthfully, "The writer's first, and perhaps only, responsibility is to be true to her or his own characters, human individuals that the writer cares about very deeply. If I had Christie Logan, the garbage man in Manawaka, speaking in the same terms in which I am now addressing you, which is my natural mode of speech, it would have been a betrayal of him. Christie did not speak as I speak. Christie spoke as *he* spoke. I had to set that down."

The audience nodded in understanding and agreement. I was vastly relieved. I was also exhausted and badly needed a cigarette. I thought I could have one, surreptitiously, using an empty cough-drop tin for an ashtray. I stooped down, lit up, took a quick puff, and held the cigarette below the level of the tabletop. I suddenly became aware of a burning smell and saw a tiny line of flames as a voice literally rang out. It was mine, as I realized a second later while beating out the flames with my bare hands: "My God! I've set fire to the bloody tablecloth!"

There was a moment of deep silence. Then, mercifully, the whole audience of women, young, middle-aged, and old, broke out in laughter.

My books were attacked again in 1985, at which time not only was *The Diviners* vilified but also *A Jest of God* and, for the first time, *The Stone Angel,* which was called demeaning to human nature. In 1985, unlike nine years earlier, I decided that it was no longer appropriate for me to maintain a dignified silence. I spent about three months at the beginning of 1985 doing interviews on radio and TV, with newspapers and magazines, and writing articles on the whole subject. On both occasions my books were vindicated and restored to the high-school courses. On both occasions I received an enormous number of supportive letters, and in 1985, I received letters of support from people all over Canada. I still find this subject very difficult to talk about, however, even though I realize that the people who are convinced they have the only answers, and who feel they have the right to impose their wishes and views on everyone else, will probably always be with us, and we must remain on guard. What troubles me perhaps more than anything else is that so many of the people who would like certain books banned are the same people who don't believe in sex education for young people, who are always anti-abortion under any circumstances, and who yet maintain they believe in Christian love. It seems to me that what they're in fact preaching is hatred, authoritarianism, and a suppression of humankind's thoughts, queries, and aspirations. I absolutely hate, despise, and loathe real pornography, films or porn magazines that make use of actual women and children in situations that are horribly degrading and demeaning. I cannot really believe, though, that the printed word should ever be censored, however terrible it may be.

I don't know how I would have managed to withstand the attacks on my books were it not for the support expressed in readers' letters and the support given to me by family, friends, and by so many people in my village. They certainly kept me going through the difficult times. It is very hard to read letters about oneself in the *Peterborough Examiner* such as, "We know that Margaret Laurence's aim in life is to destroy the home and the family." I said to myself that the people who wrote and thought those things didn't know me and had certainly not read my books with understanding, but it still hurt that anybody could feel that way.

Among the expressions of support I received, I think particularly of Joan Johnston. We met at the home of Alice and Doug Williams around the time of the 1976 attack. Joan was outraged at what was being said about my books and at the personal attacks on me. She began to keep a file, and to send me photocopies for my own files, of all the correspondence, editorials, and so forth on the whole subject. We became firm friends. In the 1985 attack, Joan also made copies of the various TV interviews, news broadcasts, everything pertaining to what we still jokingly call "the controversy." This year, 1986, I suggested to Joan that York University in Toronto, which has most of my papers, would probably like that whole file. It turned out that indeed York would. I told Joan, "Whatever they give us, kid, we'll split the proceeds." A few days later, she came by and said, "I can't do that, Margaret. I don't want to profit from your pain." She made a wonderful suggestion: We would use the money to put on a big birthday party for my sixtieth birthday. So we did. It was one of the happiest events of my life. We had a lot of laughs, thinking of appropriate toasts like, "To the people who want to ban Margaret Laurence's books, without whom this party would not have been possible."

Since I came to live in Lakefield, I have published four books. The first was a collection of essays, *Heart of a Stranger*, in 1976. Most of these essays had been printed before, but a few had never been published. The three books I have actually written in Lakefield have all been children's books. In 1979, *Six Darn Cows* was published by Lorimer. I had been asked to do a small book for a series the company was doing on the real lives of real kids and I agreed to try. I based my story on things I knew from the life of children on small farms. I was delighted that Ann Blades, a talented artist and writer, agreed to do the pictures.

When the book was finally done, I decided to do a tape of a song I had written for the ending. The tune, of course, doesn't appear in the book, but I had a little tune in my head. I sang it in my awful voice and sent it to James Lorimer as a joke. He responded by suggesting I sing it for a promotional record. I said, "Never! Why don't you sing it, Jim?" The story and the song ended up as a small record done for promotional purposes. I read the story and Bob Bossin, of Stringband, sang the song with my tune, accompanied by a nifty arrangement on his banjo. Marie-Lynn Hammond helped us do the recording. It was one of the most enjoyable times I remember about the publication of any of my books. I had enormous fun, and thought, for a moment, that I might have a new career – but then I'd thought that when I did the songs for *The Diviners,* too.

The first winter in Lakefield brought a nice surprise that also had pleasant repercussions. Dr. Gastle, who owns a farm north of the village and has an impressive collection of antique sleighs, asked me if I'd like to go out for a ride in one of his old cutters. I agreed instantly. I hadn't been in a cutter since I was a kid in Neepawa. My companion was Kay Douglas, who had once owned the farm with her husband, the explorer George Douglas, and had sold it to Dr. Gastle after her husband's death.

That ride gave me an idea for the story that later became *The Olden Days Coat.* It was first published in brief form in *Weekend Magazine,* and later I felt I wanted to improve and expand it. I rewrote it and it was accepted by McClelland and Stewart. Muriel Wood did the pictures and I could hardly have been more fortunate in having such an artist illustrate this book. Some years after the story was published, Atlantis Films, a young Canadian film company, made a half-hour film of the book, in which Megan Follows did a stunning job playing Sal. Studio D, the women's studio of the National Film Board, also did a short film of still photography on *The Olden Days Coat,* to be used in schools and libraries. The film shows me reading part of the story, with photographs of some of Muriel Wood's illustrations.

In my years in my Lakefield home, a great deal has happened, so much that it's impossible to put down even a fraction of it. The National Film Board made a documentary on me, *First Lady of Manawaka*. I participated in Terri Nash and Bonnie Klein's film *Speaking Our Peace*. I joined and served on the board of Energy Probe and have taken as active a part as I could in the entire peace movement. I have often felt, in fact, that as one grows older, one should take not fewer risks, but more.

I was also chancellor of Trent University for three years. While I was there, it was my privilege to give honorary degrees to some people who were my heroes – Tommy Douglas and Malcolm Ross, among others – and to deliver, the year after I ceased to be chancellor, a citation for Lois Wilson, first woman moderator of the United Church of Canada, with whom I had gone to college so long ago and for whom I have such love and admiration.

The last book I published, in 1980, was called *The Christmas Birthday Story*, brought out in Canada by McClelland and Stewart and in America by Knopf, with art work by Helen Lucas. As so often in my writing life, this book was a kind of gift. When my children were young, before my first novel was published, we attended the Unitarian Church in Vancouver. I agreed with many of the concepts of the Unitarian Church and still do, despite the joking definition of a Unitarian as someone who believes in one God – at most. During one parents' meeting, it was suggested that our children shouldn't be told the Nativity story because we knew that angels weren't actually flitting around the sky. I was horrified. I didn't want my children denied that part of their heritage, nor that story, which has such basic truths, whatever the interpretation. I rashly offered to try to write a version of the Nativity that would be acceptable. Since I had two young children going to the Sunday school, I wrote the story with both of them in mind. It was used in the church, but when we left

Vancouver, I lost the only copy I had. A few years after I moved to Lakefield, I went out to a friend's house for dinner and was introduced to a woman who had attended the same church and said she had a copy. She sent it to me and so the story finally came back after having been lost for so long.

The return of the story seemed to mean something. I had met, not long before, the artist Helen Lucas, who has since become one of my closest friends. I approached her tentatively, and showed her the story. I needn't have worried. She liked the story and was delighted to give the gift of her art to it. Her joyous, beautiful, and wise pictures are now a part of that book. I think Helen felt, as I have always felt, that it is *our* book.

As usual, it came out to mixed reviews. Many reviewers didn't deign to notice it because it was a children's book. Many people wrote to me about it, however, telling me they liked it for exactly the reasons I had originally written it for my own children. Fredelle Maynard, a well-known magazine writer and author of *Raisins and Almonds*, the autobiographical chronicle of a Jewish girl's childhood in small prairie towns, told me it was the only retelling of the Christian Nativity story that she would wish to give to a Jewish child. I felt honoured and grateful.

Some Christians (and I can understand their attitude although I do not agree with it) hated the book because they thought it was blasphemous, for the same reasons that others liked and welcomed it. I had thought the story ought to be understood by young children. I had not, therefore, written of the divinity of Jesus or the Virgin Birth or any of those thorny theological matters, which I as an adult have found difficult, and sometimes quite impossible, to believe in, and which I felt would confuse young children totally. The story has been told thousands of times over two thousand years, according to the perceptions and historical era of the teller. I retold it in a way that I myself understand it and believe in it. Jesus is spoken of as a beloved child, born into a loving family, a child who grew up to be a wise teacher, and a friend to all people. That is really how I think of our Lord.

Of course, another thing that bothered some Christians was that in my retelling, I wrote, "Joseph and Mary were happy because soon they were going to have a baby. They didn't mind at all whether it turned out to be a boy or a girl. Either kind would be fine with them. They just hoped their baby would be strong and healthy." Those few and, as it turned out, controversial sentences express much of my own life view and my faith, with its need to recognize both the female and male principles in the Holy Spirit.

It is difficult to retain faith in our present world. It is difficult to feel that world leaders *are* leaders. If they keep on as they are, they might, either wittingly or inadvertently, succeed in destroying all life on earth, not only humankind, but all creatures who share this planet with us, with arrogant humankind who must learn humility and responsibility before it is too late. I cannot really believe that this total negation of life will happen, but I know it could, unless the forces of the superpowers, and all the benighted powers of the world, can be turned away from hostility and hatred. Life has become so dangerous and so complex that it frightens me to know a few fallible, and indeed often ignorant and unimaginative, so-called leaders have it in their power to blow us all to bits.

We do have to keep on, in every way we can, saying, "This must not happen." Can we stop this slide into the destruction of us all? I have often felt helpless and depressed, but I do not feel so helpless or depressed as to give up the struggle. The struggle is *not* lost. I believe we have to live, as long as we live, in the expectation and hope of changing the world for the better. That may sound naïve. It may even sound sentimental. Never mind: I believe it. What are we to live for, except life itself? And, with all our doubts, with all our flaws, with all our problems, I believe that we *will* carry on, with God's help.

221

I have been blessed, with my children, with my work, with a mate of many years and a parting that was mutually respecting, with enduring friends, with my families and my places of home.

I know now, as I did not know when I wrote the first draft of these memoirs, that my own dance of life has not much longer to last. It will continue in my children, and perhaps for a while in my books. It has been varied, sometimes anguished, always interesting. I rejoice in having been given it.

May the dance go on.

VI
AFTERWORDS

OLD WOMEN'S SONG

I see old women dancing
dancing on the earth
I hear old women singing
singing children's birth

        great is their caring
        strong is their measure
        dancing and singing
        life's frail treasure

I see old women dancing
dancing even here
bleakworld and wanworld
world of fear

        great is their hoping
        great is their longing
        may all the children
        stay in life belonging

I see old women dancing
dancing children's breath
I hear old women mourning
mourning children's death

for death of children
where is any answer?
where are words' meanings
for the sorrow dancer?

I see old women dancing
dancing in their grief
singing of the sorrow
singing of belief

so did the prophetess
Miriam of old days
dance for all the people
dance in holy praise

I see old women dancing
dancing on the earth
I hear old women singing
singing death and birth

for young ones taken
without any reason
love has no ending
mourning has no season

through all the ages
children have been taken
accidents, diseases,
parents left forsaken

may the holy spirit
teach us to know why
but may we not conspire
in wars to let them die

I see old women dancing
strongly on the earth
I hear old women singing
life's holy worth

> great is their anger
> their resolve to try –
> must children needlessly
> in wars burn and die?

I see old women dancing
dancing eons past
each one a prophetess
praying life may last

> this is another world
> yet it is the old
> the powers and the nations
> death-dreaming death untold

I see young women dancing
dancing through the fire
proclaiming, praising, hoping,
speaking life's desire

> may all the children
> who are not yet born
> come into a home place
> not the terror-torn

I see old women dancing
dancing through all lands
foremothers with them joining
all of their hands

dance on, old women,
dance amidst the strife,
sing out, old women,
sing for life

I am one among them,
dancing on the earth,
mourning, grieving, raging,
yet jubilating birth.

"Old Women's Song"
Tune by Margaret Laurence
Transcribed by Shelley Brown

Jan. 3 / 1984

A CONSTANT HOPE:
WOMEN IN THE NOW AND FUTURE HIGH TECH AGE

From *Canadian Woman Studies / Les Cahiers de la Femme* (1985)

Any speculation about women in the future must be preceded by a question. Will there be a future, not only for women but for everyone, for the planet itself? Unless the nuclear arms race can be halted, unless the nations that possess nuclear weapons, and especially the two superpowers, can be persuaded to make genuine efforts to end this lunacy, the prospects do not look promising. Women have taken a large part in the growing peace and disarmament movement, and I believe we must take an even greater part in the future and on behalf of the future. For this article, I am assuming there will be a future for life itself, and this is no longer something we can take for granted.

We are living in an age of high technology, an age in which computers and other intricate machines are seen as humankind's salvation. The new religion comes to us complete with its own priesthood and even its own language. Those who have not yet learned this language, and who do not own or have access to these pieces of sophisticated equipment, are made to feel inadequate and threatened. If we do not have a computer, or cannot afford one, will we not become obsolete, irrelevant? This issue affects women deeply now, and will continue to do so, as does the use to which a lot of the high-tech stuff is being put and will be put in the future. The new technology can do some marvellous things, but it cannot take the place of human wisdom, compassion, common sense and conscience, and these values now seem to be at risk in the face of the ubiquitous machines. The technology is still largely male-dominated. I believe that women must take a very level look at the problems of the new technology before they overwhelm us. We must not be intimidated by the sales pitches that imply that everyone must buy a home computer or be left far behind. On the other hand, as many women are realizing, we need to be informed about these tools, because otherwise we will be at an even greater disadvantage in the work force than we are now, and the machines will be used to control us, our bodies and lives, and the minds of our children. In cases where possession of machinery isn't the question, and learning their use isn't possible for most women, as with much hospital equipment, we must familiarize ourselves with procedures, so we can have much more of a voice in the use of these wonderful but by no means miraculous or infallible machines.

Women have already learned, to their sorrow, that a pregnant woman's prolonged explosure to video display terminals may damage her unborn child. Women of all ages must not look passively on while even a few of our sisters and daughters run the risk of either losing their jobs or bearing damaged babies. Nothing has yet been conclusively proved, but any risk is outrageous if it is preventable. Another and related area of risk is the enormous array of high tech devices now routinely used during childbirth, by doctors who often seem to put more faith in machinery than in the mother's ability and right to deliver her own child, with as much encouragement and human help as medical staff can provide, and as little mechanical intervention as possible. "Labour" means hard work. Too often, now, in childbirth, it means passivity and even total unconsciousness. Male doctors, especially, have long tried, with much success, alas, to make the birth of children *their* achievement, as though the mother were simply a vessel, full of child but soon to be emptied efficiently by the doctor and his machinery, instead of an active participant in what can be one of the most awesome experiences of life. When the Caesarian section is necessary, obviously it saves the lives of children and mothers. No one would deny or fail to be grateful for the magnificent accomplishments of modern medical science. But there are many occasions now when the C-section is not necessary and is performed more for the convenience (and monetary reward) of the doctor than for the safety and well-being, physical and emotional, of mother and child. This will continue and even escalate in the future unless women take a very active part in informing themselves and in proclaiming their rights. The thought of routinely monitoring the foetal heart by fancy machinery, in normal deliveries, or putting electrodes into the nearly-born infant's skull, fills me with doubts and questions. Not all women want to have their children by natural childbirth, of course, but in cases where the pregnancy has been normal and the delivery promises to be so, mothers must surely have the option of a natural delivery, with the child's father supportedly present if both parents wish it. More women are now opting for a home delivery, with a trained midwife, but the medical profession is still overwhelmingly hostile to this practice, although these births are known to be, on an average, as safe as hospital births with all the machinery.

What about bringing up children in the future? That future is now with us, and its effect, in terms of certain aspects of technology, can only increase in a negative way unless women (and more and more men, it is to be hoped and prayed) take a strong stand. In an article in the Toronto *Globe and Mail* (August 9, 1984) entitled "The Awful Price of the Computer Age," Marian Kester, a freelance journalist based in Washington, said: "If children are separated from their parents by hours of TV, from their playmates by video games and from their teachers by teaching machines, where are they supposed to learn how to be human? Maybe that's just it. There's no percentage in being human any more." I understand her feelings of dismay, and yet I believe that we must not now or in the future give way to this awful feeling of helplessness. There was a time when TV was regarded (and still is, by some parents) as a handy baby-sitter. We are beginning to know just how dire can be the effect of children's growing up watching countless hours of TV violence. We have yet fully to see the effects of countless hours of their playing video war and violence games. These games don't make children smarter, and certainly not kinder and wiser. They tend to make kids (and the games are said to be more popular with male children) oriented towards winning at the expense of everything else. They encourage an attitude of "good guys" and "bad guys" in an absolute sense, and often the so-called good guys are performing acts of horrendous brutality. The war games encourage and sanctify cruelty, especially towards women and minority groups. They separate a child from the real world of family and friends, of beauty and tragedy. What appears to be action is really passivity. Hit all those little buttons and save the world from the monsters! Advertising, of course, is making these games super-popular among the young. Meantime, outside, the powers are preparing for war. If it happens, it will not be the first time in our era for the young to stride off to war, whistling a merry tune, in the belief that it is all happening on the screen, and they can't get hurt because they're the good guys. Later, they learn otherwise, when it's too late. This softening-up process of the young, in preparing them to accept readily the idea of war, will not cease until and unless we do something about it. Of course, if nuclear war happens, our children won't be conscripted or recruited. There will be no time or need. For both sides it will be game over. Forever.

Many young people have resisted and will resist being turned into zombies in the glitzy world of the video games and films, and are only too aware of the terrible possibility of nuclear destruction. Sometimes I think that many kids are more aware than their parents. Doesn't anyone wonder why the suicide rate among *children* is now so high? Counsellors and commentators speak about broken homes, worry over studies, unhappy loves. But another factor must be that many kids don't feel there will be a future. If they feel despair, we must tell them we understand and are afraid, too, but have to struggle for the survival of the world and all of us.

Vileness and violence threaten women and children in much of the media. As with pornography, so with the really bad video games or whatever, we must now and in the future take legal action and fight these things openly in the courts, not by censorship boards operating without sufficient accountability. Above all, the alienation from other people, fostered by these machines that make billions of bucks for their producers and distributors, must be countered by the human values of love, tolerance, individual worth, compassion, responsibility.

I ponder the situation of women writers in the future. Marian Kester's article also said: ". . . a boom in word processor sales has been occurring among writers. Some say they couldn't function without their Apple II. The belief seems to be that the machine, if it will not actually write the material, is at least conducive to writing. That's like saying a crutch is conducive to walking." The point is well taken. Nevertheless, I don't think it's correct. I know a number of writers, including women writers, who have word processors. I don't think they feel that the machines make *writing* easier but rather that they make copying and inserting revisions a less arduous task. For women writers, with all too often a limited time to spend on their work, this could be a godsend. Over some thirty years, I have typed many books and stories and articles and lectures and book reviews, in manuscript, many times over, on a manual typewriter, doing revisions and ending up by doing two or more fair copies with carbons, in the days when the xerox machine was not widely present, or even if it was, when I couldn't afford xerox copies. A long and laborious job. I don't have a word processor now, although I have an electric typewriter. I don't feel that at this point in my professional life I really need a word processor, but I welcome their use by my younger sisters. All I hope is that in the future women

233

writers will be able to afford such technical aids as they need.

Home computers may, at least in the near future, be another matter for women writers. In an article by Ann Silversides, entitled "Literature Goes Electronic from Coast to Coast," in the Toronto *Globe and Mail* (July 13, 1984), we were told that "about 35 Canadian writers who own their own home computers will begin sending their work electronically across the country to be criticized, revised or simply read by other members of the new network." Based at York University, Toronto, and founded by Professor Frank Davey, the venture is called "Swift Current" and it is "described variously as a Canadian literary data base or an electronic literary magazine." There will be some writing available to subscribers, for public viewing and print-outs, and subscribers will be mainly libraries and universities. This seems to me to be an interesting experiment, although I would question some of its aims (*revising* other writers' work? Can this really be what is intended?). The comment that specially interested me, however, was this: ". . . there already is one group of writers – women writers – who are almost entirely absent from the project. Davey said he approached a number of women 'who just couldn't see themselves in the project.' He offered the explanation that most women writers are more privately focussed on their writing, have less money and hence can't afford home computers, and also are 'conditioned not to participate in the machinery of a culture.'" I was one of the women writers who was approached, and I declined for a variety of reasons, one of which was certainly my lack of familiarity with computers. There were other reasons, however, and perhaps I can make a guess about the reasons other women had.

I don't think women writers are any more "privately focussed" on their writing than male writers, and I certainly hope not, out of concern for the quality of writing by either sex. I always thought all writers were privately focussed on their writing; this in no way implies an obsession with self. I agree that women writers tend to have less money. Not so many of us teach in universities or have other well-paid jobs outside the home. It is to be hoped that the financial situation of women writers, and women in general, will improve in the future, but it seems likely that a home computer will be relatively low on the list of priorities for some time. A Canadian woman writer of real distinction once told me that when her children were young, she spent most of her first and quite modest Canada Council grant on a washing machine. I understood perfectly. I wonder how many male writers would understand. As for being "'conditioned not to participate in the machinery of a culture,'" I admit that I do find the world of computers mysterious and daunting, but at this stage in my life I'm not highly motivated to learn that world. If I were, I imagine I would be able to do it. I do not think this conditioning, if it really exists, would prove a stumbling block for most women writers. I would guess that a more relevant reason for women writers' almost complete absence is *lack of time*. As in so many other professions, women in my profession have often been expected to choose between career and children, and we have often refused to choose and have opted for both. Women writers, like women in other areas of work, have usually had numerous other jobs – child-rearing with its vast emotional needs gladly given, shopping, cleaning, cooking, laundry, and a host of others, including doing their own business correspondence, without the access to typing and secretarial services that male writers, especially if associated with a university, have frequently enjoyed. Many women writers, if they have been single parents, separated or divorced, have also had to supplement meagre incomes with freelance journalism. Male writers who don't hold teaching positions have done freelance journalism as well, but not in addition to child-rearing and housework – their wives have seen to that. I don't know who originally said that every writer needs a good wife, but my own addition to the saying has always been that if you are a female heterosexual writer it's not so easy to find an understanding and unpaid housekeeper. My own children have been adults for some years, but even now I simply would not have the time to plug in to all or even some of the work being done by the writers in this experiment, and as for commenting on it and pondering other writers' comments on my work, heaven forbid. In addition to doing my writing, I am still my own housekeeper, secretary and business manager. I would like to see more women taking part in such projects as "Swift Current" because I think the voices of women are needed in every area. All I can hope is that in the future my younger sisters will be able to solve that persistent problem – lack of time. A more equitable distribution of housework and child care may ultimately be a partial solution, but it won't help single mothers and won't take care of the domestic work or business work for women writers living alone, who can't afford secretarial or domestic help. More and better day care centres, at affordable prices, are of course a top priority for women with young children, anywhere in the work force. We need not deceive ourselves that this is a top priority for men in our society. Perhaps in the future men may really come to understand that child care is their responsibility, too, and that good child care is important because children are important, as well as the fact that mothers working at other jobs not only need help but have a *right* to it.

Quite apart from the electronic experiment I've been discussing, I want to take another look at the statement that women writers are "'conditioned not to participate in the machinery of a culture.'" I am certainly not taking issue with Professor Davey here. Indeed, when I first read those words, I thought, sadly, *how true.* The statement is thought-provoking because it is almost universally believed, not only about women writers but about women in general, all women, and it is believed both by men and by women themselves. In an abstract sense, women have all too often had a self-image of being a *klutz* as far as machinery is concerned, and men have all too often believed that women just aren't very good at learning any kind of technology. A quick look at history and reality shows otherwise. For a long time, and even now, the operation of such machines as typewriters, washing machines, vacuum cleaners, has been seen as "women's work," as have the jobs of telephone operators and many other jobs involving complex machinery. What people operate the computers in your neighbourhood bank? Not the (male) manager. The tellers, who are almost all women. Women have operated machinery in factories since the industrial revolution. For many years, it was difficult for women to get into medical schools, but it was acceptable for them to become lab technicians, working with highly sophisticated machines. During World Wars I and II, women in their tens of thousands went into heavy industries and also into work involving an understanding of the most intricate technology, and at the end of those wars, were told to get back into the kitchen (which they'd never left, having done, as usual, more than one full-time job). The prairie farm women of my generation and older worked alongside their men and were no strangers to the operation of machines. What is the common denominator here? It is, I believe, that women have always operated machinery of all kinds, *when it was to the advantage of society for them to do so,* while at the same time believing in the abstract, a myth (women aren't much good with machinery) that in particular ways *they knew to be untrue.* Secondly, the jobs women have done, involving machinery, have almost always been *lower paid and of lower prestige than those held by men.*

I hope in the future this situation will change radically, as it is already beginning to do, although not rapidly enough.

I hope women will have the confidence and the strength of purpose to learn the operation of whatever kinds of technical equipment they choose, and will assert vigorously their right to whatever opportunities the technology may offer. Finally, and most of all, I hope that women will take a decisive part in choosing how and when the machinery of the future is to be used, and for what purposes, in order that machines of increasing intricacy may be used for human benefit and convenience but never seen as gods, and in order that the human values of caring and compassion and conscience will prevail. I am not in any way excluding men from this difficult struggle, but men, whatever their stances or philosophies, are already involved with the new technology, at higher levels and in greater numbers than women are at the present time. I hope for a greater balance in the future.

Who will teach our children what it means to be human? Humans will.

In my novel, *The Diviners*, the protagonist, Morag, receives a symbol of her ancestors, a symbol that also points to the future, a Scots plaid pin with the motto: "My Hope Is Constant In Thee."

To women in the future, I have to say: *My Hope Is Constant In Thee.*

Excerpts from a letter to a friend, regarding the death of Chaika Wiseman, Adele's mother.

Box 609
Lakefield, Ontario
17 Jan 80

Dearest Budge:

A very emotional and somehow kind of miraculous time here, during the period from Christmas until now. I went to Toronto for Christmas, to Adele and Dmitry's. Audrey Schultz, my young tenant (Trent student) came with me, as her people live in Philadelphia and she couldn't get home; also she is Jewish, so Hanukkah would have been the time for her to go, but it wasn't possible. Adele and I had vowed this year to keep guests to a minimum, but in fact we ended up with about 15 people. My two were there, and Jane, and several other young people who'd been there last year, plus me, Adele, Dmitry, Tamara, plus a contingent of wonderful Americans – an artist, Mary Warshaw, friend of Tillie Olsen (the terrific Amer novelist) and her grown children, plus several other friends. Adele's mother was very very frail; could hardly speak. She had not been able to be out of bed for some months, and Adele had nursed her all through what was obviously her final illness. But Budge, that woman – what a great spirit and heart! She loved seeing all the young; remembered every detail about all their current lives; insisted that they all group around her bed, with the rest of us, while Dmitry and Adele took turns taking photographs. Audrey, who knew Chaika (A's mum) only from what I had told her, plus of course *Old Woman at Play*, had embroidered a pillowcase for her, with the Tree of Life. Chaika was delighted, and this reminded her that she had not seen her own "cutwork" embroidered tablecloths for a long time. Here was a young person who could really appreciate that embroidery. So Adele got them out, or a few of them – one of them embroidered (pale beige on off-white linen) with the sheafs of wheat. Bobba whispered (she was unable to speak above a whisper) to me, "Peg . . . the wheat . . . the prairies . . . " At her instructions, near death as she so obviously was, we draped the tablecloths, plus Audrey's pillowcase, on her bed. To this she asked us to add my book *The Olden Days Coat* (dedicated, as you know, to Tamara). We then, with enormous love, grouped around her bed while the photos were taken. When that was over, and we returned to the diningroom, and the dinner was about ready to be served (I did the turkey again, and it turned out fine), Jocelyn suddenly came up to me and put her arms around me, and I put mine around her, and she cried and so did I. It seemed very natural; I guess a lot of us were crying, and yet it was not sad . . . it was a kind of celebration of a woman whom we all loved so very much. People were sort of milling about, and I went out to the kitchen. David was there, alone. He said to me, "I hadn't seen Bobba since I got back to Canada. She's dying, isn't she?" I said "Yes, she is. And Adele and Dmitry are giving her the incredible gift of being able to die at home among the people she loves." Budge . . . I can't describe how moved I was. My tall son put his arms around me, and his head on my shoulder, and cried. Then we went on with Christmas. And with Hanukkah, although that festival had been a bit earlier. Adele is Jewish. Dmitry is not – so they celebrate both festivals. After dinner, the American contingent played violins and flutes, and we all sang. It was tremendously wonderful. I stayed on in T.O. until the day after Boxing Day, then came home.

On Jan 2nd I got a phone call from Adele that her mother had died that day. I went in the next morning and stayed for 10 days, doing what I could. During the Shiva, the family is not supposed to do any work, and at least I could wash dishes and serve meals and tea, etc. The day I got there, Adele's close family also arrived . . . her brother Harry and his wife Riva with her two kids from her first marriage; her brother Mo; her sister Maryam from Montreal with her husband and their two kids. They are all like my own family to me, of course. The funeral was on the Friday, and Joss and David were there, and I felt so incredibly touched as they sat one on each side of me during the service, and at the graveside, when David gave me his arm because he saw I was shaking. Adele was marvellous; exhausted . . . but almost so exhausted she yet didn't realize how much. The cantor who took the service was the same man as had taken the service for Adele's father, nearly two years ago. He is a very special man . . . belongs to a family of rabbis and cantors whose ancestry can be traced back to the middle ages; ever since that time they have been voluntary paupers . . . they earn their living in ways other than religious, and leave any worldly goods to the poor. He takes no money for his religious services.

The Shiva goes on for one week. It was the first time I had taken part in this custom, which I think is such a good one that the Christian churches should establish it. I guess we do have some similar sort of things, but this was far from the sombre type of thing we associate with a death. After the funeral, a lot of people came back to Adele and Dmitry's, and Maryam, Adele and I had prepared quantities of food. There the family's responsibility for providing food ends . . . the rest of the week, friends came in during the days and evenings, and brought food. It was to me very moving, because during those days the emotions ranged from grief to celebration. We talked about Chaika a lot, and all of us had our special memories of her, and of how she had touched our lives and the lives of our children. I don't think I have ever known anyone who in her life exerted more of a powerful influence for love and *good*. As you know, she was like a mother to me for some 33 years, and like a grandmother to my kids. And she was that to so many!

At one point during the Shiva, Jocelyn dropped in – people just dropped in when they could – and some of us were sitting in the kitchen, talking, laughing about some of the things we remembered, and so on. Joss suddenly said to me, "Mum, how long did you know Bobba?" And I said "Thirty-three years." Joss said, "You probably felt about her then just as you do now?" And I said "Yes, I did." My daughter said, "Bobba then would have been the same age you and Adele are now, more or less. I just want to tell you I think you and Adele are in Chaika's class." Oh Budge, gifts, gifts. One doesn't think of time like that, except at such times. Chaika died when she was 83. In fact, as I realized with astonishment, when I first met Adele and her family, Chaika would have been 50.

Adele's brothers and sisters and their families had to go home on the Sunday, and would continue the Shiva in their own homes. I wanted to stay because of practical things but also because I felt there would be a sudden letdown when the family had to go. I had spoken of all this to Adele and Dmitry last summer and they had agreed. I cannot tell you how much I felt it was my privilege to be there during those days. I came home last Friday, a week ago now. It seemed to me that the time was approaching for Adele, Dmitry and Tamara to be by themselves, as a family. Adele's exhaustion will take some considerable time to get over, but there *is* time. Tamara had been prepared for her Bobba's death, but it still hit very hard. The kid was terrific, as always, but not surprisingly on the Monday after the relatives left, developed a nosebleed and a sore throat. She stayed home from school a few days, and Adele and Tamara were constantly together . . . a mutual assurance and affirmation for them both, and a mutual comfort. Harry, A's brother, who teaches Engineering at the University of Miami, did a super thing (he is a pretty super person, as they all are). He gave Adele, Dmitry and Tamara 3 tickets to the New York Met Opera for this coming weekend, so that will be good and a chance to get away for a few days and to rejoice. Budge . . .

I can see how our Catholic sisters feel, in a peculiar way . . . Adele and her family are not Orthodox Jews, just as I'm not really an orthodox Christian, but some of the same impulses are there. One mourns, but one also celebrates life. And no one taught many of us more about that than Chaika.

Much love,
Margaret

P.S. A few days after the family departed, Adele was looking through her mother's papers for Chaika's will. I was in the kitchen, messing about. Adele came out and silently handed me a paper. I looked at it with deep astonishment. It was a letter I had written to Adele's mother and father in November of 1950, from England, when Jack and I were just preparing to go off on the Great Adventure, to Somaliland. Adele was then in London, working for the Stepney Jewish Girls' Hostel, and writing *The Sacrifice*. I was 24; Adele was 22. The letter is incredibly touching . . . messages from our younger selves. I told of how Jack and I had been buying all the china, pots and pans etc that we would need in Somaliland . . . mostly at Woolworth's, I said! I described in detail . . . for Chaika, the seamstress . . . the formal evening gown I had bought; glazed chintz patterned in butterflies of all colours! I recall that formal exactly . . . it was the nicest I ever owned! And I said that Adele and I had been reading each other's manuscripts . . . I can't now remember what mine *were* . . . not much, I suspect; hers was the early draft of *The Sacrifice*. I said words to this effect . . . "We have decided we are going to write the two great novels of the century. . . "!! So much for young enthusiasm; we long ago stopped thinking in terms of "great," and I always recall Adele's wise remark, made some years later . . . "We're not in it for the immortality stakes, kid." So true. But all things considered, looking at the 30 years that divide or connect me with that letter from my young self, we weren't so very far off the mark.

"Great" is a totally meaningless term, of course, but we both had a vocation then and knew it, even if we then didn't know at all what it might mean in our lives or what it might cost us. What touched both Adele and me was that her mum had kept that letter all these years. Adele returned it to me, and I got xerox copies for her and for my children.

P.S.2. Budge, this seems a strange request, but do you think you could at some point return this letter to me? I have not written all this out before, and really wanted and needed to tell you. But I'm not sure I'll have the psychic energy to do it all again, and I guess I'd like to have it to pass on, perhaps.

Again, much love,
M

FOR ADELE WISEMAN STONE ON HER FIFTIETH BIRTHDAY . . . 1978

At my half century
beside the river flowing
both ways
timely and timeless
you were there
friend
for nearly thirty years then

        Now two years on
        at your half century
        we've been friends
        for more than the thirty

And let's proclaim it
an accomplishment
among our many
(such a time spurns modesty)
yet I'm thinking of private things
the laughter   a saving grace
and the mourning   and the rising
from mourning
of whatever kind.

        It's been some time
        when you come to think of it
        as we do from time to time
        when realizing we've talked
        about our work and our kids
        since both began.

The work and the children
the children and the work
letters   phones   sessions
as is our wont
no want or need stronger
in each of us than the prayers
we say for them
our talk of them being
a kind of prayer itself.

        Talk of family!
        talk of family
        has been there
        even before the children
        were.
        Your family almost my own
        your mother another one to me
        and my children calling her
        Baba
        and your father *Zeyda*
        and my caring about the child
        you and your good man have borne
        my caring as family
        as all of you care for me
        and mine

Remember the starting years?
each of us the only writer
the other knew
and yet maintaining some sense
of common sense and tribe

        Two prairie kids
        green as the Manitoba maples' leaves
        wondering
        if anyone would ever read us

(do you read me? you read me?
typewriters as radio transmitters)
or if anyone would hear
our proclamation
differently shaped and sculptured
intricately
yet at heart so common
to both
the awe and wonder
and the other coin side
outrage at hurts to children
of any age

It is from nature
your mother says
of all things –
pain of departures
the river terrifying and wonderful
as the voice out of the wind,
your mother teaching life by dolls
for the child heart in humans,
teaching courage
by being.

Now
none of it seems long ago
the paths we've taken
the different routes
home

And yet home encompasses that tribe
in which we now
astonished somewhat
bemused   amused
find ourselves the elders
wisewomen

(*Wiseman, yes,*
I can hear you say,
but wisewomen — me
already?)

It seems as though
it's that way
kid
and life is passing
strange
and wonderful in the strangeness
of the river and the children and our being
travellers and strangers
(always remembering
some land of egypt
some exile)

And yet
both of us mothers
of our own
and of the tribal children

                    At this landmark
                    this day's mark on your life's land,
                    watermark placed by the river,
                    only one line truly fits
                    of course
                    and is fitting to the time,
                    only one course
                    with which we've braced
                    the shifting fortress
                    staved off dark   dispelled demons
                    lit fires for warmth and
                    both weak and strong
                    risen to new   days

CORAGGIO   AVANTI

        a bravery given to you long ago
        by strange beloved people
        and passed on
        our slogan through the years

And it's not easy
but we will

sister   friend

May 21, 1978

FOR MY DAUGHTER
ON HER TWENTY-SIXTH
BIRTHDAY . . . AUGUST 1978

Twenty six years are
between us   two women
connected   related
but not bound
by blood   by love

twenty six years
since I birthed you
and this year   this once
I'm twice your age

My firstborn
you entered your life
with pain
one of your slight new bones
broken
before you first breathed
your own unknown life

You were strong
and are
you meant to be
and became
a woman in whom
strength   gentleness   wit
comeliness   combine

That time
holding you in my arms
turning away
from the South Atlantic's

ferocity of breakers
both of us almost broken
taken by the sea
And my man   your father
drew us to shore and breath
a quarter century ago
and still I waken at times
still
with terror at what might have been
still with wonder   with thanks
at lives continuing   breathing
at lives learning
that given life's ongoing
most saving is of ourselves
given grace

Times sometimes
were hard for us both
talk between us
uneasy
yet we've learned
from each other
these twenty-six years
between us both
breathing easier
speaking out some common language
for some time now

my years   my life
you glimpse only
and yet know entire
as I know
who have known you
your life entire
only glimpses of your life
Well, that's as well

we take on trust what's given
and give thanks
knowing each life's its own

You're graceful, lady
you're tough   too
in the way tree roots are tough
enduring
rising to new growth
encompassing pain
knowing no other way to be
possible
reaching for what you know
to be possible
true equality
the truth of love
every kind of love

My prayer for you
for all your life –
heart's warmth, wisdom's growth,
grace abounding.

FOR MY SON
ON HIS TWENTY-FIRST
BIRTHDAY . . . AUGUST 1976

Everything is always
beginning
again
and again
everything is always

We learn the above
and what's above
from trees and the river
and children
who become
man   woman
mother   father
ancestor

Nothing is lost
if we remember
to remember
and tell our children
old tales
and pass on to them
mysteries   strengths
before we pass on
and become the tales
never lost

Among our people
twenty one
is a beginning
but you've known many
and will know more

knowing with each
knowing
something more

For you I pray
grace   sureness   honour
and the gift of acceptance
of joy

Well, you're getting there
hitching
through pain
your lands and families
and you're going on well
so far
and that's so far
as I know
because I've known you
at least somewhat
all your life
so far

        I and the others
        of your blood people
        must leave you
        must leave you alone
        but never alone

FOR A SANSEI WOMAN
BORN ON THE FIFTH DAY OF
THE FIFTH MONTH

for Mary

Spring greeted you
At birth, and proud loving lovely
Your mother must have been
With you   firstborn   Spring-born
Spring-borne   springing forth

She did not know what witness
You would have to bear
What pain   she would have wished
To spare you   as mothers wish
To spare their children pain
A gaunt spare wish   impossible

You've struggled your life entire
Against the once-rejection   no reason
Loving   knowing   the only land   yours
No seasons knowing
Limits on anguish
Speaking as you must and not speaking
Family   families   the hurts
Knowing in hearts' dwellings the ancestors
To be freed from and yet to honour
Forever for they are ourselves

Sister, Spring-born,
When trees make life and leaves
When life declares itself
And we leave winter behind   for now
I bring you word of your mother
Gone but never gone

She might have been me
For we were much of an age
And in a different age you might
Have been daughter to me.

She might now say, with might,
With mightily caring voice,
And I dare to speak because I care,
"Gardens abandoned and left will die;
Trees, strong-seeming, need respect and care.
So with justice, and you will be
For life, one of the gardeners, and indeed
One of the living leaves on trees.
Oh hard, my child, but try."

Spring is your emblem for life.
Your and your age-old mothers' hope.

1986

FOR LORNE (1976)

That sounds like
forlorn
but it's not
You were braver by far
that was your name
lorne
maybe still is
I haven't heard
or enquired for years

                    we were far cousins
                    we could have loved
                    wed

Lorne   I'm no poet
but these lines are for you
who won't see them
but if you did
you wouldn't mind
jagged edges
you know about those
and I don't mean the knife
you all of a terrifying sudden
raised to our great-aunt Carrie
the ending of that summer
the ending of all your summers
when you helped harvest her son's farm
and the old woman said
there, there
quietly   and took that edge
out of your hand

and you cried
because you loved her
and because of the greyplace
you'd have to exist in
again   again

        What might have happened
        if that hadn't
        if I'd become your woman?
        The feckless farm on the vast lake
        the salt marshes
        north of prairie   the loser lands
        memories of dinosaurs   the lake monsters
        and the other one
        threatening inside you
        and my life   my love
        soon done in
        even though done in love
        it wouldn't have done for me

You were ten years older
an aeon's difference
when I was six
and you lived in my grandfather's house
stern house   stern brick house
there being no high school
near the worthless farm
north   by the lake like a sea
where your half-wild tribe
(and yes that's so unfair I'm shamed)
subsisted   survived
You weren't wild though
you told me stories
the two horses   yours
the graceful ones
swifting through fields of summer

(and it wasn't a lie   it was not
just that no eyes but yours could see them)
I believed and loved you
I married a man
ten years older than myself.

> No jobs
> depression   drought
> you sold magazines
> you wanted to be an engineer
> your best friend did become one
> his father was a doctor
> you had no father
> only a saltmarsh farm
> and fear
> to return to
> back home

One year
before the war
one summer before
I became woman
visiting your landplace
your strange place
far from my knownplace   homeplace
I went   childcousin   with you
to wildfields   weirdfields
I had known only the wildplaces
already tamed when I was born

The black north lake at night
after the day's haying   and the horses
stolid   working ones   not with wild mettle
breathing quietly
and a skydom of white stars
you talked of God   lorne
you wanted to know

how come so much pain hereabouts?
I couldn't answer
I couldn't say a word
I was too young then
and now I'm fifty
I still can't answer
I don't think God could either
I don't know who to blame
for what happened to you
and the others.

I couldn't imagine   you
in green England   lorne
in dark embattled England
in uniform
the letter you sent to me
saying they could command you
but you weren't there
in your body now
that letter told me
        you couldn't imagine it either
They sent you home
but not to home

Seventeen, I'd be
in love with an airman
who later left me
not for death
but for the wife I didn't know he had
that Saturday night at the dance hall
I wore a blue dress and still;
sometimes in stillness I can see
that colour exact
I looked up and saw you   lorne
released from the greyplace
working that summer as harvester

I used to imagine this
you said
coming back and finding you
grownup

> We danced so carefully,
> so carefully distantly,
>> maybe I know now
>> what you were thinking
>> and maybe I don't
> My thought was my airman
> and yet hovering
> unwillingly   loving you afraid
> of that grendel still in your mindcave?

The music said *I'll be seeing you*
>> *In all the old familiar places*
but it wasn't true
I never did again

> Thirty years ago a friend
> worked in the greyplace
> where you were
> she told me then
> you wore a grey dressing-gown
> you knew when the dark god
> was going to possess
> your hands   clenched hard
> against it   willing it away
> battling it   until
> your scream

They said it would be for life
an odd phrase
I wonder if you're   still   alive
I wonder what kind of death

I mourn you
not always
not even often
but sometimes
whcn I've been seeing you
in all the old familiar places
in sleep's other world
I want to rush back and back
to then
and at least speak
my love
make it all happen
differently

PRAYER FOR PASSOVER AND EASTER

May our eyes and hearts be opened
To all faiths that praise
And protect life
May our lives be committed
To honouring and saving life
May we struggle all our lives
For lives of us all
For all the children
And may we strive with all our lives
Against destroyers   against wars
Against those whose distortions
Have taken and would take again
Beloved children to untimely death
May we oppose those hatreds
With every strength and word
In all our lives as long as life
Shall last, and may at last
Our fears be brave and may we praise
Life given   life lived   with hope
May our symbols of faith
Of caring and respect and love
Become one symbol
As our children are
Our mutual children
As the Holy Spirit
Breathes in us all
And may we learn
Not to hurt

May we lean
One upon another
Give and receive loving strength
And may we learn

We are one
People   in our only home
Earth.
AMEN.

1985

THE GREATER EVIL
From *Toronto Life* (September 1984)

I have a troubled feeling that I may be capable of double-think, the ability to hold two opposing beliefs simultaneously. In the matter of censorship, doublethink seems, alas, appropriate. As a writer, my response to censorship of any kind is that I am totally opposed to it. But when I consider some of the vile material that is being peddled freely, I want to see some kind of control. I don't think I am being hypocritical. I have a sense of honest bewilderment. I have struggled with this inner problem for years, and now, with the spate of really bad video films and porn magazines flooding the market, my sense of ambiguity grows. I am certain of one thing, though. I cannot be alone in my uncertainty.

I have good reason to mistrust and fear censorship. I have been burned by the would-be book censors. Not burned in effigy, nor suffered my books being burned, not yet anyhow. But burned nonetheless, scorched mentally and emotionally. This has happened in more than one part of Canada, but the worst experience for me was in my own county of Peterborough a few years ago, when a group of people, sincere within their limited scope, no doubt, sought to have my novel *The Diviners* banned from the Grade 13 course and the school libraries. The book was attacked as obscene, pornographic, immoral and blasphemous. It is, I need hardly say, none of these things. Open meetings of the school board were held. Letters, pro and con, appeared in the local newspaper. Some awful things were said about the book and about me personally, mostly by people who had not read the book or met me. In retrospect, some of the comments seem pretty funny, but at the time I was hurt and furious. One person confidently stated that "Margaret Laurence's aim in life is to destroy the home and the family." In an interview, another person claimed that the novel contained a detailed account, calculated to titillate, of the sex life of the housefly. I couldn't recollect any such scene. Then I remembered that when Morag, as a child, is embarrassed by the sad, self-deprecating talk of her stepmother, the gentle, obese Prin, the girl seeks anything at all to focus on, so she need not listen. "She looked at two flies fucking, buzzing as they did it." Beginning and end of sensational scene. The reporter asked if the fundamentalist minister himself had found the scene sexually stimulating. "Oh no," was the reply. "I'm a happily married man." At one open meeting, a man rose to condemn the novel and said that he spoke for a delegation of seven: himself, his wife, their four children – and God. In another county, a bachelor pharmacist accused me of adding to the rate of venereal disease in Canada by writing my books. He claimed that young people should not be given any information about sex until they are physically mature – "at about the age of 21." I hope his knowledge of pharmacy was greater than his knowledge of biology.

Many readers, teachers and students did speak out for the novel, which was ultimately restored to the Grade 13 course. But the entire episode was enough to make me come down heavily against censorship, and especially against self-appointed groups of vigilantes. At the time I made a statement, which said, in part: "Surely it cannot do other than help in the growing toward a responsible maturity, for our young people to read novels in which many aspects of human life are dealt with, by writers whose basic faith is in the unique and irreplaceable value of the human individual."

I hold to that position. Artists of all kinds have been persecuted, imprisoned, tortured and killed, in many countries and at many times throughout history, for portraying life as they honestly saw it. Artistic suppression and political suppression go hand in hand, and always have. I would not advocate the banning of even such an evil and obscene book as Hitler's *Mein Kampf.* I think we must learn to recognize our enemies, to counter inhuman ranting with human and humane beliefs and practices. With censorship, the really bad stuff would tend to go underground and flourish covertly, while works of genuine artistic merit might get the axe (and yes, I know that "genuine artistic merit" is very difficult to define). I worry that censorship of any kind might lead to the suppression of anyone who speaks out against anything in our society, the suppression of artists, and the eventual clamping down on ideas, human perceptions, questionings. I think of our distinguished constitutional lawyer and poet F.R. Scott. In an essay written in 1933, he said: " 'The time, it is to be hoped, has gone by,' wrote John Stuart Mill, 'when any defence would be necessary of the principle of freedom of speech.' His hope was vain. The time for defending freedom never goes by. Freedom is a habit that must be kept alive by use."

And yet – my ambiguity remains. The pornography industry is now enormous, and includes so-called "kiddie porn." Most of us do not look at this stuff, nor do we have any notion how widespread it is, nor how degrading and brutal toward women and children, for it is they who are the chief victims in such magazines and films. Let me make one thing clear. I do not object to books or films or anything else that deals with sex, if those scenes are between two adults who are entering into this relationship of their own free will. (You may well say – what about *Lolita*? I hated the book, as a matter of fact, and no, I wouldn't advocate banning Nabokov. Ambiguity.) I do not object to the portrayal of social injustice, of terrible things done to one human by another or by governments or groups of whatever kind, as long as this is shown for what it is. But when we see films and photographs, *making use of real live women and children,* that portray horrifying violence, whether associated with sex or simply violence on its own, as being acceptable, on-turning, a thrill a minute, then I object.

The distinction must be made between erotic and pornographic. Eroticism is the portrayal of sexual expression between two people who desire each other and who have entered this relationship with mutual agreement. Pornography, on the other hand, is the portrayal of coercion and violence, usually with sexual connotations, and like rape in real life, it has less to do with sex than with subjugation and cruelty. Pornography is not in any sense life-affirming. It is a denial of life. It is a repudiation of any feelings of love and tenderness and mutual passion. It is about hurting people, mainly women, and having that brutality seen as socially acceptable, even desirable.

As a woman, a mother, a writer, I cannot express adequately my feelings of fear, anger and outrage at this material. I have to say that I consider visual material to be more dangerous than any printed verbal material. Possibly I will be accused of being elitist and of favoring my own medium, the printed word, and possibly such a charge could be true. I just don't know. The reason I feel this way, however, is that these films and photographs make use of living women and children – not only a degradation of them, but also a strong suggestion to the viewer that violence against women and children, real persons, is acceptable. One of the most sinister aspects of these films and photographs is that they frequently communicate the idea that not only is violence against women OK – women actually *enjoy* being the subject of insanely brutal treatment, actually enjoy being chained, beaten, mutilated and even killed. This aspect of pornography, of course, reinforces and purports to excuse the behavior of some men who do indeed hate women. I could weep in grief and rage when I think of this attitude. As for the use of children in pornography, this is unspeakable and should be forbidden by law. The effect of this material is a matter of some dispute, and nothing can be proved either way, but many people believe that such scenes have been frighteningly re-enacted in real life in one way or another.

But is censorship, in any of the media involved, the answer? I think of John Milton's *Areopagitica; A Speech for the Liberty of Unlicensed Printing, to the Parliament of England,* in 1644, in which these words appear: "He that can apprehend and consider vice with all her baits and seeming pleasures, and yet abstain, and yet distinguish, and yet prefer that which is truly better, he is the true wayfaring Christian. I cannot praise a fugitive and cloistered virtue, unexercised and unbreathed, that never sallies out and sees her adversary, but slinks out of the race, where that immortal garland is to be run for, not without dust and heat." Obviously, Milton was not thinking of the sort of video films that anyone can now show at home, where any passing boy child can perhaps get the message that cruelty is OK and fun, and any passing girl child may wonder if that is what will be expected of her, to be a victim. All the same, we forget Milton's words at our peril.

The situation is not without its ironies. It has created some very strange comrades-in-arms. We find a number of feminists taking a strong stand *for* censorship, and being praised and applauded by people whose own stance is light-years away from feminism, the same people who would like my books, Alice Munro's books, W.O. Mitchell's books, banned from our high schools. We see civil libertarians who are *against* censorship and for free expression arguing that "anything goes," a view that must rejoice the hearts of purveyors of this inhumane material, but certainly distresses mine.

I consider myself to be both a feminist and a strong supporter of civil liberties and free speech, but there is no way I want to be on the same team as the would-be book-banning groups who claim that no contemporary novels should be taught or read in our schools. There is no way, either, that I want to be on the same team as the pornographers.

What position can a person like myself honestly take? The whole subject is enormously complex, but I must finally come down against a censorship board, whether for the visual media or for the printed word. I think that such boards tend to operate by vague and ill-defined standards. What can "acceptable community standards" possibly mean? It depends on which community you're talking about, and within any one community, even the smallest village, there are always going to be wide differences. Censorship boards tend to be insufficiently accountable. I believe that in cases of obscenity, test cases have to be brought before the courts and tried openly in accordance with our federal obscenity laws. The long-term solution, of course, is to educate our children of both sexes to realize that violence against women and children, against anyone, is not acceptable, and to equalize the status of women in our society.

What about Section 159 of the Criminal Code, "Offences Tending to Corrupt Morals"? My impression of federal law in this area is that its intentions are certainly right, its aims are toward justice, and it is indeed in some ways woefully outdated and in need of clarification. Clarification and amendment have not been and will not be easy. The clause that is most widely known to the general public is Section 159(8): "For the purpose of this Act, any publication a dominant characteristic of which is the undue exploitation of sex, or of sex and any one or more of the following subjects, namely, crime, horror, cruelty and violence, shall be deemed to be obscene." I think the first use of the words "of sex" could be deleted. How much sex between consenting adults is too much? Are three scenes OK but ten excessive? Frankly, among the many things I worry about in my life, as a citizen and as a writer, this is not one of them. But how are we to enshrine in our laws the idea that the degradation and coercion of women and children, of anyone, is dreadful, without putting into jeopardy the portrayal of social injustice seen as injustice? How are we to formulate a law that says the use of real women and children in situations of demeanment and violence, shown as desirable fun stuff, is not acceptable, while at the same time not making it possible for people who don't like artists questioning the status quo to bring charges against those who must continue to speak out against the violation of the human person and spirit?

In one case cited in the Criminal Code, the judge declares: "The onus of proof upon the Crown may be discharged by simply producing the publication without expert opinion evidence. Furthermore, where, although the book has certain literary merit particularly for the more sophisticated reader, it was available for the general public to whom the book was neither symbolism nor a psychological study the accused cannot rely on the defence of public good." "Public good" is later defined as "necessary or advantageous to religion or morality, to the administration of justice, the pursuit of science, literature or art, or other objects of general interest." If this precedent means what it appears to say, it alarms me. It appears to put works of "literary merit" into some jeopardy, especially as expert opinion evidence need not be heard. If a book of mine were on trial, I would certainly want expert opinion evidence. I do not always agree with the views of the literary critics, or of teachers, but at least, and reassuringly, many of them know how to read with informed skill.

Realizing the difficulty of accurate definitions, I think that violence itself, shown as desirable, must be dealt with in some way in this law. It is *not* all right for men to beat and torture women. *It is wrong.* I also think that the exploitation of real live children for "kiddie porn" should be dealt with as a separate issue in law and should not be allowed, ever.

The more I think about it, the more the whole question becomes disturbingly complicated. Yet I believe it is a question that citizens, Parliament and the legal profession must continue to grapple with. It is not enough for citizens to dismiss our obscenity laws as inadequate and outdated, and then turn the whole matter over to censorship boards. Our laws are not engraved on stone. They have been formulated carefully, although sometimes not well, but with a regard to a general justice. The law is not perfect, but it *is* public. It can be changed, but not upon the whim of a few. An informed and alert public is a necessary component of democracy. When laws need revisions, we must seek to have them revised, not toward any narrowing down but toward a greater justice for all people, children, women and men, so that our lives may be lived without our being victimized, terrorized or exploited. Freedom is more fragile than any of us in Canada would like to believe. I think again of F.R. Scott's words: "Freedom is a habit that must be kept alive by use." Freedom, however, means responsibility and concern toward others. It does not mean that unscrupulous persons are permitted to exploit, demean and coerce others. It is said, correctly, that there is a demand for pornography. But should this demand be used to justify its unchallenged existence and distribution? Some men are said to "need" pornography. To me this is like saying some men "need" to beat up their wives or commit murder. Must women and children be victims in order to assuage the fears and insecurities of those men who want to feel they are totally powerful in a quite unreal way? I don't think so. If some men "need" pornography, then I as a woman will never be a party to it, not even by the tacit agreement of silence. We and they had better try together to control and redirect those needs. I think that citizens can and should protest in any nonviolent way possible against the brutalities and callousness of pornography, including one area I haven't even been able to deal with here, the demeanment of women in many advertisements.

In the long run, it is all-important to raise our children to know the reality of others; to let them know that sex can and should be an expression of love and tenderness and mutual caring, not hatred and domination of the victor / victim kind; to communicate to our daughters and our sons that to be truly human is to try to be loving and responsible, strong not because of power but because of self-respect and respect for others.

In *Areopagitica*, Milton said: "That which purifies us is trial, and trial is by what is contrary." In the final analysis, we and our society will not stand or fall by what we are "permitted" to see or hear or read, but by what we ourselves choose. We must, however, have some societal agreement as to what is acceptable in the widest frame of reference possible, but still within the basic concept that *damaging people is wrong*. Murder is not acceptable, and neither is the abasement, demeanment and exploitation of human persons, whatever their race, religion, age or gender. Not all of this can be enshrined in law. Laws can never make people more understanding and compassionate toward one another. That is what individual people try to do, in our imperfect and familial ways. What the law *can* do is attempt to curb, by open process in public courts, the worst excesses of humankind's always-in-some-way-present inhumanity to humankind.

This is as close as I can get to formulating my own beliefs. It is an incomplete and in many ways a contradictory formulation, and I am well aware of that. Perhaps this isn't such a bad thing. I don't think we can or should ever get to a point where we feel we know, probably in a simplistic way, what all the answers are or that we ourselves hold them and no one else does. The struggle will probably always go on, as it always has in one way or another. The new technology has brought its own intricacies. I doubt that the human heart and conscience will ever be relieved of their burdens, and I certainly hope they are not. This particular struggle, *for* human freedom and *against* the awfulness that seeks to masquerade as freedom but is really slavery, will not ever be easy or simple, but it is a struggle that those of us who are concerned must never cease to enter into, even though it will continue to be, in Milton's words, "not without dust and heat."

VIA RAIL AND VIA MEMORY

the train is always moving
west

for us   always west
for my people   west
is the direction
our lives take
west is here   in us

I hadn't seen my heartland
for years and years
at this time
the fields of fall   greengold
nearly ready for harvest
and wind-fingers ruffling
wheat oats barley
as though the fields
were the goddess's hair

sounds swell eh?
I wasn't fooled
even from the safety of a train
because a train
of consequences binds me
like long-ago binder twine
twining lives and land together

I knew the same tender wind
could turn destroyer
and what relief
when the crops are in

even for those young farmers now
who don't know
Relief's other meaning
their parents knew
the thirties years
when proud people had to take
shame for the paltry dollars
the government dole   doled out
the guilt they felt   the ruined lands
when the rain did not come and the banks
foreclosed

I know this all
I grew up with it
it is in my blood
the Depression
and how many themselves
in their own depression?

I know and remember
though I was a child then
I recall and yet I sing
this land ˌ mine
I cry for that past
and yet love
this openness of sky
these waiting fields
these bluffs   scrub-oak poplar maple
these damn tough trees like farmers
like women   men
survivors
against all odds

the train   moves west
the American lady says
"are you native-born Canadian?"
Yes, I say, I'm surely that.

Well, she says, can I tell her
and her friend, Vancouver-bound,
when we'll reach
the more interesting country?

I smile   gently I hope
because she couldn't have known
and say
"I was born and grew up
hereabouts
and for me this is
the more interesting country."

August 1983

CONVOCATION ADDRESS
York University, Toronto, June 1980

Mr. Chancellor, Mr. President, members of the faculty, graduating students, ladies and gentlemen:

I graduated from university thirty-three years ago, in 1947. I am tempted to say that it was a very different world from the present one. I'm not sure that such a statement would be true. In some ways it *was* a very different world, but it was by no means the cosy, optimistic, jitterbugging world that some of the purveyors of late 1940s and early 1950s nostalgia would have us believe.

My world had emerged two years earlier from a six-year period of world war. Most of us had lost a member of our family, or friends and schoolmates. These were the young men of my generation who died on the beaches at Dieppe or in France and Italy in the final stages of the European war, or in North Africa or Hong Kong, or in the ruins of their shot-down planes or torpedoed ships. Some of them were the boys from my town and surrounding towns, the kids I'd grown up with, several years older than I was. When Dieppe happened, in 1942, and so many of them were killed or spent the rest of the war in prison camps, I was sixteen years old. That was when I first realized – really realized – what war meant. It meant that many of the people you had known were dead, dead at a very young age, and had died horribly.

Those of my generation who were Jewish had, almost without exception, lost entire branches of their families – grandparents, uncles and aunts, cousins – in the Holocaust, in which all but a fraction of the European Jewish communities were exterminated in the gas chambers of death camps such as Auschwitz and Belsen. Innocence was no longer a possibility. The gates of whatever Eden our childhoods might have contained had clanged shut forever. We did not want to recognize, but we *had* to recognize, that humankind is indeed capable of an evil so all-encompassing that no words could possibly describe it. No mourning for those millions of murdered innocent people will ever be enough, will ever be complete.

There was, of course, one other trauma that all those of my generation underwent. We had grown up taking totally for granted that the generations of mankind and of all creatures are like the leaves on a tree; they fall but a new generation arises, and the earth endures forever. August 6th, 1945, made it impossible ever again to take that reassuring belief for granted. That was the day the first atomic bomb was dropped by the Allies on Hiroshima. Eight days later the Second World War ended. My generation had the dubious distinction of being the first in the whole history of mankind to emerge into young adulthood knowing that our species had the technological power to destroy all life on earth and possibly our earth itself.

In the face of this knowledge, it was difficult not to give way to depression or despair, not to give up entirely to the draining feeling that we were helpless. Some people I knew did indeed give up, and I mourn those casualties of peace as much as I mourn the casualties of war. Most of us have had to struggle intermittently through the years with the awful temptation to give up the struggle, to cease caring. But a great many of us have in fact gone on amidst struggles that are both inner and outer, and have tried to do our work as best we can, to raise our children as caringly as we could, and in our extremely flawed and imperfect ways to express our beliefs in social justice, in human relationships of love and value, and in the possibility and *necessity* of peoples of different cultures communicating with one another and trying to understand one another. We have proclaimed the insanity of wars, and the necessity of defending civil liberties. To our voices have been joined the voices of many of a younger generation. It cannot be said that in any world sense we have met with spectacular success. In more than thirty years there has not been a time when peace has prevailed everywhere. Still, I cannot believe we have entirely failed, either. Without these voices, it is possible that the world might be in a worse way than it is.

Today you are graduating into a world that is truly terrifying. It is difficult not to give way to despair. Not long ago, we were told by an official of the Federal Energy Management Agency in Washington that the "good news" is that in a nuclear war, not *all* the population of America (and presumably Canada) would die. Only *half* would be killed. The audacity, the blindness, of calling this "good news"! One of the candidates in the American presidential nominations some time ago was reported to have said that he could visualize a nuclear war in which America could declare itself the victor – with *two-thirds* of its population dead. Have these men absolutely no feelings or simply no imagination? Do they not consider what such statements really *mean*? And if they have no concern for the lives of so-called "ordinary" men, women and children – that is, all of us – does it not ever occur to the hawks everywhere, in all parts of the world, to wonder what kind of a world they would emerge back into, from their protected bunkers, at the end of such an unthinkable global war? In Ontario, our film censorship board is fussing about the possibility of offending public morals with such a film as *The Tin Drum*. It seems to me that the real obscenities of our age are the irresponsible and brutal statements on the acceptability of a global war, statements that treat human individuals as numbers, statistics, figures on a graph, worthless and unvalued as living creatures. How far is this from the thinking that instituted the genocide of the Holocaust? Not far, I think. Have people so soon forgotten the horrors of the Vietnam war?

In Argentina, hundreds of thousands of men and women have "disappeared" – that is, they have been tortured and killed, and in the name of "Western Christian civilization."

To me, it is an obscenity to use the word "Christian" in connection with such gruesome wholesale murder. The leaders in that greatly afflicted country have presumably never given thought to the commandment of Jesus: "Thou shalt love thy neighbour as thyself." At the other side of the political spectrum, in Russia countless victims who dared protest the system have also been imprisoned or killed, in the name of socialism and the brotherhood of man. The last thirty years have seen an increasing demeanment of language itself, as words and slogans denoting freedom and justice and brotherhood and faith are being used to practise the precise opposite. This is, of course, not a new phenomenon. It has always been true that integrity must be judged not only by what people *say*, but more importantly by what they do, how they live their lives in relation to others.

We are not immune, in Canada, to these injustices and acts of inhumanity. Racism, violence, oppression, violations of civil liberties . . . all these exist in some measure or other here, too. We should never deceive ourselves into smugness on these issues. Lastly, and individually, the enemy is always to some extent within. We are all prey to anger; we are all capable of hurting other people and of violating our own principles of integrity and humanity. We are all capable of giving way to self-righteousness, to spiritual pride. And yes, we are all too capable of giving way to despair. I believe that the early church fathers were quite right in designating despair as one of the deadly sins. In our present and threatening world, it is only too easy to feel hopeless and helpless, to withdraw into lethargy or a concern only with our own personal lives, forgetting that we are an integral part of all humanity everywhere. It is my profound belief that we must not yield to such a withdrawal.

It is my hope for you that you will sustain hope within yourselves. I think we must take responsibility for our own individual selves. We must take on responsibilities for the work we have chosen to do. We must try to honour whatever gifts of talent and ability we have been given, and whatever gifts of knowledge we have acquired. I believe we must also not ever forget our responsibilities as citizens of our own land and citizens of the world. We must continue in every way we can to protest non-violently against social injustice, infringement of civil liberties, cruelties, and the indifference of governments . . . wherever these occur. We must continue to proclaim those things we believe in – the possibility of true communication between human individuals and between people of all cultures; the responsibility of those of us in lands rich in food and natural resources to help people in lands suffering from famine and deprivation; the sheer *necessity* – if life on earth and our earth itself are to survive – of peoples to live in peaceful co-existence with one another and with the other creatures that share our planet, and our responsibility to protect and restore the earth itself.

F.R. Scott, our most distinguished constitutional lawyer and one of our very best writers and poets, once wrote an essay called "Freedom of Speech in Canada." This essay was reprinted in his book *Essays on the Constitution*, published in 1977 and winner of the Governor General's Award for non-fiction that year. In it he said:

> "The time, it is to be hoped, has gone by," wrote John Stuart Mill, "when any defence would be necessary of the principle of freedom of speech." His hope was vain. The time for defending freedom never goes by. Freedom is a habit that must be kept alive by use.

Those words were written in 1932. My generation inherited the legacy of a world war, of the Holocaust, of Hiroshima. We also inherited the legacy of all the men and women who have throughout the centuries stood up and struggled for those human values in which they believed. Frank Scott's words are as true and as relevant today as they were when he first wrote them. They will always be true and relevant. The struggles for justice, the necessity to proclaim – in the words of St. Paul – the qualities of faith, hope and love – these are never over. They go on from one generation to another. They are passed on to our inheritors.

You, my generation's inheritors, inherit a deeply troubled world. We are certainly not passing on a secure heritage to you. But I hope we *are* passing on to you, even in the midst of a terrifying world, some sense of hope, some sense that these lifelong struggles are worthwhile because life itself is worthwhile, and is given to each of us for a short time – to protect, to honour, and to celebrate.

WHEN YOU WERE FIVE
AND I WAS FOURTEEN
From *Quill & Quire* (April 1985)

It was my good luck to be born into a family of readers. It was my fate to be born in 1926, when the drought and the Depression were about to strike, and to grow up during that time and during the Second World War in a small town in Manitoba. Our house was full of books. I read Kipling, Dickens, and Mark Twain at a young age. I also read, less illuminatingly, *The Boy's Own Annual* and *The Girl's Own Annual,* books that my parents and my aunts and uncles had read when they were young, collections mainly of adventure stories (the boys got to do all the most exciting things) that told us the British Empire was the best thing in the world. Amazingly, I survived those books relatively unscathed and grew up to be vigorously anticolonialist.

My father was a lawyer, and during the Depression he got paid in eggs and chickens and produce. There was not much money, but there was always a book for me and my brother at Christmas and birthdays. During my early years there was no library in our town. The first library was started when I was 14, in 1940. My Dad had died some years before, and my Mum was bringing up my brother and myself by herself. She had been a high-school teacher of English and was determined that her kids would have the chance to read good books. She and a few others in our town, including the splendid teacher of English Miss Mildred Musgrove and Mr. Rey, the principal, started the first library. It was first housed in a room over the post office and moved quite a lot in the years to come – to the basement of the drugstore, and so on.

My mother had decided on her policy for her children's reading. We could read anything that came our way, but discussion about books was encouraged. Well do I recall myself reading *Laddie* by Gene Stratton-Porter and my mother saying, "Well, some people think it is sentimental, but I felt the same as you do now about *Tess of the D'Urbervilles*. Let's look at that." (I adopted this same policy of discussion with my own children when they were young.) In those days, recently published books such as *The Grapes of Wrath* by John Steinbeck and *Gone With the Wind* by Margaret Mitchell were thought by some parents to be unsuitable reading for the young prairie violets I and my girlfriends were then (how innocent those books seem now). My mother disagreed. I read them, and we talked about them.

From 1940, until 1944, when I was 18 and went away to college, my mother and I used to ponder on a Canadian publication to which our newly hatched library had a subscription. Called *Quill & Quire,* it told us about the Canadian books that were being published. Canadian books then? You bet. My mother was a staunch supporter of having Canadian books in our library; she was, as I realized only much later, an early evangelist for Canadian writing. She did not, of course, realize that her daughter would one day write out of our land and townspeople and that tradition, but perhaps she suspected it, for she gave me a serious critique of everything I wrote.

Quill & Quire then, as I recall, had a smaller format and was a much slimmer magazine. Mum and I read it avidly, and at 14, 15, and 16 I actually had some input about which books the town library would buy with its very limited resources. I recall those evenings now with such affection, Mum and I reading *Quill & Quire* and my practical Mum trying to figure out how we could get the maximum number of books for the minimum amount of money. It was only years later that I knew how privileged I had been. I recall one book especially – Sinclair Ross's *As for Me and My House*. It was published first in 1941, when I was 15, and we read the write-up in *Q&Q* and got it for the library.

I learned from that book that one could write about where one *was*, even a small prairie town. I never forgot that.

Quill & Quire probably gave me a lifelong addiction to book reviews and perhaps a lifelong addiction to buying books when I could.

When I left Canada, I didn't read *Q&Q* for some time, although I read it whenever I was back. When I came home to stay, in 1973, one of the first subscriptions I took out was to this magazine.

I may possibly be one of the earlier readers of *Q&Q*, and that gives me pleasure. I don't suppose too many people began to read it when they were 14 years old and *Q&Q* was five.

Foreword to *Canada and the Nuclear Arms Race,*
ed. Ernie Regehr (Toronto: Lorimer, 1983).

Our lives and the lives of all generations as yet unborn are
being threatened, as never before, by the increasing possibility of nuclear war. I believe that the question of disarmament is the most pressing practical, moral and spiritual
issue of our times. If we value our own lives and the lives of
our children and all children everywhere, if we honour
both the past and the future, then we must do everything in
our power to work non-violently for peace. These beliefs
are not only an integral part of my social and moral stance
but of my religious faith as well. Human society now
possesses the terrible ability to destroy all life on earth, and
our planet itself. Can anyone who has ever marvelled at the
miracle of creation fail to feel concerned and indeed
anguished, every single day, at this thought?

A central disagreement, of course, exists between those
who think that more and yet more nuclear arms will ensure
that nuclear arms will never be used, and those of us who
believe that the proliferation of nuclear weapons brings us
closer all the time to the actuality of nuclear war – a war
that no side could possibly win; a war that would be so
devastating that we cannot begin to imagine that horror.
Whatever we are being told about a "limited" or a "win-
nable" nuclear war, the fact remains that such a war could
destroy all that we, as humankind, have aspired to, all that
we have achieved. It could destroy the future, not only of
the world's peoples but of all creatures that share our planet
with us.

As both America and the Soviet Union develop more and
more nuclear arms, so the other inevitably responds in
kind. Both America and the Soviet Union now possess

nuclear weapons capable of wiping out all life on earth many times over. The jargon word is "overkill." Do the hawks on either side imagine that life can be "overkilled"? We die but once. Why, then, the continuing buildup of nuclear weapons? These have long since ceased to be a "deterrent," if, indeed, they were ever so, and have become by their very existence a monstrous threat. Daily, the chances are increasing for a nuclear war to break out by accident, by a failure of the intricate control and warning systems, or simply by human panic and a mutual mistrust between the superpowers.

In our own land, Canada, what can we do?

Canada could and must, I believe, have a real impact in bringing about world disarmament. We are not powerless and we are not without significance in a world sense. Yet our government has agreed to the cruise missile being tested above Alberta. The Litton plant in Ontario is producing, with the aid of millions of *our* tax dollars, guidance systems for that missile. Canada has sold nuclear reactors to such unstable and repressive regimes as Argentina, and is delivering the fuel for those reactors, despite the fact that our government is aware that nuclear weapons could soon be within Argentina's capability. These are only a few examples of Canada's complicity in the nuclear arms race.

Our prime minister, in 1978, at the United Nations Special Session on Disarmament, put forth the theory of "suffocation" of nuclear arms, and many of us took heart from that statement. Yet on 10 December 1982, in the *Globe & Mail*, a report on the cruise missile testing agreement said that ". . . External Affairs Minister Allan MacEachen has said growing public pressure against the tests has no bearing on the Government's thinking." I find the implications of that statement very chilling indeed. Prime Minister Trudeau, in his New Year's 1983 message to our nation, was reported as saying that although there are undoubtedly some gloomy aspects in our present situation, there are also positive signs, among them the growth of the anti-nuclear-weapons movement. I would certainly agree that the growth of disarmament and peace groups is a cause for hope. But how are we to interpret this statement, made by the very man whose government the peace and disarmament groups are seeking to communicate with? How does this statement jibe with MacEachen's earlier pronouncement on the cruise testing? These conflicting messages suggest that we must keep on pressuring our government in every possible non-violent way to make Canada's voice heard as a strong voice speaking for practical and achievable steps towards world disarmament.

I believe that our land should be declared a nuclear-weapons-free zone, with absolutely no testing of nuclear arms or production of parts for those arms allowed in our country. I believe Canada could do a great deal to bring about a gradual and verifiable reduction of nuclear arms by both sides, monitored by neutral countries, and to bring about a freeze on the production and testing of nuclear weapons. Canada could be a powerful influence for a "no-first-use" agreement among nations, for multilateral disarmament and for world peace. To me, this goes far beyond any political party views – indeed it goes beyond any national feelings. It means, in the most profound sense, survival. It means the future. We must not give way to despair, or to what Dr. Helen Caldicott, that courageous worker in the cause of peace, calls "psychic numbing," the sense that we cannot do anything, that we are helpless. We cannot afford passivity. We must take responsibility for our lives and our world, and be prepared to make our government listen and act. To do this, we must be informed. We must not shrink from the terrible and terrifying knowledge of what could happen and what is at stake.

This collection of articles gives us much of that necessary information. It gives us a knowledge of our own land in a nuclear-weapons world. I wish that every adult Canadian could read this book. I hope that a very great many will do so, and will learn from it.

If we will not speak out for our children, and their children and their children's children, if we will not speak out for the survival of our own land and our wider home Earth, in God's name what will move us? May our hearts be touched, our minds opened, our voices raised.

Margaret Laurence
Lakefield, Ontario
1983

A FABLE –
FOR THE WHALING FLEETS

From *Whales – A Celebration,* edited by Greg Gatenby
(Toronto: Prentice-Hall and
Lester & Orpen Dennys, 1983)

Imagine the sky creatures descending to our earth. They are very different from humankind. We have known of their existence, although we cannot truly conceive of the realms in which they live. Sometimes a tiny thing has fallen to earth violently, lifeless when we found it, like a lost bird with wings broken and useless. But the sky creatures are not birds. They are extremely intelligent beings. Their brains, although not as large as ours, have been developed for complex and subtle use. They bear their young live from the mothers' bodies, as humans do, and nourish them from the breast. Although they live in the highest heights, we breathe the same air. Like us, they have language, and like humankind they have music and song. They care for their young, love them and teach them in the ways of their species. But when they loom low over our lands in their strong air vessels, they hunt humanity with the death sticks. At first there are only a few of them, then more and more. There are fewer and fewer human beings. The sky creatures make use of the dead bodies of our children, of our hunted young women and young men, of our elders. The flesh of our dead children is eaten by the sky creatures and their slaves. The fat from the bodies of our loved children gives oil which is used by the sky creatures in various ways – most of it goes to make unguents and creams for their vanity. They do not need to hunt humans in order to survive. They continue to slaughter us out of greed. Some of their number believe the slaying is wrong. Some of them sing their songs to us, and we in return answer with our songs. Perhaps we will never be able to speak in our human languages to those who speak the sky creatures' languages. But song is communication, respectful touch and trust are

291

ways of knowing. Too many of them, however, do not think in this manner, do not have these feelings. Too many of them hear the sounds and songs of humanity but do not sense our meanings. Too many do not see our beauty as beauty, our music as music, our language as language, our thoughts as thoughts, for we are different from the sky creatures. Our songs are lost to their ears, and soon may be lost even to our own earth, when the last of humankind is hunted and slain and consumed. If that terrifying time should come, then our love, our mirth, our knowledge, our joy in life, will disappear forever, and God will mourn, for the holy spirit that created the sky creatures and gave them the possibility of the knowledge of love, also created us with the same possibilities, we who are the earthlings, humankind.

PSALMS: 39:12 – *"Hear my prayer, O Lord,
and give ear unto my cry; hold not thy peace
at my tears, for I am a stranger with thee,
and a sojourner, as all my fathers were."*

FOR MY SISTERS

My mothers' families ran to sisters
In every way
I was spared and denied.

I never had a sister
Yet have many   some close
Reached for at all times
Some reached for a time   at times
All in heartspace remaining
My life's time
And others unknown but known
To be in all lands

My close sisters
I speak with often   and know
Something of their lives   selves
As they know of mine
Speaking concern worry love
For close ones   for entire worlds
Speaking despair and the lifting
Of despair to some hoping

Unheroic heroines   saintly we aren't
We can be mean   we can snarl and do
From tiredness   anger at fates and powers
Damage to us and ours
Or knowing our powers to hurt
Sometimes used   uselessly.
We mean to try   and do

But life's trying
And yet life *is* trying.

We don't mean children, all endeavours,
To fuel the furnaces of war;
We speak our meanings plain
And cannot cease   for peace
Means life and lives we care for.
Means must be found   and will
We will it   pray it   try
Mourn   cry   refuse to die
Before our time and in time rise up
Even passing on meanings   and will
Even when passing on.

My first my lifelong sister   born
Two weeks before me   same small town
We've known all our lives   left it
But bear it within us   have known
Ourselves as sisters sixty years now
Shared secrets families fears exultances
Needs and rages   news of childrren
From births to now-adulthoods
We survive   my sister comrade
More or less whole   wholly alive.

My second sister   younger
By two years   forty years
We've been sisters
Families one another's
Vocations one another's
Our children near-relatives
Our sisterhood chosen yet committed
Nearly as near as family.
My sister's mother   wisewoman   long ago
Spoke to us what we've learned   earned –
We've chosen   people   work

We're chosen people
Our work   our own people
Giving us no choice   gifting us
These hard and blessed commitments
In families' and words' meanings
Our meanings   our abodes
Abiding.

These, my earliest sisters
Cherished so long   so well
And there are others as well
All my fond sisters   found
Through travails   travels   through years
Finding we matter
In all matters   news   lifeviews
Words of work   the young   the aged
Tragedies   gladness   encompassed
In our lives' compasses
Giving some direction.

My most close sisters
Savers of live   savourers of life
Life's saviours   giving receiving
A saving grace.

One different   dearer than any –
Costlier and more valued to my heart,
My protector as once I was hers
And still am   keeping that need
Yet keeping still   I hope
When still-ness needs to mean
Both quiet and continuing
Silent yet heard shouts
Speaking support   faith –
The woman who is most close
Is the woman I birthed.
Can one be mother   sister   both

Daughter   sister?   I believe   so
Our talk's a river   active   still
Flowing in currents of laughter   pain
Torrents of hope
Flowing both ways.

My son, so much beloved
No difference of caring
For my part   my heart
Undivided between the two
Son Daughter   Daughter Son
I love both best.

But there are paths of yours,
My son, I cannot walk   and maps
Of your worlds I cannot read
And grieve some times for this
My necessary lack and yet I honour
Your man-life   your life-honouring self
More than my words can ever say.
I know you know.

My daughter, woman as I am,
You who have no sisters
Have many and close, as I have.
You are my sister-sojourner here
As all my mothers were
And in memory remain.

February 1986

LIST OF PHOTOGRAPHS

1. Great-grandmother Wemyss.
2. Great-grandmother Wemyss, in Scotland, with three of her children. Grandfather Wemyss is on left.
3. Great-grandparents, D.H. Harrison and wife, Grandmother Wemyss' parents.
4. My paternal grandmother, Maggie Harrison Wemyss.
5. Grandfather John Wemyss at college in Scotland.
6. Jack Wemyss and my father, Bob Wemyss (right).
7. Jack Wemyss and Bob Wemyss (right) just after joining up in W.W.I.
8. Jack (left) and Bob Wemyss after they had fought in the trenches.
9. The Simpson girls – (left to right) Margaret, Verna, Ruby, Velma – c.1913.
10. My mother, Verna Simpson, as a young woman.
11. Margaret Simpson, my stepmother, about age 16.
12. Myself at 5 months.
13. Four generations: Great-grandmother Wemyss, my dad, Grandmother Wemyss, and myself.
14. My father, Bob Wemyss, 1932.
15. Grandfather John Simpson.
16. Myself (left) and my friend Mona, both of us about 2 years old.
17. Myself, age 6, on my first day of school.
18. Mum, myself, and Dad, 1933.
19. My brother, Robert, in his highchair, and myself, 1933.
20. Myself, my brother, Bob, and Rufty, 1939.
21. My brother, Bob, and Mum.
22. Myself, age 17.
23. Our cottage at Clear Lake, Riding Mountain National Park.
24. My friends Louise and Mona, and myself (age 17), at Clear Lake.

25. Jack Laurence in RCAF uniform, 1945.

26. Aunt Ruby Simpson and Mum, the year Mum died.

27. Elsie Fry as a child.

28. Elsie Fry Laurence as a young woman.

29. John and Elsie Laurence (my father-in-law and my mother-in-law), with one of their children.

30. Jocelyn and myself, Tema Beach, Ghana, 1953.

31. Jocelyn with her father, Jack Laurence. Accra, Ghana, 1953.

32. David, age about 5 months.

33. Jocelyn (age 3½), myself (29), and David (6 months), Ghana, 1955.

34. Myself, Jocelyn, David, and Jack, in Victoria, B.C., 1959.

35. David (age 6), Jocelyn (age 9), with their dad and Granddad Laurence, Vancouver.

36. Elm Cottage, Buckinghamshire, England, c.1967.

37. Myself, London, 1963.

38. My study in Elm Cottage.

39. Our guide, Hanafy Bashir, and David, in Egypt, 1967.

40. Myself, at our village grocery shop, Penn, Buckinghamshire, c.1967.

41. Myself at my cottage on the Otonabee River, near Peterborough, Ont., 1970.

42. A repainted Elm Cottage around the time of my return to Canada in the early '70s.

43. David, age 11.

44. Age 17.

45. Age 20.

46. Jocelyn, age 15.

47. Age 21.

48. Age 24, with Al Purdy in Ameliasburgh, Ont., 1976.

49. Moving into the Lakefield house, May 1, 1974.

50. The Lakefield house.

51. Adele Wiseman, 1978. *Photo by David Laurence.*

52. In my study, c.1984. *Photo by Doug Boult.*